The Diary of Xenophon's Anabasis

A Chronological Retrospect

Hutan Ashrafian

DEDICATION

To my wonderful wife Leanne and delightful son Persie.

CONTENTS

ACKNOWLEDGMENTS

The calculated chronology of the diary here-in has been scaffolded onto the original English translation of the Anabasis of Xenophon by H. G. Dakyns (1897).

META-CHRONOLOGY SERIES PREFACE

There seems to be a grand disparity in the world of historians. Whilst the concept of history is relatively robust in society, there is a rift between *Modern* and *Ancient* Historians. Such a dichotomy seems to be artificial, for both study events in the past and both are aim to apply as much objectivity as possible to clarify the causal determinants of past effects; and as a result, to educate and inform contemporaneous society of these facts; ideally to minimize future societal mistakes and to guide beneficial future decisions. Nevertheless, the dichotomy between Ancient and Modern historians seems a pervading distinction that seems largely driven by the very nature of the sources each group has to study.

For example, a very modern historian may have access to *real-time* notes, emails, newspaper articles, television interviews, social media yield and a whole trench of other online media that are contextualized by major world timelines or a *macro-chronology* (such as leadership eras and major calendar events) in addition to a micro-chronology (specific day-to-day, hour-by-hour, minute-by-minute or even second-by-second events). Conversely, an ancient historian may have a few 2nd or 3rd hand sources written in an archaic language, sometimes many centuries after the occurrence of ancient events that predominantly only offer macro-chronological information. Such differences not only seem to affect the analysis of the past but also our interpretation. This seems to limit the interpretation of ancient sources that are treated as having a miasma of 2nd hand source bias, which is not considered to equate with the presumed clarity of modern sources due to their lack of an accepted micro-chronology of events.

My goal therefore has been to offer a micro-chronology of ancient events or an acuity of day-to-day real-time actuality to some ancient individuals and subjects. The integration between both macro- and micro-chronological views can therefore act as a method to cut through the presumed miasma of ancient sources. Sometimes it seems that studying ancient sources offers an encylopaedic appreciation of past events, but this may be tinted with a tone and timing that has a rather ethereal flavor rather than the likely reality of day-to-day events; which were just as real thousands of years ago as they are today. Studying the ancients without the cloak of romanticism, but rather one of scientific daily chronology may offer the reader of ancient sources the context of real-time impetus in decisions and actions. By doing so, it will allow the conceptual bridging of how ancient subjects were actually subjects living in another time, but nonetheless human subjects with comparative sentience and intelligence to their ancient contemporaries in the context of their day-to-day events.

The *real politic* of yester-year was just as real 20,000 years ago as it is today. Sometimes assessing ancient events devoid of time or place can lead to exaggeration and bias, particularly through each iteration of news dissemination. This is one source from which legends can come to exist; for example, there may have been a skirmish between several Mediterranean states and their leaders, which in today's world would be viewed as simply that. The same story devoid of time and place could lead to embellishment to scale in the time of events and size of actions. One could see the origins of Homer's Trojan Wars with demi-gods such as Achilles and magical depictions of Olympian Gods participating in human events. It is interesting to note that Homer by himself may have been aware of loss of time information, for there is a symmetrical chronology of events in the Iliad with times taking from one night to nine nights then to twelve nights then to one night then twelve nights and so on. Additionally the journey of the Odyssey is identical to that of the Trojan War in the Iliad, both ten years; though Odysseus' journey should only take the order of weeks. This likely synthetic approximation of time detracts form the reality of activity that in turn can spawn disinformation. Other examples include those of the Sumerian King List; here we know that some of the kings in this list existed, but clearly their reign length, some at 36,000 years is clearly unfeasible and has obscured analysis of Sumerian regnal time and events.

One classical example at an attempt to quantify the chronology of the past is that of Archbishop James Ussher (1581 – 1656). As a cleric, he expressed his deep devotion to the Bible by considering it as an incontrovertibly factual document. He applied scientific arithmetic to calculate his eponymous Chronology identifing the age of the world according to that text. Others such as Lightfoot, Ben Halafta, Bede and Newton also tried to create their own chronology. Independent to the consideration of the text in question, these attempts offered a quantifiable list of events by which to compare other models of chronology for ancient occurrences and offered a yardstick for which to allow a deeper timeline scrutiny for past events.

It is with this notion, that I have studied the ancient sources for prevailing characters from the ancient world and added a diary-like chronology to them for this 'Meta-Chronology' series (integrating both macro- and micro-chronology) on the most studied events of the most prominent ancient leaders (including the life and leadership of Alexander the Great and Xenophon's Anabasis who of interest where students of amongst the greatest philosophers of all time, Alexander-Aristotle and Xenophon-Socrates). By doing so I aim to discard the shackles of *'Ancient vs. Modern'* or

'Legendary vs. Contemporary', but rather to offer anyone interested a common chronological yardstick by which to cover both modern and ancient world events. Here, metaphorically, I have aimed to clarify the nature of each individual's timeline in the same vein that the *Alexander Mosaic* has been reconstructed to give the viewer a sense of its completeness of the original piece of art. Whilst I am aware there may be some inaccuracies in this method, I feel that the bigger picture may offer a stronger sense of existence in the characters discussed, particularly to give a feel of the urgency in decisions and actions as well as times of inaction. A method therefore to directly compare their ancient world with the modern one.

For these works, I have utilised accounts from established ancient sources on day-to-day activities of individuals and have super-imposed a *real-time* date on to those known events. To do this, I calculated specific days using set-dates from accepted or validated known-time points existing in the history of each individual and imputing of extrapolating the remaining dates in an individuals life based on the ancient sources in the texts listed. On occasion I have also imputed some figures based on the description of times, places and travel times (for example if it took 10 days to march from A to B and the distance form C to D resembles that of A to B and the journey speed or impetus was similar then I deduced the journey time would also follow). I have also added to the translation of ancient-to-modern chronology by converting ancient seasons into their modern ones through conversion of the ancient dates into their Julian calendar counterpart. For consistency, I have applied the Julian Calendar in year-month-day (YMD) format. For clarification of my personal comments in the text, I have utilized curly braces {}. These have been used to include relevant travel distances, travel information and the coupling of ancient locations to their current or hypothesized modern-day counterparts. Furthermore, where necessary, other sources have been utlised to clarify dates and events. Specifically for lunar, solar, or astronomical data, sources from NASA (National Aeronautics and Space Administration) or accepted modern astronomical tables/software (including Alcyone) have been applied.

In this series, I have also categorized the listed ancient dates according to modern day designations (Sunday to Saturday utilizing the Computer Support Group [CSGNetwork.com] Calendar Converter and Translator). Whilst these days are based on a cyclical mathematical progression that is arbitrary (these day names did not exist in ancient times) and do not take into account the many calendars (of differing lengths, months and days) applied in the ancient world, the robustness of a continuous mathematically calculated sequential seven day system allows the reader to discern any seven day trends that may have occurred in the chronology of the book. For example, if person A went to war on Monday August 5th in one year and had a celebratory feast on a Monday in August the next year, this may offer an insight regarding the timing and association between these two events. Possibly the 'Monday' or that day in a rolling calendar represented something of note. Additionally it offers the reader an additional sense of tangibility and context within the modern-world calendar timeframe regarding events that occurred thousands of years ago. Significantly however, this *virtual diary* format does carry some limitations. The dates listed are not fact but calculations aiming to offer the most likely factual times. As a result, they cannot be taken as verbatim, but rather they represent the best educated guess as to when the specified ancient events actually took place.

My ultimate aim is therefore to offer a deeper perception of *'real-time'* for ancient events that to-date have suffered from being morphed to exist in an abstract space-time of their own devoid of scale and measure. It is with this I wish the reader a tangibly timely appreciation of ancient historical events.

Hutan Ashrafian
Primrose Hill, London
2017

PREFACE

The Anabasis of Xenophon is acknowledged as one of the greatest classical adventures of all time. Written by Xenophon himself at approximately 370 BC, the term Anabasis (translated from the ancient Greek as "expedition up from") is popularly translated as an "expedition up country"; relating his journey with a troop of ten thousand fellow Greek mercenary soldiers through the lands of enemy Persian territory some 30 years earlier. The book recounts how the Greeks were mercenaries on behalf of a Persian Achaemenid prince (Cyrus the Younger) hoping to usurp his older brother's (Artaxerxes II Mnemon) throne to become Emperor of the Persian Empire himself. The Greeks therefore fought alongside the Prince's own troops against the Persian army at the battle of Cunaxa (within modern day Iraq) and whilst having succeeded in technical military success, the death of their leader Cyrus the Younger resulted in isolation in the middle of the Persian Empire. What follows is a pseudo-truce between the Persian's and the Greeks resulting in assassination of the Greek generals. In order to survive, the Greek mercenary army was obliged to select new leaders including Xenophon himself to support the army with leadership and decision-making capacity as a means to save the soldiers and guide them throughout their retreat back home.

Xenophon was a Greek aristocrat who would have been approximately thirty years old during the expedition and sixty years old when having completed his book. The fact that his work remains a classic can be attributed to several reasons. First, the narrative falls into the category of classic adventure, where the Greeks are 'up against all the odds' having to get home, whilst stranded thousands of miles in enemy lands. Second, the description of this incredibly long journey acts as an extraordinary 'travel guide' for the ancient Persian Empire and therefore remains a core source for historians of this time and place. Third, the book also forms a foundation of the socio-political climate of the era, one that considers both the role of the Greeks, Persians and their interactions in an era between the times of the Greek-Persian Wars and that of Alexander the Great. This period consisted of the reign of the Achaemenid Empire in Persia at its mid-point whilst in Ancient Greece there was a period of philosophical and cultural enlightenment corresponding with luminaries such as Socrates and his followers (of which Xenephon himself was a notable student). Different Greek states had differing and multi-faceted relationships between each other and with the Persians, some of which can be discerned throughout Xenophon's text. In addition, the story is a classical example of spontaneous organisational leadership generation that remains a time-honoured source for military, business and leadership experts who characterise the process of leadership generation within leaderless institutions. Finally, Xenophon was an able author (having written several other books) and his style and usage of Ancient Greek remains accessible for scholars of this language.

The Anabasis remains a prominent cultural inspiration for the current era but has nevertheless been marred by a lack of chronological context. Historians continue to debate the exact nature and utility of the Anabasis, and how biased Xenophon was in his descriptions (with few other sources outside that of Diodorus Siculus in existence). Exactly how long was the whole journey of the Anabasis? When was the battle of Cunaxa? How much did the army rest and how fast did it travel at different times? As a result, exactly how feasible and how incredible was their journey? What was the climate and the duration spent at different locations? This issue of time and chronology therefore can fundamentally guide our understating of Xenophon's narrative.

Scholars have been unable to agree on a chronology for the Anabasis. This has been a question of continued scrutiny and debate for centuries, with the most recent tradition following a battle of Cunaxa to September 3rd 401 BC. The difficulty in Xenophon's Anabasis lies in that until now there were no known set time points described in the text. As a comparison, the life of Alexander the Great (also a book in this series) was confirmed according to given dates based on multiple sources giving dates in the Attic Calendar; which in turn have also been corroborated and clarified with concomitant archaeological finds from Ancient Egypt (kingly hieroglyphs and subsequent writers describing the date of Alexandria's founding) as well as Babylonian Astronomical Tables describing his travel, and dates of wars. These were further supported with known dates of known Astronomical events such as the well-described and clearly dated lunar eclipse before the battle of Gaugamela. Unfortunately, Xenophon's anabasis has none of these set points on which to base its chronology such that pevious historians have relied upon:

A. Internal measures of date within the text including (i) The listed dates of marching and rest in the text and (ii) Statements of time (for example 'it took six months between Sardis and Cunaxa')
B. Measures of validation, includding (i) Dating according to the description of climate variables (snow on mountains etc.), and (ii) Dating according to biological factors such as the approximate timing of the honey madness episode.

Both internal measures (A) and measures of validation (B) are utilized with a best guestimate of known or start dates.

The ultimate result is that this approach has been inconclusive with unreliable guestimates and non-specific sources of biological validation. As an example, honey madness can occur anywhere in spring to autumn and whilst this condition might be somewhat more probable in spring this is not a clear defining point. At the same time, climate variables are notoriously chaotic and as such do not provide robust date points.

Attempts have been made to date the text, for example, using the hypothesis that the description of the Arcadian festival of Lycaea, celebrated by the Greeks at Peltae occurred at the vernal or spring equinox; although this is simply a guess (K. Glombiowski. The Campaign of Cyrus the Younger and the Retreat of the Ten Thousand: Chronology, Pomoerium 1, 1994 37–44.) and not based on any rigorous fact. Others have reviewed the whole literature for Xenophon's chronology to list the various 'traditional', 'early start' and 'proposed' (or later start) dates for the commencement of the Anabasis (I. K. Paradeisopoulos. A Chronology Model for Xenophon's Anabasis, Greek, Roman, and Byzantine Studies 53, 2013 645–686). These however all remain based on speculation.

Furthermore, many of these established models aim to measure the chronology between two dates by simply measuring differences in dates and summing these up. This methodology is susceptible to inaccuracy, as the discrepancy between arrival day, stay/event duration and subsequent leave day is not always correctly accommodated for in their calculations.

In this book, I have analysed Xenophon's text to calculate all listed arrival days, stay/event durations and leave days to generate a day-by-day account of Xenophon's Anabasis. Furthermore, I have identified a clear anchor-point for the text (see below) and listed all subsequent and prior events chronologically in diary format. These have been scaffolded onto the corresponding English text translated originally by Henry Graham Dakyns (1897). Where times or durations are not explicitly stated, time lengths have been imputed from the text. Where this has not been possible, realistic travel times have been calculated from other comparable times in the text and additional context from a strategic military viewpoint added. The conversion of all dates into the Julian Calendar has been applied (the predominant method of assessing ancient sources with consistency), as this will allow the easiest assessment of time comparisons within the modern world.

Whilst the book is in diary format, there is some discrepancy in the retreat phase of Xenophon's journey times when compared to those of Diodorus Siculus. As a result, I have listed the ancient dates of events according to Xenophon himself, but also concurrently the ancient dates according to the time modification suggested for Diodorus, which finally results in approximately 29 days difference in times. It is left for the reader to select the times they feel most appropriate associated with each event where both dates are listed.

For this book, I have defined an actual calculable date that offers an anchor point for which to compute the diary chronology for the march of the Ten Thousand. This is based on the entry en route to the battle of Cunaxa where "Xenias, the Arcadian, celebrated the Lycaea". The date for this in the past had been guestimated as occurring on the spring (vernal) equinox. As there had been no evidence of validity for this date, the utility of using this time-point in the journey is refuted.

The approach in this text differs in that it is based on the recent finding of a previously unknown Bronze Tablet from circa 500 BC from the Lykaion (Johannes Heinrichs: Military Integration in Late Archaic Arkadia: New Evidence from a Bronze Pinax (ca. 500 BC) of the Lykaion in The Many Faces of War in the Ancient World Eds: Waldermar Heckel, Sabine Müller and Graham Wrightson, Cambridge Scholars Publishing, 2015). This tablet offers the description on which to calculate the date in 401 BC that Xenias the Arcadian likely celebrated the Lycaea or Lykaion:

The Lykaion was on Day 7 of the month with full moon after the summer solstice. In Arcadia as in Athens, each month began with new moon. Using established astronomical and lunar charts, I have identified the following:
(i) The summer solstice in 401 BC was June 22
(ii) The first full moon after this is July 17
(iii) The month of that full moon begins on July 02
(iv) So that the 7th day of that month = Lykaion = July 08
(v) Any mistakes in the calculation of dates within this text are the sole responsibility of the author.

The aim of this book is to offer the reader new insights in the much overlooked day-to-day events within the Anabasis. The events of time added to the description of location through its diary format is aimed to offer a wholly fresh perspective with which to enjoy, analyse and consider the amazing march of ten thousand stranded souls in enemy territory thousands of miles from home. The survival of these individuals has resonated through time in overcoming the odds to succeed. As a result, it is hoped that this book will offer a reinvigorated message of courage and hope for those immersed in Xenophon's ancient Anabasis journey or exposed to metaphorically similar situations.

Hutan Ashrafian
Primrose Hill, London
2017

1 PRELUDE AND TRAVEL TO BATTLE

Chapter 1 (Start of Book 1)

Darius and Parysatis had two sons: the elder was named Artaxerxes, and the younger Cyrus.

405 BC

21 December, Monday

Now, as Darius lay sick and felt that the end of life drew near, he wished both his sons to be with him. The elder, as it chanced, was already there, but Cyrus he must needs send for from the province over which he had made him satrap, having appointed him general moreover of all the forces that muster in the plain of the Castolus. Thus Cyrus went up, taking with him Tissaphernes as his friend, and accompanied also by a body of Hellenes, three hundred heavy armed men, under the command of Xenias the Parrhasian (1).

404 BC

25 March, Thursday

Now when Darius was dead, and

{Darius II's death and Artaxerxes reign began between the Egyptian New Year (26 Nov 405) and the Babylonian New Year (4 Apr 404) according to these respective sources. Additionally the latest death of Darius II's death was the 4th March 404 BC and according to the Egyptian calendar, this would have occurred approximately 4 months after the New Year on the 26th November.}

Artaxerxes was established in the kingdom, Tissaphernes brought slanderous accusations against Cyrus before his brother, the king, of harbouring designs against him. And Artaxerxes, listening to the words of Tissaphernes, laid hands upon Cyrus, desiring to put him to death; but his mother made intercession for him, and sent him back again in safety to his province.

403 BC

June

He then, having so escaped through peril and dishonour, fell to considering, not only how he might avoid ever again being in his brother's power, but how, if possible, he might become king in his stead. Parysatis, his mother, was his first resource; for she had more love for Cyrus than for Artaxerxes upon his throne. Moreover Cyrus's behaviour towards all who came to him from the king's court was such that, when he sent them away again, they were better friends to himself than to the king his brother. Nor did he neglect the barbarians in his own service; but trained them, at once to be capable as warriors and devoted adherents of himself. Lastly, he began collecting his Hellenic armament, but with the utmost secrecy, so that he might take the king as far as might be at unawares. The manner in which he contrived the levying of the troops was as follows: First, he sent orders to the commandants of garrisons in the cities (so held by him), bidding them to get together as large a body of picked Peloponnesian troops as they severally were able, on the plea that Tissaphernes was plotting against their cities; and truly these cities of Ionia had originally belonged to Tissaphernes, being given to him by the king; but at this time, with the exception of Miletus, they had all revolted to Cyrus. In Miletus, Tissaphernes, having become aware of similar designs, had forestalled the conspirators by putting some to death and banishing the remainder. Cyrus, on his side, welcomed these fugitives, and having collected an army, laid siege to Miletus by sea and land, endeavouring to reinstate the exiles; and this gave him another pretext for collecting an armament. At the same time he sent to the king, and claimed, as being the king's brother, that these cities should be given to himself rather than that Tissaphernes should continue to govern them; and in furtherance of this end, the queen, his mother, co-operated with him, so that the king not only failed to see the design against himself, but concluded that Cyrus was spending his money on armaments in order to make war on Tissaphernes. Nor did it pain him greatly to see the two at war together, and the less so because Cyrus was careful to remit the tribute due to the king from the cities which belonged to Tissaphernes. A third army was being collected for him in the Chersonese, over against Abydos, the origin of which was as follows: There was a Lacedaemonian exile, named Clearchus, with whom Cyrus had become associated. Cyrus admired the man, and made him a present of ten thousand darics (2). Clearchus took the gold, and with the money raised an army, and using the Chersonese as his base of operations, set to work to fight the Thracians north of the Hellespont, in the interests of the Hellenes, and with such happy result that the Hellespontine cities, of their own accord, were eager to contribute funds for the support of his troops. In this way, again, an armament was being secretly maintained for Cyrus.

Then there was the Thessalian Aristippus, Cyrus's friend (3), who, under pressure of the rival political party at home, had come to Cyrus and asked him for pay for two thousand mercenaries, to be continued for three months, which would enable him, he said, to gain the upper hand of his antagonists. Cyrus replied by presenting him with six months' pay for four thousand mercenaries--only stipulating that Aristippus should not come to terms with his antagonists without final consultation with himself. In this way he secured to himself the secret maintenance of a fourth armament.

Further, he bade Proxenus, a Boeotian, who was another friend, get together as many men as possible, and join him in an expedition which he meditated against the Pisidians (4), who were causing annoyance to his territory. Similarly two other friends, Sophaenetus the Stymphalian (5), and Socrates the Achaean, had orders to get together as many men as possible and come to him, since he was on the point of opening a campaign, along with Milesian exiles, against Tissaphernes. These orders were duly carried out by the officers in question.

401 BC

II

February

But when the right moment seemed to him to have come, at which he should begin his march into the interior, the pretext which he put forward was his desire to expel the Pisidians utterly out of the country; and he began collecting both his Asiatic and his Hellenic armaments, avowedly against that people. From Sardis in each direction his orders sped: to Clearchus, to join him there with the whole of his army; to Aristippus, to come to terms with those at home, and to despatch to him the troops in his employ; to Xenias the Arcadian, who was acting as general-in-chief of the foreign troops in the cities, to present himself with all the men available, excepting only those who were actually needed to garrison the citadels. He next summoned the troops at present engaged in the siege of Miletus, and called upon the exiles to follow him on his intended expedition, promising them that if he were successful in his object, he would not pause until he had reinstated them in their native city. To this invitation they hearkened gladly; they believed in him; and with their arms they presented themselves at Sardis. So, too, Xenias arrived at Sardis with the contingent from the cities, four thousand hoplites; Proxenus, also, with fifteen hundred hoplites and five hundred light-armed troops; Sophaenetus the Stymphalian, with one thousand hoplites; Socrates the Achaean, with five hundred hoplites; while the Megarion Pasion came with three hundred hoplites and three hundred peltasts (6). This latter officer, as well as Socrates, belonged to the force engaged against Miletus. These all joined him at Sardis.

March

But Tissaphernes did not fail to note these proceedings. An equipment so large pointed to something more than an invasion of Pisidia: so he argued; and with what speed he might, he set off to the king, attended by about five hundred horse. The king, on his side, had no sooner heard from Tissaphernes of Cyrus's great armament, than he began to make counter-preparations.

May 23, Thursday
Leaves Sardis (modern day Sart in Turkey)

Thus Cyrus, with the troops which I have named, set out from Sardis, and marched on and on through Lydia three stages,

May 26, Sunday
Arrives at the River Maeander

making two-and-twenty parasangs (7), to the river Maeander. That river is two hundred feet (8) broad, and was spanned by a bridge consisting of seven boats.

May 27, Monday
Arrives at Colossae (corresponds to an area north of Honaz in Denizli Province of the Aegean Region of modern day Turkey)

Crossing it, he marched through Phrygia a single stage, of eight parasangs, to Colossae, an inhabited city (9), prosperous and large. Here he remained seven days, and was joined by Menon the Thessalian, who arrived with one thousand hoplites and five hundred peltasts, Dolopes, Aenianes, and Olynthians.

June 03, Monday
Leaves Colossae

From this place he marched three stages, twenty parasangs in all,

June 06, Thursday
Arrives at Celaenae

to Celaenae, a populous city of Phrygia, large and prosperous. Here Cyrus owned a palace and a large park (10) full of wild beasts, which he used to hunt on horseback, whenever he wished to give himself or his horses exercise. Through the midst of the park flows the river Maeander, the sources of which are within the palace buildings, and it flows through the city of Celaenae. The great king also has a palace in Celaenae, a strong place, on the sources of another river, the Marsyas, at the foot of the acropolis. This river also flows through the city, discharging itself into the Maeander, and is five-and-twenty feet broad. Here is the place where Apollo is said to have flayed Marsyas, when he had conquered him in the contest of skill. He hung up the skin of the conquered man, in the cavern where the spring wells forth, and hence the name of the river, Marsyas. It was on this site that Xerxes, as tradition tells, built this very palace, as well as the citadel of Celaenae itself, on his retreat from Hellas, after he had lost the famous battle. Here Cyrus remained for thirty days, during which Clearchus the Lacedaemonian arrived with one thousand hoplites and eight hundred Thracian peltasts and two hundred Cretan archers. At the same time, also, came Sosis the Syracusian with three thousand hoplites, and Sophaenetus the Arcadian (11) with one thousand hoplites; and here Cyrus held a review, and numbered his Hellenes in the park, and found that they amounted in all to eleven thousand hoplites and about two thousand peltasts.

July 06, Saturday

From this place he continued his march two stages--ten parasangs-

July 08, Monday
Arrives at Peltae

to the populous city of Peltae, where he remained three days; while Xenias, the Arcadian, celebrated the Lycaea (12) with sacrifice, and instituted games. The prizes were headbands of gold; and Cyrus himself was a spectator of the contest.

{date calculated by the author based on a recently discovered bronze tablet.

The celebration would be between 7th-9th of the month corresponding to July 08-July 10 401 BC of the Julian calendar (please refer to the preface).}

July 11, Thursday
Leaves Peltae

From this place the march was continued two stages--twelve parasangs--

July 13, Saturday
Arrives at Ceramon-agora

to Ceramon-agora, a populous city, the last on the confines of Mysia. Thence a march of three stages--thirty parasangs--

July 16, Tuesday
Arrives at Caystru-pedion

brought him to Caystru-pedion (13), a populous city. Here Cyrus halted five days; and the soldiers, whose pay was now more than three months in arrear, came several times to the palace gates demanding their dues; while Cyrus put them off with fine words and expectations, but could not conceal his vexation, for it was not his fashion to stint payment, when he had the means. At this point Epyaxa, the wife of Syennesis, the king of the Cilicians, arrived on a visit to Cyrus; and it was said that Cyrus received a large gift of money from the queen. At this date, at any rate, Cyrus gave the army four months' pay. The queen was accompanied by a bodyguard of Cilicians and Aspendians; and, if report speaks truly, Cyrus had intimate relations with the queen.

July 21, Saturday
Leaves Caystru-pedion

From this place he marched two stages--ten parasangs--

{Via Thymbrion at half way through this}

July 25, Thursday
Arrives at Tyriaeum

to Tyriaeum, a populous city. Here he halted three days; and the Cilician queen, according to the popular account, begged Cyrus to exhibit his armament for her amusement. The latter being only too glad to make such an exhibition, held a review of the Hellenes and barbarians in the plain. He ordered the Hellenes to draw up their lines and post themselves in their customary battle order, each general marshalling his own battalion. Accordingly they drew up four-deep. The right was held by Menon and those with him; the left by Clearchus and his men; the centre by the remaining generals with theirs. Cyrus first inspected the barbarians, who marched past in troops of horses and companies of infantry. He then inspected the Hellenes; driving past them in his chariot, with the queen in her carriage. And they all had brass helmets and purple tunics, and greaves, and their shields uncovered (14).

After he had driven past the whole body, he drew up his chariot in front of the centre of the battle-line, and sent his interpreter Pigres to the generals of the Hellenes, with orders to present arms and to advance along the whole line. This order was repeated by the generals to their men; and at the sound of the bugle, with shields forward and spears in rest, they advanced to meet the enemy. The pace quickened, and with a shout the soldiers spontaneously fell into a run, making in the direction of the camp. Great was the panic of the barbarians. The Cilician queen in her carriage turned and fled; the sutlers in the marketing place left their wares and took to their heels; and the Hellenes meanwhile came into camp with a roar of laughter. What astounded the queen was the brilliancy and order of the armament; but Cyrus was pleased to see the terror inspired by the Hellenes in the hearts of the Asiatics.

July 28, Sunday
Leaves Tyriaeum

From this place he marched on three stages--twenty parasangs--

July 31, Wednesday
Arrives at Iconium (corresponds to Konya in Turkey)

to Iconium, the last city of Phrygia, where he remained three days.

August 03, Saturday
Leaves Iconium

Thence he marched through

August 08, Thursday
Arrives and Leaves Lycaonia travelling through Cappadocia

Lycaonia five stages--thirty parasangs. This was hostile country, and he gave it over to the Hellenes to pillage. At this point Cyrus sent back the Cilician queen to her own country by the quickest route; and to escort her he sent the soldiers of Menon, and Menon himself. With the rest of the troops he continued his march through Cappadocia four stages--twenty-five parasangs--

August 12, Monday
Arrives at Dana (also known as Tyana or Tyanna, corresponds to modern Kemerhisar, Niğde Province in Turkey)

to Dana, a populous city, large and flourishing. Here they halted three days, within which interval Cyrus put to death, on a charge of conspiracy, a Persian nobleman named Megaphernes, a wearer of the royal purple; and along with him another high dignitary among his subordinate commanders.

August 15, Thursday
Leaves Dana

From this place they endeavoured to force a passage into Cilicia. Now the entrance was by an exceedingly steep cart-road, impracticable for an army in face of a resisting force; and report said that Syennesis was on the summit of the pass guarding the approach.

August 16, Friday
Cilician Plain

Accordingly they halted a day in the plain;

August 17, Saturday
Crosses Cilicia (The Gates of Cilicia or Cilician Gates or Gülek Pass is a pass running in the Taurus Mountains; Alexander the Great also passed through here)

but next day came a messenger informing them that Syenesis had left the pass; doubtless, after perceiving that Menon's army was already in Cilicia on his own side of the mountains; and he had further been informed that ships of war, belonging to the Lacedaemonians and to Cyrus himself, with Tamos on board as admiral, were sailing round from Ionia to Cilicia. Whatever the reason might be, Cyrus made his way up into the hills without let or hindrance, and came in sight of the tents where the Cilicians were on guard. From that point he descended gradually into a large and beautiful plain country, well watered, and thickly covered with trees of all sorts and vines. This plain produces sesame plentifully, as also panic and millet and barley and wheat; and it is shut in on all sides by a steep and lofty wall of mountains from sea to sea. Descending through this plain country, he advanced four stages--twenty-five parasangs--

August 21, Wednesday
Arrives at Tarsus (centre of the Çukurova region of modern Turkey's Mersin Province. Alexander the Great also passed through here)

to Tarsus, a large and prosperous city of Cilicia. Here stood the palace of Syennesis, the king of the country; and through the middle of the city flows a river called the Cydnus, two hundred feet broad. They found that the city had been deserted by its inhabitants, who had betaken themselves, with Syennesis, to a strong place on the hills. All had gone, except the tavern-keepers. The sea-board inhabitants of Soli and Issi also remained. Now Epyaxa, Syennesis's queen, had reached Tarsus five days in advance of

Cyrus. During their passage over the mountains into the plain, two companies of Menon's army were lost. Some said they had been cut down by the Cilicians, while engaged on some pillaging affair; another account was that they had been left behind, and being unable to overtake the main body, or discover the route, had gone astray and perished. However it was, they numbered one hundred hoplites; and when the rest arrived, being in a fury at the destruction of their fellow soldiers, they vented their spleen by pillaging the city of Tarsus and the palace to boot. Now when Cyrus had marched into the city, he sent for Syennesis to come to him; but the latter replied that he had never yet put himself into the hands of any one who was his superior, nor was he willing to accede to the proposal of Cyrus now; until, in the end, his wife persuaded him, and he accepted pledges of good faith. After this they met, and Syennesis gave Cyrus large sums in aid of his army; while Cyrus presented him with the customary royal gifts--to wit, a horse with a gold bit, a necklace of gold, a gold bracelet, and a gold scimitar, a Persian dress, and lastly, the exemption of his territory from further pillage, with the privilege of taking back the slaves that had been seized, wherever they might chance to come upon them.

III

At Tarsus Cyrus and his army halted for twenty days; the soldiers refusing to advance further, since the suspicion ripened in their minds, that the expedition was in reality directed against the king; and as they insisted, they had not engaged their services for that object. Clearchus set the example of trying to force his men to continue their march; but he had no sooner started at the head of his troops than they began to pelt him and his baggage train, and Clearchus had a narrow escape of being stoned to death there and then. Later on, when he perceived that force was useless, he summoned an assembly of his own men; and for a long while he stood and wept, while the men gazed in silent astonishment. At last he spoke as follows: "Fellow soldiers, do not marvel that I am sorely distressed on account of the present troubles. Cyrus has been no ordinary friend to me. When I was in banishment he honoured me in various ways, and made me also a present of ten thousand darics. These I accepted, but not to lay them up for myself for private use; not to squander them in pleasure, but to expend them on yourselves. And, first of all, I went to war with the Thracians, and with you to aid, I wreaked vengeance on them in behalf of Hellas; driving them out of the Chersonese, when they wanted to deprive its Hellenic inhabitants of their lands. But as soon as Cyrus summoned me, I took you with me and set out, so that, if my benefactor had any need of me, I might requite him for the good treatment I myself had received at his hands.... But since you are not minded to continue the march with me, one of two things is left to me to do; either I must renounce you for the sake of my friendship with Cyrus, or I must go with you at the cost of deceiving him. Whether I am about to do right or not, I cannot say, but I choose yourselves; and, whatever beside, I mean to share your fate. Never shall it be said of me by any one that, having led Greek troops against the barbarians (15), I betrayed the Hellenes, and chose the friendship of the barbarian. No! since you do not choose to obey and follow me, I will follow after you. Whatever beside, I will share your fate. I look upon you as my country, my friends, my allies; with you I think I shall be honoured, wherever I be; without you I do not see how I can help a friend or hurt a foe. My decision is taken. Wherever you go, I go also."

Such were his words. But the soldiers, not only his own, but the rest also, when they heard what he said, and how he had scouted the idea of going up to the great king's palace (16), expressed their approval; and more than two thousand men deserted Xenias and Pasion, and took their arms and baggage-train, and came and encamped with Clearchus. But Cyrus, in despair and vexation at this turn of affairs, sent for Clearchus. He refused to come; but, without the knowledge of the soldiers, sent a message to Cyrus, bidding him keep a good heart, for that all would arrange itself in the right way; and bade him keep on sending for him, whilst he himself refused to go. After that he got together his own men, with those who had joined him, and of the rest any who chose to come, and spoke as follows: "Fellow soldiers, it is clear that the relations of Cyrus to us are identical with ours to him. We are no longer his soldiers, since we have ceased to follow him; and he, on his side, is no longer our paymaster. He, however, no doubt considers himself wronged by us; and though he goes on sending for me, I cannot bring myself to go to him: for two reasons, chiefly from a sense of shame, for I am forced to admit to myself that I have altogether deceived him; but partly, too, because I am afraid of his seizing me and inflicting a penalty on the wrongs which he conceives that I have done him. In my opinion, then, this is no time for us to go to sleep and forget all about ourselves, rather it is high time to deliberate on our next move; and as long as we do remain here, we had better bethink us how we are to abide in security; or, if we are resolved to turn our backs at once, what will be the safest means of retreat; and, further, how we are to procure supplies, for without supplies there is no profit whatsoever in the general or the private soldier. The man with whom we have to deal is an excellent friend to his friends, but a very dangerous enemy to his foes. And he is backed by a force of infantry and cavalry and ships such as we all alike very well see and know, since we can hardly be said to have posted ourselves at any great distance from him. If, then, any one has a suggestion to make, now is the time to speak." With these words he ceased.

Then various speakers stood up; some of their own motion to propound their views; others inspired by Clearchus to dilate on the hopeless difficulty of either staying, or going back without the goodwill of Cyrus. One of these, in particular, with a make-believe of anxiety to commence the homeward march without further pause, called upon them instantly to choose other generals, if Clearchus were not himself prepared to lead them back: "Let them at once purchase supplies" (the market being in the heart of the Asiatic camp), "let them pack up their baggage: let them," he added, "go to Cyrus and ask for some ships in order to return by sea: if he refused to give them ships, let them demand of him a guide to lead them back through a friendly district; and if he would not so much as give them a guide, they could but put themselves, without more ado, in marching order, and send on a detachment to occupy the pass--before Cyrus and the Cilicians, whose property," the speaker added, "we have so plentifully pillaged, can anticipate us." Such were the remarks of that speaker; he was followed by Clearchus, who merely said: "As to my acting personally as general at this season, pray do not propose it: I can see numerous obstacles to my doing so. Obedience, in the fullest, I can render to the man of your choice, that is another matter: and you shall see and know that I can play my part, under command, with the best of you." After Clearchus another spokesman stood up, and proceeded to point out the simplicity of the speaker, who proposed to ask for vessels, just as if Cyrus were minded to renounce the expedition and sail back again. "And let me further point out," he said, "what a simple-minded notion it is to beg a guide of the very man whose designs we are marring. If we can trust any guide whom Cyrus may vouchsafe to us, why not order Cyrus at once to occupy the pass on our behoof? For my part, I should think twice before I set foot on any ships that he might give us, for fear lest he should sink them with his men-of-war; and I should equally hesitate to follow any guide of his: he might lead us into some place out of which we should find it impossible to escape. I should much prefer, if I am to return home against the will of Cyrus at all, to give him the slip, and so begone: which indeed is impossible. But these schemes are simply nonsensical. My proposal is that a deputation of fit persons, with Clearchus, should go to Cyrus: let them go to Cyrus and ask him: what use he proposes to make of us? and if the business is at all similar to that on which he once before employed a body of foreigners--let us by all means follow: let us show that we are the equals of those who accompanied him on his much up formerly. But if the design should turn out to be of larger import than the former one--involving more toil and more danger--we should ask him, either to give us good reasons for following his lead, or else consent to send us away into a friendly country. In this way, whether we follow him, we shall do so as friends, and with heart and soul, or whether we go back, we shall do so in security. The answer to this shall be reported to us here, and when we have heard it, we will advise as to our best course." This resolution was carried, and they chose and sent a deputation with Clearchus, who put to Cyrus the questions which had been agreed upon by the army. Cyrus replied as follows: That he had received news that Abrocomas, an enemy of his, was posted on the Euphrates, twelve stages off; his object was to march against this aforesaid Abrocomas: and if he were still there, he wished to inflict punishment on him, "or if he be fled" (so the reply concluded), "we will there deliberate on the best course." The deputation received the answer and reported it to the soldiers. The suspicion that he was leading them against the king was not dispelled; but it seemed best to follow him. They only demanded an increase of pay, and Cyrus promised to give them half as much again as they had hitherto received--that is to say, a daric and a half a month to each man, instead of a daric. Was he really leading them to attack the king? Not even at this moment was any one apprised of the fact, at any rate in any open and public manner.

September 10, Tuesday
Leaves Tarsus

IV

From this point he marched two stages--ten parasangs--

September 12, Thursday
Arrives at Psarus River

to the river Psarus, which is two hundred feet broad, and from the Psarus he marched a single stage--five parasangs--

{via the Pyramus river or Ceyhan River in Anatolia in the south of Turkey}

September 15, Sunday
Arrives at Issi (Alexander the Great fought the battle of Issus near here. Corresponds to modern day iskenderun and also near the Payas River in Turkey)

to Issi, the last city in Cilicia. It lies on the seaboard--a prosperous, large and flourishing town. Here they halted three days, and here Cyrus was joined by his fleet. There were thirty-five ships from Peloponnesus, with the Lacedaemonian admiral Pythagoras on board. These had been piloted from Ephesus by Tamos the Egyptian, who himself had another fleet of twenty-five ships belonging to Cyrus. These had formed Tamos's blockading squadron at Miletus, when that city sided with Tissaphernes; he had also used them in other military services rendered to Cyrus in his operations against that satrap. There was a third officer on board the fleet, the Lacedaemonian Cheirisophus, who had been sent for by Cyrus, and had brought with him seven hundred hoplites, over whom he was to act as general in the service of Cyrus. The fleet lay at anchor opposite Cyrus's tent. Here too another reinforcement presented itself. This was a body of four hundred hoplites, Hellenic mercenaries in the service of Abrocomas, who deserted him for Cyrus, and joined in the campaign against the king.

September 18, Wednesday
Leaves Issi

From Issi, he marched a single stage--five parasangs--

September 19, Thursday
Arrives at the Gates of Cilicia and Syria

to the gates of Cilicia and Syria. This was a double fortress: the inner and nearer one, which protects Cilicia, was held by Syennesis and a garrison of Cilicians; the outer and further one, protecting Syria, was reported to be garrisoned by a body of the king's troops. Through the gap between the two fortresses flows a river named the Carsus, which is a hundred feet broad, and the whole space between was scarcely more than six hundred yards. To force a passage here would be impossible, so narrow was the pass itself, with the fortification walls stretching down to the sea, and precipitous rocks above; while both fortresses were furnished with gates. It was the existence of this pass which had induced Cyrus to send for the fleet, so as to enable him to lead a body of hoplites inside and outside the gates; and so to force a passage through the enemy, if he were guarding the Syrian gate, as he fully expected to find Abrocomas doing with a large army. This, however, Abrocomas had not done; but as soon as he learnt that Cyrus was in Cilicia, he had turned round and made his exit from Phoenicia, to join the king with an army amounting, as report said, to three hundred thousand men. From this point Cyrus pursued his march, through Syria a single stage-

-five parasangs--

September 20, Friday
Arrives at Myriandus

to Myriandus, a city inhabited by Phoenicians, on the sea-coast. This was a commercial port, and numerous merchant vessels were riding at anchor in the harbour. Here they halted seven days, and here Xenias the Arcadian general, and Pasion the Megarian got on board a trader, and having stowed away their most valuable effects, set sail for home; most people explained the act as the outcome of a fit of jealousy, because Cyrus had allowed Clearchus to retain their men, who had deserted to him, in hopes of returning to Hellas instead of marching against the king; when the two had so vanished, a rumour spread that Cyrus was after them with some ships of war, and some hoped the cowards might be caught, others pitied them, if that should be their fate. But Cyrus summoned the generals and addressed them: "Xenias and Pasion," he said, "have taken leave of us; but they need not flatter themselves that in so doing they have stolen into hiding. I know where they are gone; nor will they owe their escape to speed; I have men-of-war to capture their craft, if I like. But heaven help me! if I mean to pursue them: never shall it be said of me, that I turn people to account as long as they stay with me, but as soon as they are minded to be off, I seize and maltreat them, and strip them of their wealth. Not so! let them go with the consciousness that our behaviour to them is better than theirs to us. And yet I have their children and wives safe under lock and key in Tralles; but they shall not be deprived even of these. They shall receive them back in return for their former goodness to me." So he spoke, and the Hellenes, even those who had been out of heart at the thought of marching up the country, when they heard of the nobleness of Cyrus, were happier and more eager to follow him on his path.

September 27, Friday
Leaves Myriandus

After this Cyrus marched onwards four stages--twenty parasangs--

October 01,
Arrives at the River Chalus

to the river Chalus. That river is a hundred feet broad, and is stocked with tame fish which the Syrians regard as gods, and will not suffer to be injured--and so too the pigeons of the place. The villages in which they encamped belonged to Parysatis, as part of her girdle money (17). From this point he marched on five stages--thirty parasangs--

October 06, Tuesday
Arrives at the River Dardas

to the sources of the river Dardas, which is a hundred feet broad. Here stood the palace of Belesys, the ruler of Syria, with its park--which was a very large and beautiful one, and full of the products of all the seasons in their course. But Cyrus cut down the park and burnt the palace. Thence he marched on three stages--fifteen parasangs--

October 09, Wednesday
Arrives at Thapsacus on the Euphrates River (possibly Carchemish, on the modern Turkey-Syria border)

to the river Euphrates, which is nearly half a mile broad. A large and flourishing city, named Thapsacus, stands on its banks. Here they halted five days, and here Cyrus sent for the generals of the Hellenes, and told them that the advance was now to be upon Babylon, against the great king; he bade them communicate this information to the soldiers and persuade them to follow. The generals called an assembly, and announced the news to the soldiers. The latter were indignant and angry with the generals, accusing them of having kept secret what they had long known; and refused to go, unless such a bribe of money were given them as had been given to their predecessors, when they went up with Cyrus to the court of his father, not as now to fight a battle, but on a peaceful errand--the visit of a son to his father by invitation. The demand was reported to Cyrus by the generals, and he undertook to give each man five silver minae as soon as Babylon was reached, and their pay in full, until he had safely conveyed them back to Ionia again. In this manner the Hellenic force were persuaded--that is to say, the majority of them. Menon, indeed, before it was clear what the rest of the soldiers would do--whether, in fact they would follow Cyrus or not--collected his own troops apart and made them the following speech; "Men," he said, "if you will listen to me, there is a method by which, without risk or toil, you may win the special favour of Cyrus beyond the rest of the soldiers. You ask what it is I would have you to do? I will tell you. Cyrus at this instant is begging the Hellenes to follow him to attack the king. I say then: Cross the Euphrates at once, before it is clear what answer the rest will make; if they vote in favour of following, you will get the credit of having set the example, and Cyrus will be grateful to you. He will look upon you as being the heartiest in his cause; he will repay, as of all others he best knows how; while, if the rest vote against crossing, we shall go back again; but as the sole adherents, whose fidelity he can altogether trust, it is you whom Cyrus will turn to account, as commandants of garrisons or captains of companies. You need only ask him for whatever you want, and you will get it from him, as being the friends of Cyrus."

The men heard and obeyed, and before the rest had given their answer, they were already across. But when Cyrus perceived that Menon's troops had crossed, he was well pleased, and he sent Glus to the division in question, with this message: "Soldiers, accept my thanks at present; eventually you shall thank me. I will see to that, or my name is not Cyrus." The soldiers therefore could not but pray heartily for his success; so high their hopes ran. But to Menon, it was said, he sent gifts with lordly liberality. This done, Cyrus proceeded to cross; and in his wake followed the rest of the armament to a man. As they forded, never a man was wetted above the chest: nor ever until this moment, said the men of Thapascus, had the river been so crossed on foot, boats had always been required; but these, at the present time, Abrocomas, in his desire to hinder Cyrus from crossing, had been at pains to burn. Thus the passage was looked upon as a thing miraculous; the river had manifestly retired before the face of Cyrus, like a courtier bowing to his future king.

October 14, Monday
Leaves Thapsacus

From this place he continued his march through Syria nine stages--fifty parasangs--

October 23, Wednesday
Arrives at the River Araxes

and they reached the river Araxes. Here were several villages full of corn and wine; in which they halted three days, and provisioned the army.

October 26, Saturday
Leaves the River Araxes

V

Thence he marched on through Arabia, keeping the Euphrates on the right, five desert stages--thirty-five parasangs.

October 31, Thursday
Arrives at Corsote on the River Mascas (possibly Baghuz on the Euphrates on the Turkey-Syria border)

In this region the ground was one long level plain, stretching far and wide like the sea, full of absinth; whilst all the other vegetation, whether wood or reed, was sweet scented like spice or sweet herb; there were no trees; but there was wild game of all kinds--wild asses in greatest abundance, with plenty of ostriches; besides these, there were bustards and antelopes. These creatures were occasionally chased by the cavalry. The asses, when pursued, would run forward a space, and then stand still--their pace being much swifter than that of horses; and as soon as the horses came close, they went through the same performance. The only way to catch them was for the riders to post themselves at intervals, and to hunt them in relays, as it were. The flesh of those they captured was not unlike venison, only more tender. No one was lucky enough to capture an ostrich. Some of the troopers did give chase, but it had soon to be abandoned; for the bird, in its effort to escape, speedily put a long interval between itself and its pursuers; plying its legs at full speed, and using its wings the while like a sail. The bustards were not so hard to catch when started suddenly; for they only take short flights, like partridges, and are soon tired. Their flesh is delicious. As the army wended its way through this region, they reached the river Mascas, which is one hundred feet in breadth. Here stood a big deserted city called Corsote, almost literally environed by the stream, which flows round it in a circle. Here they halted three days and provisioned themselves.

November 03, Sunday
Leaves Corsote

Thence they continued their march thirteen desert stages--ninety parasangs--with the Euphrates still on their right,

November 16, Saturday
Arrives at the Gates (Pylae, or Amanian Gate or Bahçe Pass; a mountain pass Osmaniye and Gaziantep provinces in south-central Turkey)

until they reached the Gates. On these marches several of the baggage animals perished of hunger, for there was neither grass nor green herb, or tree of any sort; but the country throughout was barren. The inhabitants make their living by quarrying millstones on the river banks, which they work up and take to Babylon and sell, purchasing corn in exchange for their goods. Corn failed the army, and was not to be got for money, except in the Lydian market open in Cyrus's Asiatic army; where a kapithe of wheat or barley cost four shekels; the shekel being equal to seven and a half Attic obols, whilst the kapithe is the equivalent of two Attic choeneces (18), dry measure, so that the soldiers subsisted on meat alone for the whole period. Some of the stages were very long, whenever they had to push on to find water or fodder; and once they found themselves involved in a narrow way, where the deep clay presented an obstacle to the progress of the wagons. Cyrus, with the nobles about him, halted to superintend the operation, and ordered Glus and Pigres to take a body of barbarians and to help in extricating the wagons. As they seemed to be slow about the business, he turned round angrily to the Persian nobles and bade them lend a hand to force the wagons out. Then, if ever, what goes to constitute one branch of good discipline, was to be witnessed. Each of those addressed, just where he chanced to be standing, threw off his purple cloak, and flung himself into the work with as much eagerness as if it had been a charge for victory. Down a steep hill side they flew, with their costly tunics and embroidered trousers--some with the circlets round their necks, and bracelets on their arms--in an instant, they had sprung into the miry clay, and in less time than one could have conceived, they had landed the wagons safe on terra firma.

Altogether it was plain that Cyrus was bent on pressing on the march, and averse to stoppages, except where he halted for the sake of provisioning or some other necessary object; being convinced that the more rapidly he advanced, the less prepared for battle would he find the king; while the slower his own progress, the larger would be the hostile army which he would find collected. Indeed, the attentive observer could see, at a glance, that if the king's empire was strong in its extent of territory and the number of inhabitants, that strength is compensated by an inherent weakness, dependent upon the length of roads and the inevitable dispersion of defensive forces, where an invader insists upon pressing home the war by forced marches. On the opposite side of the Euphrates to the point reached on one of these desert stages, was a large and flourishing city named Charmande. From this town the soldiers made purchases of provisions, crossing the river on rafts, in the following fashion: They took the skins which they used as tent coverings, and filled them with light grass; they then compressed and stitched them tightly together by the ends, so that the water might not touch the hay. On these they crossed and got provisions: wine made from the date-nut, and millet or panic-corn, the common staple of the country. Some dispute or other here occurred between the soldiers of Menon and Clearchus, in which Clearchus sentenced one of Menon's men, as the delinquent, and had him flogged. The man went back to his own division and told them. Hearing what had been done to their comrade, his fellows fretted and fumed, and were highly incensed against Clearchus. The same day Clearchus visited the passage of the river, and after inspecting the market there, was returning with a few followers, on horseback, to his tent, and had to pass through Menon's quarters. Cyrus had not yet come up, but was riding up in the same direction. One of Menon's men, who was splitting wood, caught sight of Clearchus as he rode past, and aimed a blow at him with his axe. The aim took no effect; when another hurled a stone at him, and a third, and then several, with shouts and hisses. Clearchus made a rapid retreat to his own troops, and at once ordered them to get under arms. He bade his hoplites remain in position with their shields resting against their knees, while he, at the head of his Thracians and horsemen, of which he had more than forty in his army--Thracians for the most part-- advanced against Menon's soldiers, so that the latter, with Menon himself, were panic-stricken, and ran to seize their arms; some even stood riveted to the spot, in perplexity at the occurrence. Just then Proxenus came up from behind, as chance would have it, with his division of hoplites, and without a moment's hesitation marched into the open space between the rival parties, and grounded arms; then he fell to begging Clearchus to desist. The latter was not too well pleased to hear his trouble mildly spoken of, when he had barely escaped being stoned to death; and he bade Proxenus retire and leave the intervening space open. At this juncture Cyrus arrived and inquired what was happening. There was no time for hesitation. With his javelins firmly grasped in his hands he galloped up--escorted by some of his faithful bodyguard, who were present--and was soon in the midst, exclaiming: "Clearchus, Proxenus, and you other Hellenes yonder, you know not what

you do. As surely as you come to blows with one another, our fate is sealed-
-this very day I shall be cut to pieces, and so will you: your turn will follow
close on mine. Let our fortunes once take an evil turn, and these barbarians
whom you see around will be worse foes to us than those who are at
present serving the king." At these words Clearchus came to his senses.
Both parties paused from battle, and retired to their quarters: order reigned.

VI

As they advanced from this point (opposite Charmande), they came upon
the hoof-prints and dung of horses at frequent intervals. It looked like the
trail of some two thousand horses. Keeping ahead of the army, these
fellows burnt up the grass and everything else that was good for use. Now
there was a Persian, named Orontas; he was closely related to the king by
birth: and in matters pertaining to war reckoned among the best of Persian
warriors. Having formerly been at war with Cyrus, and afterwards
reconciled to him, he now made a conspiracy to destroy him. he made a
proposal to Cyrus: if Cyrus would furnish him with a thousand horsemen,
he would deal with these troopers, who were burning down everything in
front of them; he would lay an ambuscade and cut them down, or he would
capture a host of them alive; in any case, he would put a stop to their
aggressiveness and burnings; he would see to it that they did not ever get a
chance of setting eyes on Cyrus's army and reporting its advent to the king.
The proposal seemed plausible to Cyrus, who accordingly authorised
Orontas to take a detachment from each of the generals, and be gone. He,
thinking that he had got his horsemen ready to his hand, wrote a letter to
the king, announcing that he would ere long join him with as many troopers
as he could bring; he bade him, at the same time, instruct the royal cavalry
to welcome him as a friend. The letter further contained certain reminders
of his former friendship and fidelity. This despatch he delivered into the
hands of one who was a trusty messenger, as he thought; but the bearer
took and gave it to Cyrus. Cyrus read it. Orontas was arrested. Then Cyrus
summoned to his tent seven of the noblest Persians among his personal
attendants, and sent orders to the Hellenic generals to bring up a body of
hoplites. These troops were to take up a position round his tent. This the
generals did; bringing up about three thousand hoplites. Clearchus was also
invited inside, to assist at the court-martial; a compliment due to the
position he held among the other generals, in the opinion not only of
Cyrus, but also of the rest of the court. When he came out, he reported the
circumstances of the trial (as to which, indeed, there was no mystery) to his
friends. He said that Cyrus opened the inquiry with these words: "I have
invited you hither, my friends, that I may take advice with you, and carry
out whatever, in the sight of God and man, it is right for me to do, as

concerning the man before you, Orontas. The prisoner was, in the first instance, given to me by my father, to be my faithful subject. In the next place, acting, to use his own words, under the orders of my brother, and having hold of the acropolis of Sardis, he went to war with me. I met war with war, and forced him to think it more prudent to desist from war with me: whereupon we shook hands, exchanging solemn pledges. After that," and at this point Cyrus turned to Orontas, and addressed him personally-- "after that, did I do you any wrong?" Answer, "Never." Again another question: "Then later on, having received, as you admit, no injury from me, did you revolt to the Mysians and injure my territory, as far as in you lay?"-- "I did," was the reply. "Then, once more having discovered the limits of your power, did you flee to the altar of Artemis, crying out that you repented? and did you thus work upon my feelings, that we a second time shook hands and made interchange of solemn pledges? Are these things so?" Orontas again assented. "Then what injury have you received from me," Cyrus asked, "that now for the third time, you have been detected in a treasonous plot against me?"--"I must needs do so," he answered. Then Cyrus put one more question: "But the day may come, may it not, when you will once again be hostile to my brother, and a faithful friend to myself?" The other answered: "Even if I were, you could never be brought to believe it, Cyrus." At this point Cyrus turned to those who were present and said: "Such has been the conduct of the prisoner in the past: such is his language now. I now call upon you, and you first, Clearchus, to declare your opinion--what think you?" And Clearchus answered: "My advice to you is to put this man out of the way as soon as may be, so that we may be saved the necessity of watching him, and have more leisure, as far as he is concerned, to requite the services of those whose friendship is sincere."-- "To this opinion," he told us, "the rest of the court adhered." After that, at the bidding of Cyrus, each of those present, in turn, including the kinsmen of Orontas, took him by the girdle; which is as much as to say, "Let him die the death," and then those appointed led him out; and they who in old days were wont to do obeisance to him, could not refrain, even at that moment, from bowing down before him, albeit they knew he was being led forth to death. After they had conducted him to the tent of Artapates, the trustiest of Cyrus's wand-bearers, none set eyes upon him ever again, alive or dead. No one, of his own knowledge, could declare the manner of his death; though some conjectured one thing and some another. No tomb to mark his resting-place, either then or since, was ever seen.

VII

From this place Cyrus marched through Babylonia three stages--twelve parasangs.

November 19, Tuesday
Travelling through Babylonia

Now, on the third stage,

November 20, Wednesday
1st day of preparation for battle

about midnight, Cyrus held a review of the Hellenes and Asiatics in the plain, expecting that the king would arrive the following day with his army to offer battle. He gave orders to Clearchus to take command of the right wing, and to Menon the Thessalian of the left, while he himself undertook to the disposition of his own forces in person. After the review, with the first approach of day, deserters from the great king arrived, bringing Cyrus information about the royal army. Then Cyrus summoned the generals and captains of the Hellenes, and held a council of war to arrange the plan of battle. He took this opportunity also to address the following words of compliment and encouragement to the meeting: "Men of Hellas," he said, "it is certainly not from dearth of barbarians to fight my battles that I put myself at your head as my allies; but because I hold you to be better and stronger than many barbarians. That is why I took you. See then that you prove yourselves to be men worthy of the liberty which you possess, and which I envy you. Liberty--it is a thing which, be well assured, I would choose in preference to all my other possessions, multiplied many times. But I would like you to know into what sort of struggle you are going: learn its nature from one who knows. Their numbers are great, and they come on with much noise; but if you can hold out against these two things, I confess I am ashamed to think, what a sorry set of folk you will find the inhabitants of this land to be. But you are men, and brave you must be, being men: it is agreed; then if you wish to return home, any of you, I undertake to send you back, in such sort that your friends at home shall envy you; but I flatter myself I shall persuade many of you to accept what I will offer you here, in lieu of what you left at home." Here Gaulites, a Samian exile, and a trusty friend of Cyrus, being present, exclaimed: "Ay, Cyrus, but some say you can afford to make large promises now, because you are in the crisis of impending danger; but let matters go well with you, will you recollect? They shake their heads. Indeed, some add that, even if you did recollect, and were ever so willing, you would not be able to make good all your promises, and repay." When Cyrus heard that, he answered: "You forget, sirs, my father's empire stretches southwards to a region where men cannot dwell by reason of the heat, and northwards to a region uninhabitable through cold; but all the intervening space is mapped out in satrapies belonging to my brother's friends: so that if the victory be ours, it will be ours also to put our friends in possession in their room. On the whole my fear is, not that I may not have enough to give to each of my friends, but lest I may not have friends enough on whom to bestow what I have to give, and to each of you Hellenes I will give a crown of gold." So they, when they heard these words, were once more elated than ever themselves, and spread the good news among the rest outside. And there came into his presence both the generals and some of the other Hellenes also, claiming to know what they should have in the event of victory; and Cyrus satisfied the expectations of each and all, and so dismissed them. Now the advice and admonition of all who came into conversation with him was, not to enter the battle himself, but to post himself in rear of themselves; and at this season Clearchus put a question to him: "But do you think that your brother will give battle to you, Cyrus?" and Cyrus answered: "Not without a battle, be assured, shall the prize be won; if he be the son of Darius and Parysatis, and a brother of mine." In the final arming for battle at this juncture, the numbers were as follows: Of Hellenes there were ten thousand four hundred heavy infantry with two thousand five hundred targeteers, while the barbarians with Cyrus reached a total of one hundred thousand. He had too about twenty scythe-chariots. The enemy's forces were reported to number one million two hundred thousand, with two hundred scythe-chariots, besides which he had six thousand cavalry under Artagerses. These formed the immediate vanguard of the king himself. The royal army was marshalled by four generals or field-marshals, each in command of three hundred thousand men. Their names were Abrocomas, Tissaphernes, Gobryas, and Arbaces. (But of this total not more than nine hundred thousand were engaged in the battle, with one hundred and fifty scythe-chariots; since Abrocomas, on his march from Phoenicia, arrived five days too late for the battle.) Such was the information brought to Cyrus by deserters who came in from the king's army before the battle, and it was corroborated after the battle by those of the enemy who were taken prisoners. From this place Cyrus advanced one stage--three parasangs--with the whole body of his troops, Hellenic and barbarian alike in order of battle. He expected the king to give battle the same day, for in the middle of this day's march a deep sunk trench was reached, thirty feet broad, and eighteen feet deep. The trench was carried inland through the plain, twelve parasang's distance, to the wall of Media (19). (Here are canals, flowing from the river Tigris; they are four in number, each a hundred feet broad, and very deep, with corn ships plying upon them; they empty themselves into the Euphrates, and are at intervals of one parasang apart, and are spanned by bridges.)

Between the Euphrates and the trench was a narrow passage, twenty feet only in breadth. The trench itself had been constructed by the great king upon hearing of Cyrus's approach, to serve as a line of defence. Through this narrow passage then Cyrus and his army passed, and found themselves safe inside the trench. So there was no battle to be fought with the king that day; only there were numerous unmistakable traces of horse and infantry in retreat. Here Cyrus summoned Silanus, his Ambraciot soothsayer, and presented him with three thousand darics; because eleven days back, when sacrificing, he had told him that the king would not fight within ten days, and Cyrus had answered: "Well, then, if he does not fight within that time, he will not fight at all; and if your prophecy comes true, I promise you ten talents." So now, that the ten days were passed, he presented him with the above sum. But as the king had failed to hinder the passage of Cyrus's army at the trench, Cyrus himself and the rest concluded that he must have abandoned the idea of offering battle,

November 21, Thursday
2nd day of preparation for battle

so that next day Cyrus advanced with less than his former caution.

2 BATTLE OF CUNAXA AND ITS AFTERMATH

November 22, Friday
Battle of Cunaxa (70 km north of Babylon, on the left bank of the Euphrates)

On the third day he was conducting the march, seated in his carriage, with only a small body of troops drawn up in front of him. The mass of the army was moving on in no kind of order: the soldiers having consigned their heavy arms to be carried in the wagons or on the backs of beasts.

VIII

It was already about full market time (20) and the halting-place at which the army was to take up quarters was nearly reached, when Pategyas, a Persian, a trusty member of Cyrus's personal staff, came galloping up at full speed on his horse, which was bathed in sweat, and to every one he met he shouted in Greek and Persian, as fast as he could ejaculate the words: "The king is advancing with a large army ready for battle." Then ensued a scene of wild confusion. The Hellenes and all alike were expecting to be attacked on the instant, and before they could form their lines. Cyrus sprang from his carriage and donned his corselet; then leaping on to his charger's back, with the javelins firmly clutched, he passed the order to the rest, to arm themselves and fall into their several ranks.

The orders were carried out with alacrity; the ranks shaped themselves. Clearchus held the right wing resting on the Euphrates, Proxenus was next, and after him the rest, while Menon with his troops held the Hellenic left. Of the Asiatics, a body of Paphlagonian cavalry, one thousand strong, were posted beside Clearchus on the right, and with them stood the Hellenic peltasts. On the left was Ariaeus, Cyrus's second in command, and the rest of the barbarian host. Cyrus was with his bodyguard of cavalry about six hundred strong, all armed with corselets like Cyrus, and cuirasses and helmets; but not so Cyrus: he went into battle with head unhelmeted (21). So too all the horses with Cyrus wore forehead-pieces and breast-pieces, and the troopers carried short Hellenic swords.

It was now mid-day, and the enemy was not yet in sight; but with the approach of afternoon was seen dust like a white cloud, and after a considerable interval a black pall as it were spread far and high above the plain. As they came nearer, very soon was seen here and there a glint of bronze and spear-points; and the ranks could plainly be distinguished. On the left were troopers wearing white cuirasses. That is Tissaphernes in command, they said, and next to these a body of men bearing wicker-shields, and next again heavy-armed infantry, with long wooden shields reaching to the feet. These were the Egyptians, they said, and then other cavalry, other bowmen; all were in national divisions, each nation marching in densely-crowded squares. And all along their front was a line of chariots at considerable intervals from one another--the famous scythe-chariots, as they were named--having their scythes fitted to the axle-trees and stretching out slantwise, while others protruded under the chariot-seats, facing the ground, so as to cut through all they encountered. The design was to let them dash full speed into the ranks of the Hellenes and cut them through. Curiously enough the anticipation of Cyrus, when at the council of war he admonished the Hellenes not to mind the shouting of the Asiatics, was not justified. Instead of shouting, they came on in deep silence, softly and slowly, with even tread. At this instant, Cyrus, riding past in person, accompanied by Pigres, his interpreter, and three or four others, called aloud to Clearchus to advance against the enemy's centre, for there the king was to be found: "And if we strike home at this point," he added, "our work is finished." Clearchus, though he could see the compact body at the centre, and had been told by Cyrus that the king lay outside the Hellenic left (for, owing to numerical superiority, the king, while holding his own centre, could well overlap Cyrus's extreme left), still hesitated to draw off his right wing from the river, for fear of being turned on both flanks; and he simply replied, assuring Cyrus that he would take care all went well. At this time the barbarian army was evenly advancing, and the Hellenic division was still riveted to the spot, completing its formation as the various contingents came up. Cyrus, riding past at some distance from the lines, glanced his eye first in one direction and then in the other, so as to take a complete survey of friends and foes; when Xenophon the Athenian, seeing him, rode up from the Hellenic quarter to meet him, asking him whether he had any orders to give. Cyrus, pulling up his horse, begged him to make the announcement generally known that the omens from the victims, internal and external alike, were good (22). While he was still speaking, he heard a confused murmur passing through the ranks, and asked what it meant. The other replied that it was the watchword being passed down for the second time. Cyrus wondered who had given the order, and asked what the watchword was. On being told it was "Zeus our Saviour and Victory," he replied, "I accept it; so let it be," and with that remark rode away to his own position. And now the two battle lines were no more than three or four furlongs apart, when the Hellenes began chanting the paean, and at the same time advanced against the enemy.

But with the forward movement a certain portion of the line curved onwards in advance, with wave-like sinuosity, and the portion left behind quickened to a run; and simultaneously a thrilling cry burst from all lips, like that in honour of the war-god--eleleu! eleleu! and the running became general. Some say they clashed their shields and spears, thereby causing terror to the horses (23); and before they had got within arrowshot the barbarians swerved and took to flight. And now the Hellenes gave chase with might and main, checked only by shouts to one another not to race, but to keep their ranks. The enemy's chariots, reft of their charioteers, swept onwards, some through the enemy themselves, others past the Hellenes. They, as they saw them coming, opened a gap and let them pass. One fellow, like some dumbfoundered mortal on a racecourse, was caught by the heels, but even he, they said, received no hurt, nor indeed, with the single exception of some one on the left wing who was said to have been wounded by an arrow, did any Hellene in this battle suffer a single hurt.

Cyrus, seeing the Hellene's conquering, as far as they at any rate were concerned, and in hot pursuit, was well content; but in spite of his joy and the salutations offered him at that moment by those about him, as though he were already king, he was not led away to join in the pursuit, but keeping his squadron of six hundred horsemen in cloe order, waited and watched to see what the king himself would do. The king, he knew, held the centre of the Persian army. Indeed it is the fashion for the Asiatic monarch to occupy that position during action, for this twofold reason: he holds the safest place, with his troops on either side of him, while, if he has occasion to despatch any necessary rider along the lines, his troops will receive the message in half the time. The king accordingly on this occasion held the centre of his army, but for all that, he was outside Cyrus's left wing; and seeing that no one offered him battle in front, nor yet the troops in front of him, he wheeled as if to encircle the enemy. It was then that Cyrus, in apprehension lest the king might get round to the rear and cut to pieces the

Hellenic body, charged to meet him. Attacking with his six hundred, he mastered the line of troops in front of the king, and put to flight the six thousand, cutting down, as is said, with his own hand their general, Artagerses. But as soon as the rout commenced, Cyrus's own six hundred themselves, in the ardour of pursuit, were scattered, with the exception of a handful who were left with Cyrus himself--chiefly his table companions, so-called. Left alone with these, he caught sight of the king, and the close throng about him. Unable longer to contain himself, with a cry, "I see the man," he rushed at him and dealt a blow at his chest, wounding him through the corselet. This, according to the statement of Ctesias the surgeon (24), who further states that he himself healed the wound. As Cyrus delivered the blow, some one struck him with a javelin under the eye severely; and in the struggle which then ensued between the king and Cyrus and those about them to protect one or other, we have the statement of Ctesias as to the number slain on the king's side, for he was by his side. On the other, Cyrus himself fell, and eight of his bravest companions lay on the top of him. The story says that Artapes, the trustiest among his wand-wearers, when he saw that Cyrus had fallen to the ground, leapt from his horse and threw his arms about him. Then, as one account says, the king bade one slay him as a worthy victim to his brother: others say that Artapates drew his scimitar and slew himself by his own hand. A golden scimitar it is true, he had; he wore also a collar and bracelets and the other ornaments such as the noblest Persians wear; for his kindliness and fidelity had won him honours at the hands of Cyrus.

IX

So died Cyrus; a man the kingliest (25) and most worthy to rule of all the Persians who have lived since the elder Cyrus: according to the concurrent testimony of all who are reputed to have known him intimately. To begin from the beginning, when still a boy, and whilst being brought up with his brother and the other lads, his unrivalled excellence was recognised. For the sons of the noblest Persians, it must be known, are brought up, one and all, at the king's portals. Here lessons of sobriety and self-control may largely be laid to heart, while there is nothing base or ugly for eye or ear to feed upon. There is the daily spectacle ever before the boys of some receiving honour from the king, and again of others receiving dishonour; and the tale of all this is in their ears, so that from earliest boyhood they learn how to rule and to be ruled.

In this courtly training Cyrus earned a double reputation; first he was held to be a paragon of modesty among his fellows, rendering an obedience to his elders which exceeded that of many of his own inferiors; and next he bore away the palm for skill in horsemanship and for love of the animal itself. Nor less in matters of war, in the use of the bow and the javelin, was he held by men in general to be at once the ablest of learners and the most eager practiser. As soon as his age permitted, the same pre-eminence showed itself in his fondness for the chase, not without a certain appetite for perilous adventure in facing the wild beasts themselves. Once a bear made a furious rush at him (26), and without wincing he grappled with her, and was pulled from his horse, receiving wounds the scars of which were visible through life; but in the end he slew the creature, nor did he forget him who first came to his aid, but made him enviable in the eyes of many.

After he had been sent down by his father to be satrap of Lydia and Great Phrygia and Cappadocia, and had been appointed general of the forces, whose business it is to muster in the plain of the Castolus, nothing was more noticeable in his conduct than the importance which he attached to the faithful fulfilment of every treaty or compact or undertaking entered into with others. He would tell no lies to any one. Thus doubtless it was that he won the confidence alike of individuals and of the communities entrusted to his care; or in case of hostility, a treaty made with Cyrus was a guarantee sufficient to the combatant that he would suffer nothing contrary to its terms. Therefore, in the war with Tissaphernes, all the states of their own accord chose Cyrus in lieu of Tissaphernes, except only the men of Miletus, and these were only alienated through fear of him, because he refused to abandon their exiled citizens; and his deeds and words bore emphatic witness to his principle: even if they were weakened in number or in fortune, he would never abandon those who had once become his friends. He made no secret of his endeavour to outdo his friends and his foes alike in reciprocity of conduct. The prayer has been attributed to him, "God grant I may live along enough to recompense my friends and requite my foes with a strong arm." However this may be, no one, at least in our days, ever drew together so ardent a following of friends, eager to lay at his feet their money, their cities, their own lives and persons; nor is it to be inferred from this that he suffered the malefactor and the wrongdoer to laugh him to scorn; on the contrary, these he punished most unflinchingly. It was no rare sight to see on the well-trodden highways, men who had forfeited hand or foot or eye; the result being that throughout the satrapy of Cyrus any one, Hellene or barbarian, provided he were innocent, might fearlessly travel wherever he pleased, and take with him whatever he felt disposed. However, as all allowed, it was for the brave in war that he reserved especial honour. To take the first instance to hand, he had a war with the Pisidians and Mysians. Being himself at the head of an expedition into those territories, he could observe those who voluntarily encountered risks; these he made rulers of the territory which he subjected, and afterwards honoured them with other gifts. So that, if the good and brave were set on a pinnacle of fortune, cowards were recognised as their natural slaves; and so it befell that Cyrus never had lack of volunteers in any service of danger, whenever it was expected that his eye would be upon them. So again, wherever he might discover any one ready to distinguish himself in the service of uprightness, his delight was to make this man richer than those who seek for gain by unfair means. On the same principle, his own administration was in all respects uprightly conducted, and, in particular, he secured the services of an army worthy of the name. Generals, and subalterns alike, came to him from across the seas, not merely to make money, but because they saw that loyalty to Cyrus was a more profitable investment than so many pounds a month. Let any man whatsoever render him willing service, such enthusiasm was sure to win its reward. And so Cyrus could always command the service of the best assistants, it was said, whatever the work might be. Or if he saw any skilful and just steward who furnished well the country over which he ruled, and created revenues, so far from robbing him at any time, to him who had, he delighted to give more. So that toil was a pleasure, and gains were amassed with confidence, and least of all from Cyrus would a man conceal the amount of his possessions, seeing that he showed no jealousy of wealth openly avowed, but his endeavour was rather to turn to account the riches of those who kept them secret. Towards the friends he had made, whose kindliness he knew, or whose fitness as fellow-workers with himself, in aught which he might wish to carry out, he had tested, he showed himself in turn an adept in the arts of courtesy. Just in proportion as he felt the need of this friend or that to help him, so he tried to help each of them in return in whatever seemed to be their heart's desire. Many were the gifts bestowed on him, for many and diverse reasons; no one man, perhaps, ever received more; no one, certainly, was ever more ready to bestow them upon others, with an eye ever to the taste of each, so as to gratify what he saw to be the individual requirement. Many of these presents were sent to him to serve as personal adornments of the body or for battle; and as touching these he would say, "How am I to deck myself out in all these? to my mind a man's chief ornament is the adornment of nobly-adorned friends." Indeed, that he should triumph over his friends in the great matters of welldoing is not surprising, seeing that he was much more powerful than they, but that he should go beyond them in minute attentions, and in an eager desire to give pleasure, seems to me, I must confess, more admirable. Frequently when he had tasted some specially excellent wine, he would send the half remaining flagon to some friend with a message to say: "Cyrus says, this is the best wine he has tasted for a long time, that is his excuse for sending it to you. He hopes you will drink it up to-day with a choice party of friends." Or, perhaps, he would send the remainder of a dish of geese, half loaves of bread, and so forth, the bearer being instructed to say: "This is Cyrus's favourite dish, he hopes you will taste it yourself." Or, perhaps, there was a great dearth of provender, when, through the number of his servants and his own careful forethought, he was enabled to get supplies for himself; at such times he would send to his friends in different parts, bidding them feed their horses on his hay, since it would not do for the horses that carried his friends to go starving. Then, on any long march or expedition, where the crowd of lookers-on would be large, he would call his friends to him and entertain them with serious talk, as much as to say, "These I delight to honour." So that, for myself, and from all that I can hear, I should be disposed to say that no one, Greek or barbarian, was ever so beloved. In proof of this, I may cite the fact that, though Cyrus was the king's vassal and slave, no one ever forsook him to join his master, if I may except the attempt of Orontas, which was abortive. That man, indeed, had to learn that Cyrus was closer to the heart of him on whose fidelity he relied than he himself was. On the other hand, many a man revolted from the king to Cyrus, after they went to war with one another; nor were these nobodies, but rather persons high in the king's affection; yet for all that, they believed that their virtues would obtain a reward more adequate from Cyrus than from the king. Another great proof at once of his own worth and of his capacity rightly to discern all loyal, loving and firm friendship is afforded by an incident which belongs to the last moment of his life. He was slain, but fighting for his life beside him fell also every one of his faithful bodyguard of friends and table-companions, with the sole exception of Ariaeus, who was in command of the cavalry on the left, and he no sooner perceived the fall of Cyrus than he betook himself to flight, with the whole body of troops under his lead. X Then the head of Cyrus and his right hand were severed from the body. But the king and those about him pursued and fell upon the Cyreian camp, and the troops of Ariaeus no longer stood their ground, but fled through their own camp back to the halting-place of the night before--a distance of four parasangs, it was said. So the king and those with him fell to ravaging right and left, and amongst other spoil he captured the Phocaean woman, who was a concubine of Cyrus, witty and beautiful, if fame speaks correctly. The Milesian, who was the younger, was also seized by some of the king's men; but, letting go her outer garment, she made good her escape to the Hellenes, who had been left among the camp followers on guard. These fell at once into line and put to the sword many of the pillagers, though they lost some men themselves; they stuck to the place and succeeded in saving not only that lady, but all else, whether chattels or human beings, which lay within their reach. At this point the king and the Hellenes were something like three miles apart; the one set were pursuing their opponents just as if their conquest had been general; the others were pillaging as merrily as if their victory were already universal. But when the Hellenes learnt that the king and his troops were in the baggage camp; and the king, on his side, was informed by Tissaphernes that the Hellenes were victorious in their quarter of the field, and had gone forward in pursuit, the effect was instantaneous. The king massed his troops and formed into line. Clearchus summoned Proxenus, who was next him, and debated whether to send a detachment or to go in a body to the camp to save it. Meanwhile the king was seen again advancing, as it seemed, from the rear; and the Hellenes, turning right about, prepared to receive his attack then and there. But instead of advancing upon them at that point, he drew off, following the line by which he had passed earlier in the day, outside the left wing of his opponent, and so picked up in his passage those who had deserted to the Hellenes during the battle, as also Tissaphernes and his division. The latter had not fled in the first shock of the encounter; he had charged parallel to the line of the Euphrates into the Greek peltasts, and through them. But charge as he might, he did not lay low a single man. On the contrary, the Hellenes made a gap to let them through, hacking them with their swords and hurling their javelins as they passed. Episthenes of Amphipolis was in command of the peltasts, and he showed himself a sensible man, it was said. Thus it was that Tissaphernes, having got through haphazard, with rather the worst of it, failed to wheel round and return the way he came, but reaching the camp of the Hellenes, there fell in with the king; and falling into order again, the two divisions advanced side by side. When they were parallel with the (original) left wing of the Hellenes, fear seized the latter lest they might take them in flank and enfold them on both sides and cut them down. In this apprehension they determined to extend their line and place the river on their rear. But while they deliberated, the king passed by and ranged his troops in line to meet them, in exactly the same position in which he had advanced to offer battle at the commencement of the engagement. The Hellenes, now seeing them in close proximity and in battle order, once again raised the paean and began the attack with still greater enthusiasm than before: and once again the barbarians did not wait to receive them, but took to flight, even at a greater distance than before. The Hellenes pressed the pursuit until they reached a certain village, where they halted, for above the village rose a mound, on which the king and his party rallied and reformed; they had no infantry any longer, but the crest was crowded with cavalry, so that it was impossible to discover what was happening. They did see, they said, the royal standard, a kind of golden eagle, with wings extended, perched on a bar of wood and raised upon a lance. But as soon as the Hellenes again moved onwards, the hostile cavalry at once left the hillock--not in a body any longer, but in fragments--some streaming from one side, some from another; and the crest was gradually stripped of its occupants, till at last the company was gone. Accordingly, Clearchus did not ascend the crest, but posting his army at its base, he sent Lycius of Syracuse and another to the summit, with orders to inspect the condition of things on the other side, and to report results. Lycius galloped up and investigated, bringing back news that they were fleeing might and main. Almost at that instant the sun sank beneath the horizon. There the Hellenes halted; they grounded arms and rested, marvelling the while that Cyrus was not anywhere to be seen, and that no messenger had come from him. For they were in complete ignorance of his death, and conjectured that either he had gone off in pursuit, or had pushed forward to occupy some point. Left to themselves, they now deliberated, whether they should stay where they were and have the baggage train brought up, or should return to camp. They resolved to return, and about supper time reached the tents. Such was the conclusion of this day. They found the larger portion of their property pillaged, eatables and drinkables alike, not excepting the wagons laden with corn and wine, which Cyrus had prepared in case of some extreme need overtaking the expedition, to divide among the Hellenes. There were four hundred of these wagons, it was said, and these had now been ransacked by the king and his men; so that the greater number of the Hellenes went supperless, having already gone without their breakfasts, since the king had appeared before the usual halt for breakfast. Accordingly, in no better plight than this they passed the night.

BOOK II (In the previous book will be found a full account of the method by which Cyrus collected a body of Greeks when meditating an expedition against his brother Artaxerxes; as also of various occurrences on the march up; of the battle itself, and of the death of Cyrus; and lastly, a description of the arrival of the Hellenes in camp after the battle, and as to how they betook themselves to rest, none suspecting but what they were altogether victorious and that Cyrus lived.)

November 23, Saturday
The day after the Battle of Cunaxa

I

With the break of day the generals met, and were surprised that Cyrus should not have appeared himself, or at any rate have sent some one to tell them what to do. Accordingly, they resolved to put what they had together, to get under arms, and to push forward until they effected junction with Cyrus. Just as they were on the point of starting, with the rising sun came Procles the ruler of Teuthrania. He was a descendant of Damaratus (27) the

Laconian, and with him also came Glus the son of Tamos. These two told them, first, that Cyrus was dead; next, that Ariaeus had retreated with the rest of the barbarians to the halting-place whence they had started at dawn on the previous day; and wished to inform them that, if they were minded to come, he would wait for this one day, but on the morrow he should return home again to Ionia, whence he came.

When they heard these tidings, the generals were sorely distressed; so too were the rest of the Hellenes when they were informed of it. Then Clearchus spoke as follows: "Would that Cyrus were yet alive! But since he is dead, take back this answer to Ariaeus, that we, at any rate, have conquered the king; and, as you yourselves may see, there is not a man left in the field to meet us. Indeed, had you not arrived, we should ere this have begun our march upon the king. Now, we can promise to Ariaeus that, if he will join us here, we will place him on the king's throne. Surely to those who conquer empire pertains." With these words he sent back the messengers and with them he sent Cheirisophus the Laconian, and Menon the Thessalian. That was what Menon himself wished, being, as he was, a friend and intimate of Ariaeus, and bound by mutual ties of hospitality. So these set off, and Clearchus waited for them. The soldiers furnished themselves with food (and drink) as best they might--falling back on the baggage animals, and cutting up oxen and asses. There was no lack of firewood; they need only step forward a few paces from the line where the battle was fought, and they would find arrows to hand in abundance, which the Hellenes had forced the deserters from the king to throw away. There were arrows and wicker shields also, and the huge wooden shields of the Egyptians. There were many targets also, and empty wagons left to be carried off. Here was a store which they were not slow to make use of to cook their meat and serve their meals that day. It was now about full market hour (28) when heralds from the king and Tissaphernes arrived. These were barbarians with one exception. This was a certain Phalinus, a Hellene who lived at the court of Tissaphernes, and was held in high esteem. He gave himself out to be a connoisseur of tactics and the art of fighting with heavy arms. These were the men who now came up, and having summoned the generals of the Hellenes, they delivered themselves of the following message: "The great king having won the victory and slain Cyrus, bids the Hellenes to surrender their arms; to betake themselves to the gates of the king's palace, and there obtain for themselves what terms they can." That was what the heralds said, and the Hellenes listened with heavy hearts; but Clearchus spoke, and his words were few; "Conquerors do not, as a rule, give up their arms"; then turning to the others he added, "I leave it to you, my fellow-generals, to make the best and noblest answer, that ye may, to these gentlemen. I will rejoin you presently." At the moment an official had

36

summoned him to come and look at the entrails which had been taken out, for, as it chanced, he was engaged in sacrificing. As soon as he was gone, Cleanor the Arcadian, by right of seniority, answered: "They would sooner die than give up their arms." Then Proxenus the Theban said: "For my part, I marvel if the king demands our arms as our master, or for the sake of friendship merely, as presents. If as our master, why need he ask for them rather than come and take them? But if he would fain wheedle us out of them by fine speeches, he should tell us what the soldiers will receive in turn for such kindness." In answer to him Phalinus said: "The king claims to have conquered, because he has put Cyrus to death; and who is there now to claim the kingdom as against himself? He further flatters himself that you also are in his power, since he holds you in the heart of his country, hemmed in by impassable rivers; and he can at any moment bring against you a multitude so vast that even if leave were given to rise and slay you could not kill them." After him Theopompus (29) the Athenian spoke. "Phalinus," he said, "at this instant, as you yourself can see, we have nothing left but our arms and our valour. If we keep the former we imagine we can make use of the latter; but if we deliver up our arms we shall presently be robbed of our lives. Do not suppose then that we are going to give up to you the only good things which we possess. We prefer to keep them; and by their help we will do battle with you for the good things which are yours." Phalinus laughed when he heard those words, and said: "Spoken like a philosopher, my fine young man, and very pretty reasoning too; yet, let me tell you, your wits are somewhat scattered if you imagine that your valour will get the better of the king's power." There were one or two others, it was said, who with a touch of weakness in their tone or argument, made answer: "They had proved good and trusty friends to Cyrus, and the king might find them no less valuable. If he liked to be friends with them, he might turn them to any use that pleased his fancy, say for a campaign against Egypt. Their arms were at his service; they would help to lay that country at his feet."

Just then Clearchus returned, and wished to know what answer they had given. The words were barely out of his mouth before Phalinus interrupting, answered: "As for your friends here, one says one thing and one another; will you please give us your opinion"; and he replied: "The sight of you, Phalinus, caused me much pleasure; and not only me, but all of us, I feel sure; for you are a Hellene even as we are--every one of us whom you see before you. In our present plight we would like to take you into our counsel as to what we had better do touching your proposals. I beg you then solemnly, in the sight of heaven--do you tender us such advice as you shall deem best and worthiest, and such as shall bring you honour of after time, when it will be said of you how once on a time Phalinus was sent by the great king to bid certain Hellenes yield up their arms, and when they had taken him into their counsel, he gave them such and such advice. You know that whatever advice you do give us cannot fail to be reported in Hellas." Clearchus threw out these leading remarks in hopes that this man, who was the ambassador from the king, might himself be led to advise them not to give up their arms, in which case the Hellenes would be still more sanguine and hopeful. But, contrary to his expectation, Phalinus turned round and said: "I say that if you have one chance, one hope in ten thousand to wage a war with the king successfully, do not give up your arms. That is my advice. If, however, you have no chance of escape without the king's consent, then I say save yourselves in the only way you can." And Clearchus answered: "So, then, that is your deliberate view? Well, this is our answer, take it back. We conceive that in either case, whether we are expected to be friends with the king, we shall be worth more as friends if we keep our arms than if we yield them to another; or whether we are to go to war, we shall fight better with them than without." And Phalinus said: "That answer we will repeat; but the king bade me tell you this besides, 'Whilst you remain here there is truce; but one step forward or one step back, the truce ends; there is war.' Will you then please inform us as to that point also? Are you minded to stop and keep truce, or is there to be war? What answer shall I take from you?" And Clearchus replied: "Pray answer that we hold precisely the same views on this point as the king."--"How say you the same views?" asked Phalinus. Clearchus made answer: "As long as we stay here there is truce, but a step forward or a step backward, the truce ends; there is war." The other again asked: "Peace or war, what answer shall I make?" Clearchus returned answer once again in the same words: "Truce if we stop, but if we move forwards or backwards war." But what he was minded really to do, that he refused to make further manifest.

II

Phalinus and those that were with him turned and went. But the messengers from Ariaeus, Procles and Cheirisophus came back. As to Menon, he stayed behind with Ariaeus, They brought back this answer from Ariaeus: "'There are many Persians,' he says, 'better than himself who will not suffer him to sit upon the king's throne; but if you are minded to go back with him, you must join him this very night, otherwise he will set off himself to-morrow on the homeward route.'" And Clearchus said: "It had best stand thus between us then. If we come, well and good, be it as you propose; but if we do not come, do whatsoever you think most conducive to your interests." And so he kept these also in the dark as to his real intention. After this, when the sun was already sinking, he summoned the generals and officers, and made the following statement: "Sirs, I sacrificed and found the victims unfavourable to an advance against the king. After all, it is not so surprising perhaps, for, as I now learn, between us and the king flows the river Tigris, navigable for big vessels, and we could not possibly cross it without boats, and boats we have none. On the other hand, to stop here is out of the question, for there is no possibility of getting provisions. However, the victims were quite agreeable to us joining the friends of Cyrus. This is what we must do then. Let each go away and sup on whatever he has. At the first sound of the bugle to turn in, get kit and baggage together; at the second signal, place them on the baggage animals; and at the third, fall in and follow the lead, with the baggage animals on the inside protected by the river, and the troops outside." After hearing the orders, the generals and officers retired, and did as they were bid; and for the future Clearchus led, and the rest followed in obedience to his orders, not that they had expressly chosen him, but they saw that he alone had the sense and wisdom requisite in a general, while the rest were inexperienced (30).

Here, under cover of the darkness which descended, the Thracian Miltocythes, with forty horsemen and three hundred Thracian infantry, deserted to the king; but the rest of the troops--Clearchus leading and the rest following in accordance with the orders promulgated--took their departure, and about midnight reached their first stage, having come up with Ariaeus and his army. They grounded arms just as they stood in rank, and the generals and officers of the Hellenes met in the tent of Ariaeus. There they exchanged oaths--the Hellenes on the one side and Ariaeus with his principal officers on the other--not to betray one another, but to be true to each other as allies. The Asiatics further solemnly pledged themselves by oath to lead the way without treachery. The oaths were ratified by the sacrifice of a bull, a wolf (31), a boar, and a ram over a shield. The Hellenes dipped a sword, the barbarians a lance, into the blood of the victims.

As soon as the pledge was taken, Clearchus spoke: "And now, Ariaeus," he said, "since you and we have one expedition in prospect, will you tell us what you think about the route; shall we return the way we came, or have you devised a better?" He answered: "To return the same way is to perish to a man by hunger; for at this moment we have no provisions whatsoever. During the seventeen last stages, even on our way hither, we could extract nothing from the country; or, if there was now and again anything, we passed over and utterly consumed it. At this time our project is to take another and a longer journey certainly, but we shall not be in straits for provisions. The earliest stages must be very long, as long as we can make them; the object is to put as large a space as possible between us and the royal army; once we are two or three days' journey off, the danger is over. The king will never overtake us. With a small army he will not dare to dog our heels, and with a vast equipment he will lack the power to march quickly. Perhaps he, too, may even find a scarcity of provisions. There," said he, "you asked for my opinion, see, I have given it." Here was a plan of the campaign, which was equivalent to a stampede: helter-skelter they were to run away, or get into hiding somehow; but fortune proved a better general.

November 24, Sunday

For as soon as it was day they recommenced the journey, keeping the sun on their right, and calculating that with the westering rays they would have reached villages in the territory of Babylonia, and in this hope they were not deceived. While it was yet afternoon, they thought they caught sight of some of the enemy's cavalry; and those of the Hellenes who were not in rank ran to their ranks; and Ariaeus, who was riding in a wagon to nurse a wound, got down and donned his cuirass, the rest of his party following his example. Whilst they were arming themselves, the scouts, who had been sent forward, came back with the information that they were not cavalry but baggage animals grazing. It was at once clear to all that they must be somewhere in the neighbourhood of the king's encampment. Smoke could actually be seen rising, evidently from villages not far ahead. Clearchus hesitated to advance upon the enemy, knowing that the troops were tired and hungry; and indeed it was already late. On the other hand he had no mind either to swerve from his route--guarding against any appearance of flight. Accordingly he marched straight as an arrow, and with sunset entered the nearest villages with his vanguard and took up quarters. These villages had been thoroughly sacked and dismantled by the royal army--down to the very woodwork and furniture of the houses. Still, the vanguard contrived to take up their quarters in some sort of fashion; but the rear division, coming up in the dark, had to bivouac as best they could, one detachment after another; and a great noise they made, with hue and cry to one another, so that the enemy could hear them; and those in their immediate proximity actually took to their heels, left their quarters, and decamped, as was plain enough next morning, when not a beast was to be seen, nor sign of camp or wreath of smoke anywhere in the neighbourhood. The king, as it would appear, was himself quite taken aback by the advent of the army; as he fully showed by his proceedings next day. During the progress of this night the Hellenes had their turn of scare--a panic seized them, and there was a noise and clatter, hardly to be explained except by the visitation of some sudden terror. But Clearchus had with him the Eleian Tolmides, the best herald of his time; him he ordered to proclaim silence, and then to give out this proclamation of the generals: "Whoever will give any information as to who let an ass into the camp shall receive a talent of silver in reward." On hearing this proclamation the soldiers made up their minds that their fear was baseless, and their generals safe and sound.

November 25, Monday

At break of day Clearchus gave the order to the Hellenes to get under arms in line of battle, and take up exactly the same position as they held on the day of the battle.

III

And now comes the proof of what I stated above--that the king was utterly taken aback by the sudden apparition of the army; only the day before, he had sent and demanded the surrender of their arms--and now, with the rising sun, came heralds sent by him to arrange a truce. These, having reached the advanced guard, asked for the generals. The guard reported their arrival; and Clearchus, who was busy inspecting the ranks, sent back word to the heralds that they must await his leisure. Having carefully arranged the troops so that from every side they might present the appearance of a compact battle line without a single unarmed man in sight, he summoned the ambassadors, and himself went forward to meet them with the soldiers, who for choice accoutrement and noble aspect were the flower of his force; a course which he had invited the other generals also to adopt. And now, being face to face with the ambassadors, he questioned them as to what their wishes were. They replied that they had come to arrange a truce, and were persons competent to carry proposals from the king to the Hellenes and from the Hellenes to the king. He returned answer to them: "Take back word then to your master, that we need a battle first, for we have had no breakfast; and he will be a brave man who will dare mention the word 'truce' to Hellenes without providing them with breakfast." With this message the heralds rode off, but were back again in no time, which was a proof that the king, or some one appointed by him to transact the business, was hard by. They reported that "the message seemed reasonable to the king; they had now come bringing guides who, if a truce were arranged, would conduct them where they would get provisions." Clearchus inquired "whether the truce was offered to the individual men merely as they went and came, or to all alike." "To all," they replied, "until the king receives your final answer." When they had so spoken, Clearchus, having removed the ambassadors, held a council; and it was resolved to make a truce at once, and then quietly to go and secure provisions; and Clearchus said: "I agree to the resolution; still I do not propose to announce it at once, but to wile away time till the ambassadors begin to fear that we have decided against the truce; though I suspect," he added, "the same fear will be operative on the minds of our soldiers also." As soon as the right moment seemed to have arrived, he delivered his answer in favour of the truce, and bade the ambassadors at once conduct them to the provisions. So these led the way; and Clearchus, without relaxing precaution, in spite of having secured a truce, marched after them with his army in line and himself in command of the rearguard. Over and over again they encountered trenches and conduits so full of water that they could not be crossed without bridges; but they contrived well enough for these by means of trunks of palm trees which had fallen, or which they cut down for the occasion. And here Clearchus's system of superintendence was a study in itself; as he stood with a spear in his left hand and a stick in the other; and when it seemed to him there was any dawdling among the parties told off to the work, he would pick out the right man and down would come the stick; nor, at the same time, was he above plunging into the mud and lending a hand himself, so that every one else was forced for very shame to display equal alacrity. The men told off for the business were the men of thirty years of age; but even the elder men, when they saw the energy of Clearchus, could not resist lending their aid also. What stimulated the haste of Clearchus was the suspicion in his mind that these trenches were not, as a rule, so full of water, since it was not the season to irrigate the plain; and he fancied that the king had let the water on for the express purpose of vividly presenting to the Hellenes the many dangers with which their march was threatened at the very start. Proceeding on their way they reached some villages, where their guides indicated to them that they would find provisions. They were found to contain plenty of corn, and wine made from palm dates, and an acidulated beverage extracted by boiling from the same fruit. As to the palm nuts or dates themselves, it was noticeable that the sort which we are accustomed to see in Hellas were set aside for the domestic servants; those put aside for the masters are picked specimens, and are simply marvellous for their beauty and size, looking like great golden lumps of amber; some specimens they dried and preserved as sweetmeats. Sweet enough they were as an accompaniment of wine, but apt to give headache. Here, too, for the first time in their lives, the men tasted the brain (32) of the palm. No one could help being struck by the beauty of this object, and the peculiarity of its delicious flavour; but this, like the dried fruits, was exceedingly apt to give headache. When this cabbage or brain has been removed from the palm the whole tree withers from top to bottom.

In these villages they remained three days,

November 28, Thursday

and a deputation from the great king arrived--Tissaphernes and the king's brother-in-law and three other Persians--with a retinue of many slaves. As soon as the generals of the Hellenes had presented themselves, Tissaphernes opened the proceedings with the following speech, through the lips of an interpreter: "Men of Hellas, I am your next-door neighbour in Hellas. Therefore was it that I, when I saw into what a sea of troubles you were fallen, regarded it as a godsend, if by any means I might obtain, as a boon from the king, the privilege of bringing you back in safety to your own country: and that, I take it, will earn me gratitude from you and all Hellas. In this determination I preferred my request to the king; I claimed it as a favour which was fairly my due; for was it not I who first announced to him the hostile approach of Cyrus? who supported that announcement by the aid I brought; who alone among the officers confronted with the Hellenes in battle did not flee, but charged right through and united my troops with the king inside your camp, where he was arrived, having slain Cyrus; it was I, lastly, who gave chase to the barbarians under Cyrus, with the help of those here present with me at this moment, which are also among the trustiest followers of our lord the king. Now, I counsel you to give a moderate answer, so that it may be easier for me to carry out my design, if haply I may obtain from him some good thing on your behalf." Thereupon the Hellenes retired and took counsel. Then they answered, and Clearchus was their spokesman: "We neither mustered as a body to make war against the king, nor was our march conducted with that object. But it was Cyrus, as you know, who invented many and divers pretexts, that he might take you off your guard, and transport us hither. Yet, after a while, when we saw that he was in sore straits, we were ashamed in the sight of God and man to betray him, whom we had permitted for so long a season to benefit us. But now that Cyrus is dead, we set up no claim to his kingdom against the king himself; there is neither person nor thing for the sake of which we would care to injure the king's country; we would not choose to kill him if we could, rather we would march straight home, if we were not molested; but, God helping us, we will retaliate on all who injure us. On the other hand, if any be found to benefit us, we do not mean to be outdone in kindly deeds, as far as in us lies." So he spoke, and Tissaphernes listened and replied: "That answer will I take back to the king and bring you word from him again. Until I come again, let the truce continue, and we will furnish you with a market."

November 29, Friday

All next day he did not come back, and the Hellenes were troubled with anxieties,

December 01, Sunday

but on the third day he arrived with the news that he had obtained from the king the boon he asked; he was permitted to save the Hellenes, though there were many gainsayers who argued that it was not seemly for the king to let those who had marched against him depart in peace. And at last he said: "You may now, if you like, take pledges from us, that we will make the countries through which you pass friendly to you, and will lead you back without treachery into Hellas, and will furnish you with a market; and wherever you cannot purchase, we will permit you to take provisions from the district. You, on your side, must swear that you will march as through a friendly country, without damage--merely taking food and drink wherever we fail to supply a market--or, if we afford a market, you shall only obtain provisions by paying for them." This was agreed to, and oaths and pledges exchanged between them--Tissaphernes and the king's brother-in-law upon the one side, and the generals and officers of the Hellenes on the other. After this Tissaphernes said: "And now I go back to the king; as soon as I have transacted what I have a mind to, I will come back, ready equipped, to lead you away to Hellas, and to return myself to my own dominion."

IV

After these things the Hellenes and Ariaeus waited for Tissaphernes, being encamped close to one another: for more than twenty days they waited, during which time there came visitors to Ariaeus, his brother and other kinsfolk. To those under him came certain other Persians, encouraging them and bearing pledges to some of them from the king himself--that he would bear no grudge against them on account of the part they bore in the expedition against him with Cyrus, or for aught else of the things which were past. Whilst these overtures were being made, Ariaeus and his friends gave manifest signs of paying less attention to the Hellenes, so much so that, if for no other reason, the majority of the latter were not well pleased, and they came to Clearchus and the other generals, asking what they were waiting for. "Do we not know full well," they said, "that the king would give a great deal to destroy us, so that other Hellenes may take warning and think twice before they march against the king. To-day it suits his purpose to induce us to stop here, because his army is scattered; but as soon as he has got together another armament, attack us most certainly he will. How do we know he is not at this moment digging away at trenches, or running up walls, to make our path impassable. It is not to be supposed that he will desire us to return to Hellas with a tale how a handful of men like ourselves beat the king at his own gates, laughed him to scorn, and then came home again." Clearchus replied: "I too am keenly aware of all this; but I reason thus: if we turn our backs now, they will say, we mean war and are acting contrary to the truce, and then what follows? First of all, no one will furnish us with a market or means of providing ourselves with food. Next, we shall have no one to guide us; moreover, such action on our part will be a signal to Ariaeus to hold aloof from us, so that not a friend will be left to us; even those who were formerly our friends will now be numbered with our enemies. What other river, or rivers, we may find we have to cross, I do not know; but this we know, to cross the Euphrates in face of resistance is impossible. You see, in the event of being driven to an engagement, we have no cavalry to help us, but with the enemy it is the reverse--not only the most, but the best of his troops are cavalry, so that if we are victorious, we shall kill no one, but if we are defeated, not a man of us can escape. For my part, I cannot see why the king, who has so many advantages on his side, if he desires to destroy us, should swear oaths and tender solemn pledges merely in order to perjure himself in the sight of heaven, to render his word worthless and his credit discreditable the wide world over." These arguments he propounded at length.

{Many authors measure this as only 20 days, however the source clearly states more than 20 days which has been factored in here.}

December 23, Monday

Meanwhile Tissaphernes came back, apparently ready to return home; he had his own force with him, and so had Orontas, who was also present, his. The latter brought, moreover, his bride with him, the king's daughter, whom he had just wedded. The journey was now at length fairly commenced. Tissaphernes led the way, and provided a market. They advanced, and Ariaeus advanced too, at the head of Cyrus's Asiatic troops, side by side with Tissaphernes and Orontas, and with these two he also pitched his camp. The Hellenes, holding them in suspicion, marched separately with the guides, and they encamped on each occasion a parasang apart, or rather less; and both parties kept watch upon each other as if they were enemies, which hardly tended to lull suspicion; and sometimes, whilst foraging for wood and grass and so forth on the same ground, blows were exchanged, which occasioned further embitterments.

December 26, Thursday
Arrival at the Wall of Media

Three stages they had accomplished ere they reached the wall of Media, as it is called, and passed within it. It was built of baked bricks laid upon bitumen. It was twenty feet broad and a hundred feet high, and the length of it was said to be twenty parasangs. It lies at no great distance from Babylon. From this point they marched two stages--eight parasangs--and crossed two canals, the first by a regular bridge, the other spanned by a bridge of seven boats. These canals issued from the Tigris, and from them a whole system of minor trenches was cut, leading over the country, large ones to begin with, and then smaller and smaller, till at last they become the merest runnels, like those in Hellas used for watering millet fields.

December 28, Saturday
Arrival at Sittace (capital of ancient Sittacene)

They reached the river Tigris. At this point there was a large and thickly populated city named Sittace, at a distance of fifteen furlongs from the river. The Hellenes accordingly encamped by the side of that city, near a large and beautiful park, which was thick with all sorts of trees. The Asiatics had crossed the Tigris, but somehow were entirely hidden from view. After supper, Proxenus and Xenophon were walking in front of the place d'armes, when a man came up and demanded of the advanced guard where he could find Proxenus or Clearchus. He did not ask for Menon, and that too though he came from Ariaeus, who was Menon's friend. As soon as Proxenus had said: "I am he, whom you seek," the man replied: "I have been sent by Ariaeus and Artaozus, who have been trusty friends to Cyrus in past days, and are your well-wishers. They warn you to be on your guard, in case the barbarians attack you in the night. There is a large body of troops in the neighbouring park. They also warn you to send and occupy the bridge over the Tigris, since Tissaphernes is minded to break it down in the night, if he can, so that you may not cross, but be caught between the river and the canal." On hearing this they took the man to Clearchus and acquainted him with his statement. Clearchus, on his side, was much disturbed, and indeed alarmed at the news. But a young fellow who was present (33), struck with an idea, suggested that the two statements were inconsistent; as to the contemplated attack and the proposed destruction of the bridge. Clearly, the attacking party must either conquer or be worsted: if they conquer, what need of their breaking down the bridge? "Why! if there were half a dozen bridges," said he, "we should not be any the more able to save ourselves by flight--there would be no place to flee to; but, in the opposite case, suppose we win, with the bridge broken down, it is they who will not be able to save themselves by flight; and, what is worse for them, not a single soul will be able to bring them succour from the other side, for all their numbers, since the bridge will be broken down."

Clearchus listened to the reasoning, and then he asked the messenger, "How large the country between the Tigris and the canal might be?" "A large district," he replied, "and in it are villages and cities numerous and large." Then it dawned upon them: the barbarians had sent the man with subtlety, in fear lest the Hellenes should cut the bridge and occupy the island territory, with the strong defences of the Tigris on the one side and of the canal on the other; supplying themselves with provisions from the country so included, large and rich as it was, with no lack of hands to till it; in addition to which, a harbour of refuge and asylum would be found for any one, who was minded to do the king a mischief. After this they retired to rest in peace, not, however, neglecting to send a guard to occupy the bridge in spite of all, and there was no attack from any quarter whatsoever; nor did any of the enemy's people approach the bridges: so the guards were able to report next morning. But as soon as it was morning, they proceeded to cross the bridge, which consisted of thirty-seven vessels, and in so doing they used the utmost precaution possible; for reports were brought by some of the Hellenes with Tissaphernes that an attempt was to be made to attack them while crossing. All this turned out to be false, though it is true that while crossing they did catch sight of Glus watching, with some others, to see if they crossed the river; but as soon as he had satisfied himself on that point, he rode off and was gone. From the river Tigris they advanced four stages--twenty parasangs--

400 BC

Leap Year

January 01, Wednesday
Arrival at Opis (near the Tigris, close to modern Baghdad). Alexander the Great also visited here in 324 BC in the year before his death. Opis is southeast of modern Baghdad and north of ancient Babylon, possibly at Tall al-Mujailat

to the river Physcus, which is a hundred feet broad and spanned by a bridge. Here lay a large and populous city named Opis, close to which the Hellenes were encountered by the natural brother of Cyrus and Artaxerxes, who was leading a large army from Susa and Ecbatana to assist the king. He halted his troops and watched the Helleens march past. Clearchus led them in column two abreast: and from time to time the vanguard came to a standstill, just so often and just so long the effect repeated itself down to the hindmost man: halt! halt! halt! along the whole line: so that even to the Hellenes themselves their army seemed enormous; and the Persian was fairly astonished at the spectacle. From this place they marched through Media six desert stages--thirty parasangs--

January 07, Tuesday

to the villages of Parysatis, Cyrus's and the king's mother. These Tissaphernes, in mockery of Cyrus, delivered over to the Hellenes to plunder, except that the folk in them were not to be made slaves. They contained much corn, cattle, and other property. From this place they advanced four desert stages--twenty parasangs--keeping the Tigris on the left. On the first of these stages, on the other side of the river, lay a large city; it was a well-to-do place named Caenae, from which the natives used to carry across loaves and cheeses and wine on rafts made of skins.

January 11, Saturday

V

After this they reached the river Zapatas (34), which is four hundred feet broad, and here they halted three days. During the interval suspicions were rife, though no act of treachery displayed itself. Clearchus accordingly resolved to bring to an end these feelings of mistrust, before they led to war. Consequently, he sent a messenger to the Persian to say that he desired an interview with him; to which the other readily consented. As soon as they were met, Clearchus spoke as follows: "Tissaphernes," he said, "I do not forget that oaths have been exchanged between us, and right hands shaken, in token that we will abstain from mutual injury; but I can see that you watch us narrowly, as if we were foes; and we, seeing this, watch you narrowly in return. But as I fail to discover, after investigation, that you are endeavouring to do us a mischief--and I am quite sure that nothing of the sort has ever entered our heads with regard to you--the best plan seemed to me to come and talk the matter over with you, so that, if possible, we might dispel the mutual distrust on either side. For I have known people ere now, the victims in some cases of calumny, or possibly of mere suspicion, who in apprehension of one another and eager to deal the first blow, have committed irreparable wrong against those who neither intended nor so much as harboured a thought of mischief against them. I have come to you under a conviction that such misunderstandings may best be put a stop to by personal intercourse, and I wish to instruct you plainly that you are wrong in mistrusting us. The first and weightiest reason is that the oaths, which we took in the sight of heaven, are a barrier to mutual hostility. I envy not the man whose conscience tells him that he has disregarded these! For in a war with heaven, by what swiftness of foot can a man escape?--in what quarter find refuge?--in what darkness slink away and be hid?--to what strong fortress scale and be out of reach? Are not all things in all ways subject to the gods? is not their lordship over all alike outspread? As touching the gods, therefore, and our oaths, that is how I view this matter. To their safe keeping we consigned the friendship which we solemnly contracted. But turning to matters human, you I look upon as our greatest blessing in this present time. With you every path is plain to us, every river passable, and of provisions we shall know no stint. But without you, all our way is through darkness; for we known nothing concerning it, every river will be an obstacle, each multitude a terror; but, worst terror of all, the vast wilderness, so full of endless perplexity. Nay, if in a fit of madness we murdered you, what then? in slaying our benefactor should we not have challenged to enter the lists against us a more formidable antagonist in the king himself? Let me tell you, how many high hopes I should rob myself of, were I to take in hand to do you mischief.

"I coveted the friendship of Cyrus; I believed him to be abler than any man of his day to benefit those whom he chose; but to-day I look and, behold, it is you who are in his place; the power which belonged to Cyrus and his territory are yours now. You have them, and your own satrapy besides, safe and sound; while the king's power, which was a thorn in the side of Cyrus, is your support. This being so, it would be madness not to wish to be your friend. But I will go further and state to you the reasons of my confidence, that you on your side will desire our friendship. I know that the Mysians are a cause of trouble to you, and I flatter myself that with my present force I could render them humbly obedient to you. This applies to the Pisidians also; and I am told there are many other such tribes besides. I think I can deal with them all; they shall cease from being a constant disturbance to your peace and prosperity. Then there are the Egyptians (35). I know your anger against them to-day is very great. Nor can I see what better force you will find to help you in chastising them than this which marches at my back to-day. Again, if you seek the friendship of any of your neighbours round, there shall be no friend so great as you; if any one annoys you, with us as your faithful servitors you shall belord it over him; and such service we will render you, not as hirelings merely for pay's sake, but for the gratitude which we shall rightly feel to you, to whom we owe our lives. As I dwell on these matters, I confess, the idea of your feeling mistrust of us is so astonishing, that I would give much to discover the name of the man, who is so clever of speech that he can persuade you that we harbour designs against you." Clearchus ended, and Tissaphernes responded thus--

"I am glad, Clearchus, to listen to your sensible remarks; for with the sentiments you hold, if you were to devise any mischief against me, it could only be out of malevolence to yourself. But if you imagine that you, on your side, have any better reason to mistrust the king and me, than we you, listen to me in turn, and I will undeceive you. I ask you, does it seem to you that we lack the means, if we had the will, to destroy you? have we not horsemen enough, or infantry, or whatever other arm you like, whereby we may be able to injure you, without risk of suffering in return? or, possibly, do we seem to you to lack the physical surroundings suitable for attacking you? Do you not see all these great plains, which you find it hard enough to traverse even when they are friendly? and all yonder great mountain chains left for you to cross, which we can at any time occupy in advance and render impassable? and all those rivers, on whose banks we can deal craftily by you, checking and controlling and choosing the right number of you whom we care to fight! Nay, there are some which you will not be able to cross at all, unless we transport you to the other side. "And if at all these points we were worsted, yet 'fire,' as they say, 'is stronger than the fruit of the field': we can burn it down and call up famine in arms against you; against which you, for all your bravery, will never be able to contend. Why then, with all these avenues of attack, this machinery of war, open to us, not one of which can be turned against ourselves, why should we select from among them all that method, which alone in the sight of God is impious and of man abominable? Surely it belongs to people altogether without resources, who are helplessly struggling in the toils of fate, and are villains to boot, to seek accomplishment of their desires by perjury to heaven and faithlessness to their fellows. We are not so unreasoning, Clearchus, nor so foolish. "Why, when we had it in our power to destroy you, did we not proceed to do it? Know well that the cause of this was nothing less than my passion to prove myself faithful to the Hellenes, and that, as Cyrus went up, relying on a foreign force attracted by payment, I in turn might go down strong in the same through service rendered. Various ways in which you Hellenes may be useful to me you yourself have mentioned, but there is one still greater. It is the great king's privilege alone to wear the tiara upright upon his head, yet in your presence it may be given to another mortal to wear it upright, here, upon his heart." Throughout this speech he seemed to Clearchus to be speaking the truth, and he rejoined: "Then are not those worthy of the worst penalties who, in spite of all that exists to cement our friendship, endeavour by slander to make us enemies?" "Even so," replied Tissaphernes, "and if your generals and captains care to come in some open and public way, I will name to you those who tell me that you are plotting against me and the army under me." "Good," replied Clearchus. "I will bring all, and I will show you, on my side, the source from which I derive my information concerning you." After this conversation Tissaphernes, with kindliest expression, invited Clearchus to remain with him at the time, and entertained him at dinner.

January 12, Sunday

Next day Clearchus returned to the camp, and made no secret of his persuasion that he at any rate stood high in the affections of Tissaphernes, and he reported what he had said, insisting that those invited ought to go to Tissaphernes, and that any Hellene convicted of calumnious language ought to be punished, not only as traitors themselves, but as disaffected to their fellow-countrymen. The slanderer and traducer was Menon; so, at any rate, he suspected, because he knew that he had had meetings with Tissaphernes whilst he was with Ariaeus, and was factiously opposed to himself, plotting how to win over the whole army to him, as a means of winning the good graces of Tissaphernes. But Clearchus wanted the entire army to give its mind to no one else, and that refractory people should be put out of the way. Some of the soldiers protested: the captains and generals had better not all go; it was better not to put too much confidence in Tissaphernes. But Clearchus insisted so strongly that finally it was arranged for five generals to go and twenty captains. These were accompanied by about two hundred of the other soldiers, who took the opportunity of marketing. On arrival at the doors of Tissaphernes's quarters the generals were summoned inside. They were Proxenus the Boeotian, Menon the Thessalian, Agias the Arcadian, Clearchus the Laconian, and Socrates the Achaean; while the captains remained at the doors. Not long after that, at one and the same signal, those within were seized and those without cut down; after which some of the barbarian horsemen galloped over the plain, killing every Hellene they encountered, bond or free. The Hellenes, as they looked from the camp, viewed that strange horsemanship with surprise, and could not explain to themselves what it all meant, until Nicarchus the Arcadian came tearing along for bare life with a wound in the belly, and clutching his protruding entrails in his hands. He told them all that had happened. Instantly the Hellenes ran to their arms, one and all, in utter consternation, and fully expecting that the enemy would instantly be down upon the camp. However, they did not all come; only Ariaeus came, and Artaozus and Mithridates, who were Cyrus's most faithful friends; but the interpreter of the Hellenes said he saw and recognised the brother of Tissaphernes also with them. They had at their back other Persians also, armed with cuirasses, as many as three hundred. As soon as they were within a short distance, they bade any general or captain of the Hellenes who might be there to approach and hear a message from the king. After this, two Hellene generals went out with all precaution. These were Cleanor the Orchomenian, and Sophaenetus the Stymphalion, attended by Xenophon the Athenian, who went to learn news of Proxenus. Cheirisophus was at the time away in a village with a party gathering provisions. As soon as they had halted within earshot, Ariaeus said: "Hellenes, Clearchus being shown to have committed perjury and to have broken the truce, has suffered the penalty, and he is dead; but Proxenus and Menon, in return for having given information of his treachery, are in high esteem and honour. As to yourselves, the king demands your arms. He claims them as his, since they belonged to Cyrus, who was his slave." To this the Hellenes made answer by the mouth of Cleanor of Orchomenus, their spokesman, who said, addressing Ariaeus: "Thou villain, Ariaeus, and you the rest of you, who were Cyrus's friends, have you no shame before God or man, first to swear to us that you have the same friends and the same enemies as we ourselves, and then to turn and betray us, making common cause with Tissaphernes, that most impious and villainous of men? With him you have murdered the very men to whom you gave your solemn word and oath, and to the rest of us turned traitors; and, having so done, you join hand with our enemies to come against us." Ariaeus answered: "There is no doubt but that Clearchus has been known for some time to harbour designs against Tissaphernes and Orontas, and all of us who side with them." Taking up this assertion,

Xenophon said: "Well, then, granting that Clearchus broke the truce contrary to our oaths, he has his deserts, for perjurers deserve to perish; but where are Proxenus and Menon, our generals and your good friends and benefactors, as you admit? Send them back to us. Surely, just because they are friends of both parites, they will try to give us the best advice for you and for us." At this, the Asiatics stood discussing with one another for a long while, and then they went away without vouchsafing a word.

VI

The generals who were thus seized were taken up to the king and there decapitated. The first of these, Clearchus, was a thorough soldier, and a true lover of fighting. This is the testimony of all who knew him intimately. As long as the war between the Lacedaemonians and Athenians lasted, he could find occupation at home; but after the peace, he persuaded his own city that the Thracians were injuring the Hellenes, and having secured his object, set sail, empowered by the ephorate to make war upon the Thracians north of the Chersonese and Perinthus. But he had no sooner fairly started than, for some reason or other, the ephors changed their minds, and endeavoured to bring him back again from the isthmus. Thereupon he refused further obedience, and went off with sails set for the Hellespont. In consequence he was condemned to death by the Spartan authorities for disobedience to orders; and now, finding himself an exile, he came to Cyrus. Working on the feelings of that prince, in language described elsewhere, he received from his entertainer a present of ten thousand darics. Having got this money, he did not sink into a life of ease and indolence, but collected an army with it, carried on war against the Thracians, and conquered them in battle, and from that date onwards harried and plundered them with war incessantly, until Cyrus wanted his army; whereupon he at once went off, in hopes of finding another sphere of warfare in his company. These, I take it, were the characteristic acts of a man whose affections are set on warfare. When it is open to him to enjoy peace with honour, no shame, no injury attached, still he prefers war; when he may live at home at ease, he insists on toil, if only it may end in fighting; when it is given to him to keep his riches without risk, he would rather lessen his fortune by the pastime of battle. To put it briefly, war was his mistress; just as another man will spend his fortune on a favourite, or to gratify some pleasure, so he chose to squander his substance on soldiering. But if the life of a soldier was a passion with him, he was none the less a soldier born, as herein appears; danger was a delight to him; he courted it, attacking the enemy by night or by day; and in difficulties he did not lose his head, as all who ever served in a campaign with him would with one consent allow. A good solder! the question arises, Was he equally good as a commander? It must be admitted that, as far as was compatible with his quality of temper, he was; none more so. Capable to a singular degree of devising how his army was to get supplies, and of actually getting them, he was also capable of impressing upon those about him that Clearchus must be obeyed; and that he brought about by the very hardness of his nature. With a scowling expression and a harshly-grating voice, he chastised with severity, and at times with such fury, that he was sorry afterwards himself for what he had done. Yet it was not without purpose that he applied the whip; he had a theory that there was no good to be got out of an unchastened army. A saying of his is recorded to the effect that the soldier who is to mount guard and keep his hands off his friends, and be ready to dash without a moment's hesitation against the foe--must fear his commander more than the enemy. Accordingly, in any strait, this was the man whom the soldiers were eager to obey, and they would have no other in his place. The cloud which lay upon his brow, at those times lit up with brightness; his face became radiant, and the old sternness was so charged with vigour and knitted strength to meet the foe, that it savoured of salvation, not of cruelty. But when the pinch of danger was past, and it was open to them to go and taste subordination under some other officer, many forsook him. So lacking in grace of manner was he; but was ever harsh and savage, so that the feeling of the soldiers towards him was that of schoolboys to a master. In other words, though it was not his good fortune ever to have followers inspired solely by friendship or goodwill, yet those who found themselves under him, either by State appointment or through want, or other arch necessity, yielded him implicit obedience. From the moment that he led them to victory, the elements which went to make his soldiers efficient were numerous enough. There was the feeling of confidence in facing the foe, which never left them, and there was the dread of punishment at his hands to keep them orderly. In this way and to this extent he knew how to rule; but to play a subordinate part himself he had no great taste; so, at any rate, it was said. At the time of his death he must have been about fifty years of age. Proxenus, the Boeotian, was of a different temperament. It had been the dream of his boyhood to become a man capable of great achievements. In obedience to this passionate desire it was, that he paid his fee to Gorgias of Leontini (36). After enojoying that teacher's society, he flattered himself that he must be at once qualified to rule; and while he was on friendly terms with the leaders of the age, he was not to be outdone in reciprocity of service (37). In this mood he threw himself into the projects of Cyrus, and in return expected to derive from this essay the reward of a great name, large power, and wide wealth. But for all that he pitched his hopes so high, it was none the less evident that he would refuse to gain any of the ends he set before him wrongfully. Righteously and honourably he would obtain them, if he might, or else forego them. As a commander he had the art of leading gentlemen, but he failed to inspire adequately either respect for himself or fear in the soldiers under him. Indeed, he showed a more delicate regard for his soldiers than his subordinates for him, and he was indisputably more apprehensive of incurring their hatred than they were of losing their fidelity. The one thing needful to real and recognised generalship was, he thought, to praise the virtuous and to withhold praise from the evildoer. It can be easily understood, then, that of those who were brought in contact with him, the good and noble indeed were his well-wishers; but he laid himself open to the machinations of the base, who looked upon him as a person to be dealt with as they liked. At the time of his death he was only thirty years of age.

As to Menon the Thessalian (38), the mainspring of his action was obvious; what he sought after insatiably was wealth. Rule he sought after only as a stepping-stone to larger spoils. Honours and high estate he craved for simply that he might extend the area of his gains; and if he studied to be on friendly terms with the powerful, it was in order that he might commit wrong with impunity. The shortest road to the achievement of his desires lay, he thought, through false swearing, lying, and cheating; for in his vocabulary simplicity and truth were synonyms of folly. Natural affection he clearly entertained for nobody. If he called a man his friend it might be looked upon as certain that he was bent on ensnaring him. Laughter at an enemy he considered out of place, but his whole conversation turned upon the ridicule of his associates. In like manner, the possessions of his foes were secure from his designs, since it was no easy task, he thought, to steal from people on their guard; but it was his particular good fortune to have discovered how easy it is to rob a friend in the midst of his security. If it were a perjured person or a wrongdoer, he dreaded him as well armed and intrenched; but the honourable and the truth-loving he tried to practise on, regarding them as weaklings devoid of manhood. And as other men pride themselves on piety and truth and righteousness, so Menon prided himself on a capacity for fraud, on the fabrication of lies, on the mockery and scorn of friends. The man who was not a rogue he ever looked upon as only half educated. Did he aspire to the first place in another man's friendship, he set about his object by slandering those who stood nearest to him in affection. He contrived to secure the obedience of his solders by making himself an accomplice in their misdeeds, and the fluency with which he vaunted his own capacity and readiness for enormous guilt was a sufficient title to be honoured and courted by them. Or if any one stood aloof from him, he set it down as a meritorious act of kindness on his part that during their intercourse he had not robbed him of existence.

As to certain obscure charges brought against his character, these may certainly be fabrications. I confine myself to the following facts, which are known to all. He was in the bloom of youth when he procured from Aristippus the command of his mercenaries; he had not yet lost that bloom when he became exceedingly intimate with Ariaeus, a barbarian, whose liking for fair young men was the explanation; and before he had grown a beard himself, he had contracted a similar relationship with a bearded favourite named Tharypas. When his fellow-generals were put to death on the plea that they had marched with Cyrus against the king, he alone, although he had shared their conduct, was exempted from their fate. But after their deaths the vengeance of the king fell upon him, and he was put to death, not like Clearchus and the others by what would appear to be the speediest of deaths--decapitation--but, as report says, he lived for a year in pain and disgrace and died the death of a felon. Agias the Arcadian and Socrates the Achaean were both among the sufferers who were put to death. To the credit, be it said, of both, no one ever derided either as cowardly in war: no one ever had a fault to find with either on the score of friendship. They were both about thirty-five years of age.

3 ESCAPE AND JOURNEY TO THE BLACK SEA

BOOK III (In the preceding pages of the narrative will be found a full account, not only of the doings of the Hellenes during the advance of Cyrus till the date of the battle, but of the incidents which befell them after Cyrus' death at the commencement of the retreat, while in company with Tissaphernes during the truce.)

I

After the generals had been seized, and the captains and soldiers who formed their escort had been killed, the Hellenes lay in deep perplexity--a prey to painful reflections. Here were they at the king's gates, and on every side environing them were many hostile cities and tribes of men. Who was there now to furnish them with a market? Separated from Hellas by more than a thousand miles, they had not even a guide to point the way. Impassable rivers lay athwart their homeward route, and hemmed them in. Betrayed even by the Asiatics, at whose side they had marched with Cyrus to the attack, they were left in isolation. Without a single mounted trooper to aid them in pursuit: was it not perfectly plain that if they won a battle, their enemies would escape to a man, but if they were beaten themselves, not one soul of them would survive? Haunted by such thoughts, and with hearts full of despair, but few of them tasted food that evening; but few of them kindled even a fire, and many never came into camp at all that night, but took their rest where each chanced to be. They could not close their eyes for very pain and yearning after their fatherlands or their parents, the wife or child whom they never expected to look upon again. Such was the plight in which each and all tried to seek repose. Now there was in that host a certain man, an Athenian (39), Xenophon, who had accompanied Cyrus, neither as a general, nor as an officer, nor yet as a private soldier, but simply

57

on the invitation of an old friend, Proxenus. This old friend had sent to fetch him from home, promising, if he would come, to introduce him to Cyrus, "whom," said Proxenus, "I consider to be worth my fatherland and more to me."

Xenophon having read the letter, consulted Socrates the Athenian, whether he should accept or refuse the invitation. Socrates, who had a suspicion that the State of Athens might in some way look askance at my friendship with Cyrus, whose zealous co-operation with the Lacedaemonians against Athens in the war was not forgotten, advised Xenophon to go to Delphi and there to consult the god as to the desirability of such a journey. Xenophon went and put the question to Apollo, to which of the gods he must pray and do sacrifice, so that he might best accomplish his intended journey and return in safety, with good fortune. Then Apollo answered him: "To such and such gods must thou do sacrifice," and when he had returned home he reported to Socrates the oracle. But he, when he heard, blamed Xenophon that he had not, in the first instance, inquired of the god, whether it were better for him to go or to stay, but had taken on himself to settle that point affirmatively, by inquiring straightway, how he might best perform the journey. "Since, however," continued Socrates, "you did so put the question, you should do what the god enjoined." Thus, and without further ado, Xenophon offered sacrifice to those whom the god had named, and set sail on his voyage. He overtook Proxenus and Cyrus at Sardis, when they were just ready to start on the march up country, and was at once introduced to Cyrus. Proxenus eagerly pressed him to stop--a request which Cyrus with like ardour supported, adding that as soon as the campaign was over he would send him home. The campaign referred to was understood to be against the Pisidians. That is how Xenophon came to join the expedition, deceived indeed, though not by Proxenus, who was equally in the dark with the rest of the Hellenes, not counting Clearchus, as to the intended attack upon the king. Then, though the majority were in apprehension of the journey, which was not at all to their minds, yet, for very shame of one another and Cyrus, they continued to follow him, and with the rest went Xenophon. And now in this season of perplexity, he too, with the rest, was in sore distress, and could not sleep; but anon, getting a snatch of sleep, he had a dream. It seemed to him in a vision that there was a storm of thunder and lightning, and a bolt fell on his father's house, and thereupon the house was all in a blaze. He sprung up in terror, and pondering the matter, decided that in part the dream was good: in that he had seen a great light from Zeus, whilst in the midst of toil and danger. But partly too he feared it, for evidently it had come from Zeus the king. And the fire kindled all around--what could that mean but that he was hemmed in by various perplexities, and so could not escape from the country of the king? The full meaning, however, is to be discovered from what happened after the dream. This is what took place. As soon as he was fully awake, the first clear thought which came into his head was, Why am I lying here? The night advances; with the day, it is like enough, the enemy will be upon us. If we are to fall into the hands of the king, what is left us but to face the most horrible of sights, and to suffer the most fearful pains, and then to die, insulted, an ignominious death? To defend ourselves--to ward off that fate-- not a hand stirs: no one is preparing, none cares; but here we lie, as though it were time to rest and take our ease. I too! what am I waiting for? a general to undertake the work? and from what city? am I waiting till I am older mysef and of riper age? older I shall never be, if to-day I betray myself to my enemies. Thereupon he got up, and called together first Proxenus's officers; and when they were met, he said: "Sleep, sirs, I cannot, nor can you, I fancy, nor lie here longer, when I see in what straits we are. Our enemy, we may be sure, did not open war upon us till he felt he had everything amply ready; yet none of us shows a corresponding anxiety to enter the lists of battle in the bravest style. "And yet, if we yield ourselves and fall into the king's power, need we ask what our fate will be? This man, who, when his own brother, the son of the same parents, was dead, was not content with that, but severed head and hand from the body, and nailed them to a cross. We, then, who have not even the tie of blood in our favour, but who marched against him, meaning to make a slave of him instead of a king--and to slay him if we could: what is likely to be our fate at his hands? Will he not go all lengths so that, by inflicting on us the extreme of ignominy and torture, he may rouse in the rest of mankind a terror of ever marching against him any more? There is no question but that our business is to avoid by all means getting into his clutches. "For my part, all the while the truce lasted, I never ceased pitying ourselves and congratulating the king and those with him, as, like a helpless spectator, I surveyed the extent and quality of their territory, the plenteousness of their provisions, the multitude of their dependants, their cattle, their gold, and their apparel. And then to turn and ponder the condition of our soldiers, without part or lot in these good things, except we bought it; few, I knew, had any longer the wherewithal to buy, and yet our oath held us down, so that we could not provide ourselves otherwise than by purchase. I say, as I reasoned thus, there were times when I dreaded the truce more than I now dread war. "Now, however, that they have abruptly ended the truce, there is an end also to their own insolence and to our suspicion. All these good things of theirs are now set as prizes for the combatants. To whichsoever of us shall prove the better men, will they fall as guerdons; and the gods themselves are the judges of the strife. The gods, who full surely will be on our side, seeing it is our enemies who have taken their names falsely; whilst we, with much to lure us, yet for our oath's sake, and the gods who were our witnesses, sternly held aloof. So that, it seems to me, we have a right to enter upon this contest with much more heart than our foes; and further, we are possessed of bodies more capable than theirs of bearing cold and heat and labour; souls too we have, by the help of heaven, better and braver; nay, the men themselves are more vulnerable, more mortal, than ourselves, if so be the gods vouchsafe to give us victory once again. "Howbeit, for I doubt not elsewhere similar reflections are being made, whatsoever betide, let us not, in heaven's name, wait for others to come and challenge us to noble deeds; let us rather take the lead in stimulating the rest to valour. Show yourselves to be the bravest of officers, and among generals, the worthiest to command. For myself, if you choose to start forwards on this quest, I will follow; or, if you bid me lead you, my age shall be no excuse to stand between me and your orders. At least I am of full age, I take it, to avert misfortune from my own head." Such were the speaker's words; and the officers, when they heard, all, with one exception, called upon him to put himself at their head. This was a certain Apollonides there present, who spoke in the Boeotian dialect. This man's opinion was that it was mere nonsense for any one to pretend they could obtain safety otherwise than by an appeal to the king, if he had skill to enforce it; and at the same time he began to dilate on the difficulties. But Xenophon cut him short. "O most marvellous of men! though you have eyes to see, you do not perceive; though you have ears to hear, you do not recollect. You were present with the rest of us now here when, after the death of Cyrus, the king, vaunting himself on that occurrence, sent dictatorially to bid us lay down our arms. But when we, instead of giving up our arms, put them on and went and pitched our camp near him, his manner changed. It is hard to say what he did not do, he was so at his wit's end, sending us embassies and begging for a truce, and furnishing provisions the while, until he had got it. Or to take the contrary instance, when just now, acting precisely on your principles, our generals and captains went, trusting to the truce, unarmed to a conference with them, what came of it? what is happening at this instant? Beaten, goaded with pricks, insulted, poor souls, they cannot even die: though death, I ween, would be very sweet. And you, who know all this, how can you say that it is mere nonsense to talk of self-defence? how can you bid us go again and try the arts of persuasion? In my opinion, sirs, we ought not to admit this fellow to the same rank with ourselves; rather ought we to deprive him of his captaincy, and load him with packs and treat him as such. The man is a disgrace to his own fatherland and the whole of Hellas, that, being a Hellene, he is what he is." Here Agasias the Stymphalian broke in, exclaiming: "Nay, this fellow has no connection either with Boeotia or with Hellas, none whatever. I have noted both his ears bored like a Lydian's." And so it was. Him then they banished. But the rest visited the ranks, and wherever a general was left, they summoned the general; where he was gone, the lieutenant-general; and where again the captain alone was left, the captain. As soon as they were all met, they seated themselves in front of the place d'armes: the assembled generals and officers, numbering about a hundred. It was nearly midnight when this took place. Thereupon Hieronymous the Eleian, the eldest of Proxenus's captains, commenced speaking as follows: "Generals and captains, it seemed right to us, in view of the present crisis, ourselves to assemble and to summon you, that we might advise upon some practicable course. Would you, Xenophon, repeat what you said to us?" Thereupon Xenophon spoke as follows: "We all know only too well, that the king and Tissaphernes have seized as many of us as they could, and it is clear they are plotting to destroy the rest of us if they can. Our business is plain: it is to do all we can to avoid getting into the power of the barbarians; rather, if we can, we will get them into our power. Rely upon this then, all you who are here assembled, now is your great opportunity. The soldiers outside have their eyes fixed upon you; if they think that you are faint-hearted, they will turn cowards; but if you show them that you are making your own preparations to attack the enemy, and setting an example to the rest--follow you, be assured, they will: imitate you they will. May be, it is but right and fair that you should somewhat excel them, for you are generals, you are commanders of brigades or regiments; and if, while it was peace, you had the advantage in wealth and position, so now, when it is war, you are expected to rise superior to the common herd--to think for them, to toil for them, whenever there be need. "At this very moment you would confer a great boon on the army, if you made it your business to appoint generals and officers to fill the places of those that are lost. For without leaders nothing good or noble, to put it concisely, was ever wrought anywhere; and in military matters this is absolutely true; for if discipline is held to be of saving virtue, the want of it has been the ruin of many ere now. Well, then! when you have appointed all the commanders necessary, it would only be opportune, I take it, if you were to summon the rest of the soldiers and speak some words of encouragement. Even now, I daresay you noticed yourselves the crestfallen air with which they came into camp, the despondency with which they fell to picket duty, so that, unless there is a change for the better, I do not know for what service they will be fit; whether by night, if need were, or even by day. The thing is to get them to turn their thoughts to what they mean to do, instead of to what they are likely to suffer. Do that, and their spirits will soon revive wonderfully. You know, I need hardly remind you, it is not numbers or strength that gives victory in war; but, heaven helping them, to one or other of two combatants it is given to dash with stouter hearts to meet the foe, and such onset, in nine cases out of ten, those others refuse to meet. This observation, also, I have laid to heart, that they, who in matters of war seek in all ways to save their lives, are just they who, as a rule, die dishonourably; whereas they who, recognising that death is the common lot and destiny of all men, strive hard to die nobly: these more frequently, as I observe, do after all attain to old age, or, at any rate, while life lasts, they spend their days more happily. This lesson let all lay to heart this day, for we are just at such a crisis of our fate. Now is the season to be brave ourselves, and to stimulate the rest by our example." With these words he ceased; and after him, Cheirisophus said: "Xenophon, hitherto I knew only so much of you as that you were, I heard, an Athenian, but now I must commend you for your words and for your conduct. I hope that there may be many more like you, for it would prove a public blessing." Then turning to the officers: "And now," said he, "let us waste no time; retire at once, I beg you, and choose leaders where you need them. After you have made your elections, come back to the middle of the camp, and bring the newly appointed officers. After that, we will there summon a general meeting of the soldiers. Let Tolmides, the herald," he added, "be in attendance." With these words on his lips he got up, in order that what was needful might be done at once without delay. After this the generals were chosen. These were Timasion the Dardanian, in place of Clearchus; Xanthicles, an Achaean, in place of Socrates; Cleanor, an Arcadian, in place of Agias; Philesius, an Achaean, in place of Menon; and in place of Proxenus, Xenophon the Athenian.

January 13, Monday

II

By the time the new generals had been chosen, the first faint glimmer of dawn had hardly commenced, as they met in the centre of the camp, and resolved to post an advance guard and to call a general meeting of the soldiers. Now, when these had come together, Cheirisophus the Lacedaemonian first rose and spoke as follows: "Fellow-soldiers, the present posture of affairs is not pleasant, seeing that we are robbed of so many generals and captains and soldiers; and more than that, our former allies, Ariaeus and his men, have betrayed us; still, we must rise above our circumstances to prove ourselves brave men, and not give in, but try to save ourselves by glorious victory if we can; or, if not, at least to die gloriously, and never, while we have breath in our bodies, fall into the hands of our enemies. In which latter case, I fear, we shall suffer things, which I pray the gods may visit rather upon those we hate." At this point Cleanor the Ochomenian stood up and spoke as follows: "You see, men, the perjury and the impiety of the king. You see the faithlessness of Tissaphernes,

professing that he was next-door neighbour to Hellas, and would give a
good deal to save us, in confirmation of which he took an oath to us
himself, he gave us the pledge of his right hand, and then, with a lie upon
his lips, this same man turned round and arrested our generals. He had no
reverence even for Zeus, the god of strangers; but, after entertaining
Clearchus at his own board as a friend, he used his hospitality to delude and
decoy his victims. And Ariaeus, whom we offered to make king, with whom
we exchanged pledges not to betray each other, even this man, without a
particle of fear of the gods, or respect for Cyrus in his grave, though he was
most honoured by Cyrus in lifetime, even he has turned aside to the worst
foes of Cyrus, and is doing his best to injure the dead man's friends. Them
may the gods requite as they deserve! But we, with these things before our
eyes, will not any more be cheated and cajoled by them; we will make the
best fight we can, and having made it, whatever the gods think fit to send,
we will accept." After him Xenophon arose; he was arrayed for war in his
bravest apparel (40): "For," said he to himself, "if the gods grant victory, the
finest attire will match with victory best; or if I must needs die, then for one
who has aspired to the noblest, it is well there should be some outward
correspondence between his expectation and his end." He began his speech
as follows: "Cleanor has spoken of the perjury and faithlessness of the
barbarians, and you yourselves know them only too well, I fancy. If then we
are minded to enter a second time into terms of friendship with them, with
the experience of what our generals, who in all confidence entrusted
themselves to their power, have suffered, reason would we should feel deep
despondency. If, on the other hand, we purpose to take our good swords in
our hands and to inflict punishment on them for what they have done, and
from this time forward will be on terms of downright war with them, then,
God helping, we have many a bright hope of safety." The words were
scarcely spoken when someone sneezed (41), and with one impulse the
soldiers bowed in worship; and Xenophon proceeded: "I propose, sirs,
since, even as we spoke of safety, an omen from Zeus the Saviour has
appeared, we vow a vow to sacrifice to the Saviour thank-offerings for safe
deliverance, wheresoever first we reach a friendly country; and let us couple
with that vow another of individual assent, that we will offer to the rest of
the gods 'according to our ability.' Let all those who are in favour of this
proposal hold up their hands." They all held up their hands, and there and
then they vowed a vow and chanted the battle hymn. But as soon as these
sacred matters were duly ended, he began once more thus: "I was saying
that many and bright are the hopes we have of safety. First of all, we it is
who confirm and ratify the oaths we take by heaven, but our enemies have
taken false oaths and broken the truce, contrary to their solemn word. This
being so, it is but natural that the gods should be opposed to our enemies,
but with ourselves allied; the gods, who are able to make the great ones

quickly small, and out of sore perplexity can save the little ones with ease, what time it pleases them. In the next place, let me recall to your minds the dangers of our own forefathers, that you may see and know that bravery is your heirloom, and that by the aid of the gods brave men are rescued even out of the midst of sorest straits." So was it when the Persians came, and their attendant hosts (42), with a very great armament, to wipe out Athens from the face of the earth--the men of Athens had the heart to withstand them and conquered them. Then they vowed to Artemis that for every man they slew of the enemy, they would sacrifice to the goddess goats so many; and when they could not find sufficient for the slain, they resolved to offer yearly five hundred; and to this day they perform that sacrifice. And at a somewhat later date, when Xerxes assembled his countless hosts and marched upon Hellas, then (43) too our fathers conquered the forefathers of our foes by land and by sea.

"And proofs of these things are yet to be seen in trophies; but the greatest witness of all is the freedom of our cities--the liberty of that land in which you were born and bred. For you call no man master or lord; you bow your heads to none save to the gods alone. Such were your forefathers, and their sons are ye. Think not I am going to say that you put to shame in any way your ancestry--far from it. Not many days since, you too were drawn up in battle face to face with these true descendants of their ancestors, and by the help of heaven you conquered them, though they many times outnumbered you. At that time, it was to win a throne for Cyrus that you showed your bravery; to-day, when the struggle is for your own salvation, what is more natural than that you should show yourselves braver and more zealous still. Nay, it is very meet and right that you should be more undaunted still to-day to face the foe. The other day, though you had not tested them, and before your eyes lay their immeasurable host, you had the heart to go against them with the spirit of your fathers. To-day you have made trial of them, and knowing that, however many times your number, they do not care to await your onset, what concern have you now to be afraid of them?

"Nor let any one suppose that herein is a point of weakness, in that Cyrus's troops, who before were drawn up by your side, have now deserted us, for they are even worse cowards still than those we worsted. At any rate they have deserted us, and sought refuge with them. Leaders of the forlorn hope of flight--far better is it to have them brigaded with the enemy than shoulder to shoulder in our ranks. But if any of you is out of heart to think that we have no cavalry, while the enemy have many squadrons to command, lay to heart this doctrine, that ten thousand horse only equal ten thousand men upon their backs, neither less nor more. Did any one ever die in battle from the bite or kick of a horse? It is the men, the real swordsmen, who do whatever is done in battles. In fact we, on our stout shanks, are better mounted than those cavalry fellows; there they hang on to their horses' necks in mortal dread, not only of us, but of falling off; while we, well planted upon earth, can deal far heavier blows to our assailants, and aim more steadily at who we will. There is one point, I admit, in which their cavalry have the whip-hand of us; it is safer for them than it is for us to run away. "May be, however, you are in good heart about the fighting, but annoyed to think that Tissaphernes will not guide us any more, and that the king will not furnish us with a market any longer. Now, consider, is it better for us to have a guide like Tissaphernes, whom we know to be plotting against us, or to take our chance of the stray people whom we catch and compel to guide us, who will know that any mistake made in leading us will be a sad mistake for their own lives? Again, is it better to be buying provisions in a market of their providing, in scant measure and at high prices, without even the money to pay for them any longer; or, by right of conquest, to help ourselves, applying such measure as suits our fancy best? "Or again, perhaps you admit that our present position is not without its advantages, but you feel sure that the rivers are a difficulty, and think that you were never more taken in than when you crossed them; if so, consider whether, after all, this is not perhaps the most foolish thing which the barbarians have done. No river is impassable throughout; whatever difficulties it may present at some distance from its source, you need only make your way up to the springhead, and there you may cross it without wetting more than your ankles. But, granted that the rivers do bar our passage, and that guides are not forthcoming, what care we? We need feel no alarm for all that. We have heard of the Mysians, a people whom we certainly cannot admit to be better than ourselves; and yet they inhabit numbers of large and prosperous cities in the king's own country without asking leave. The Pisidians are an equally good instance, or the Lycaonians. We have seen with our own eyes how they fare: seizing fortresses down in the plains, and reaping the fruits of these men's territory. As to us, I go so far as to assert, we ought never to have let it be seen that we were bent on getting home: at any rate, not so soon; we should have begun stocking and furnishing ourselves, as if we fully meant to settle down for life somewhere or other hereabouts. I am sure that the king would be thrice glad to give the Mysians as many guides as they like, or as many hostages as they care to demand, in return for a safe conduct out of his country; he would make carriage roads for them, and if they preferred to take their departure in coaches and four, he would not say them nay. So too, I am sure, he would be only too glad to accommodate us in the same way, if he saw us preparing to settle down here. But, perhaps, it is just as well that we did not stop; for I fear, if once we learn to live in idleness and to batten in luxury and dalliance with these tall and handsome Median and Persian women and maidens, we shall be like the Lotus-eaters (44), and forget the road home altogether.

"It seems to me that it is only right, in the first instance, to make an effort to return to Hellas and to revisit our hearths and homes, if only to prove to other Hellenes that it is their own faults if they are poor and needy (45), seeing it is in their power to give to those now living a pauper life at home a free passage hither, and convert them into well-to-do burghers at once. Now, sirs, is it not clear that all these good things belong to whoever has strength to hold them?

"Let us look another matter in the face. How are we to march most safely? or where blows are needed, how are we to fight to the best advantage? That is the question. "The first thing which I recommend is to burn the wagons we have got, so that we may be free to march wherever the army needs, and not, practically, make our baggage train our general. And, next, we should throw our tents into the bonfire also: for these again are only a trouble to carry, and do not contribute one grain of good either for fighting or getting provisions. Further, let us get rid of all superfluous baggage, save only what we require for the sake of war, or meat and drink, so that as many of us as possible may be under arms, and as few as possible doing porterage. I need not remind you that, in case of defeat, the owners' goods are not their own; but if we master our foes, we will make them our baggage bearers. "It only rests for me to name the one thing which I look upon as the greatest of all. You see, the enemy did not dare to bring war to bear upon us until they had first seized our generals; they felt that whilst our rulers were there, and we obeyed them, they were no match for us in war; but having got hold of them, they fully expected that the consequent confusion and anarchy would prove fatal to us. What follows? This: Officers and leaders ought to be more vigilant ever than their predecessors; subordinates still more orderly and obedient to those in command now than even they were to those who are gone. And you should pass a resolution that, in case of insubordination, any one who stands by is to aid the officer in chastising the offender. So the enemy will be mightily deceived; for on this day they will behold ten thousand Clearchuses instead of one, who will not suffer one man to play the coward. And now it is high time I brought my remarks to an end, for may be the enemy will be here anon. Let those who are in favour of these proposals confirm them with all speed, that they may be realised in fact; or if any other course seem better, let not any one, even though he be a private soldier, shrink from proposing it. Our common safety is our common need." After this Cheirisophus spoke. He said: "If there is anything else to be done, beyond what Xenophon has mentioned, we shall be able to carry it out presently; but with regard to what he has already proposed, it seems to me the best course to vote upon the matters at once. Those who are in favour of Xenophon's proposals, hold up their hands." They all held them up. Xenophon rose again and said: "Listen, sirs, while I tell you what I think we have need of besides. It is clear that we must march where we can get provisions. Now, I am told there are some splendid villages not more than two miles and a half distant. I should not be surprised, then, if the enemy were to hang on our heels and dog us as we retire, like cowardly curs which rush out at the passer-by and bite him if they can, but when you turn upon them they run away. Such will be their tactics, I take it. It may be safer, then, to march in a hollow square, so as to place the baggage animals and our mob of sutlers in greater security. It will save time to make the appointments at once, and to settle who leads the square and directs the vanguard; who will take command of the two flanks, and who of the rearguard; so that, when the enemy appears, we shall not need to deliberate, but can at once set in motion the machinery in existence. "If any one has any better plan, we need not adopt mine; but if not, suppose Cheirisophus takes the lead, as he is a Lacedaemonian, and the two eldest generals take in charge the two wings respectively, whilst Timasion and I, the two youngest, will for the present guard the rear. For the rest, we can but make experiment of this arrangement, and alter it with deliberation, as from time to time any improvement suggests itself. If any one has a better plan to propose, let him do so."... No dissentient voice was heard. Accordingly he said: "Those in favour of this resolution, hold up their hands." The resolution was carried. "And now," said he, "it would be well to separate and carry out what we have decreed. If any of you has set his heart on seeing his friends again, let him remember to prove himself a man; there is no other way to achieve his heart's wish. Or is mere living an object with any of you, strive to conquer; if to slay is the privilege of victory, to die is the doom of the defeated. Or perhaps to gain money and wealth is your ambition, strive again for mastery; have not conquerors the double gain of keeping what is their own, whilst they seize the possessions of the vanquished?"

III

The speaking was ended; they got up and retired; then they burnt the wagons and the tents, and after sharing with one another what each needed out of their various superfluities, they threw the remnant into the fire. Having done that, they proceeded to make their breakfasts. While they were breakfasting, Mithridates came with about thirty horsemen, and summoning the generals within earshot, he thus addressed them: "Men of Hellas, I have been faithful to Cyrus, as you know well, and to-day I am your well-wisher; indeed, I am here spending my days in great fear: if then I could see any salutory course in prospect, I should be disposed to join you with all my retainers. Please inform me, then, as to what you propose, regarding me as your friend and well-wisher, anxious only to pursue his march in your company." The generals held council, and resolved to give the following answer, Cheirisophus acting as spokesman: "We have resolved to make our way through the country, inflicting the least possible damage, provided we are allowed a free passage homewards; but if any one tries to hinder us, he will have to fight it out with us, and we shall bring all the force in our power to bear." Thereat Mithridates set himself to prove to them that their deliverance, except with the king's good pleasure, was hopeless. Then the meaning of his mission was plain. He was an agent in disguise; in fact, a relation of Tissaphernes was in attendance to keep a check on his loyalty. After that, the generals resolved that it would be better to proclaim open war, without truce or herald, as long as they were in the enemy's country; for they used to come and corrupt the soldiers, and they were even successful with one officer--Nicarchus (46), an Arcadian, who went off in the night with about twenty men.

After this, they breakfasted and crossed the river Zapatas, marching in regular order, with the beasts and mob of the army in the middle. They had not advanced far on their route when Mithridates made his appearance again, with about a couple of hundred horsemen at his back, and bowmen and slingers twice as many, as nimble fellows as a man might hope to see. He approached the Hellenes as if he were friendly; but when they had got fairly to close quarters, all of a sudden some of them, whether mounted or on foot, began shooting with their bows and arrows, and another set with slings, wounding the men. The rearguard of the Hellenes suffered for a while severely without being able to retaliate, for the Cretans had a shorter range than the Persians, and at the same time, being light-armed troops, they lay cooped up within the ranks of the heavy infantry, while the javelin men again did not shoot far enough to reach the enemy's slingers. This being so, Xenophon thought there was nothing for it but to charge, and charge they did; some of the heavy and light infantry, who were guarding the rear, with him; but for all their charging they did not catch a single man. The dearth of cavalry told against the Hellenes; nor were their infantry able to overhaul the enemy's infantry, with the long start they had, and considering the shortness of the race, for it was out of the question to pursue them far from the main body of the army. On the other hand, the Asiatic cavalry, even while fleeing, poured volleys of arrows behind their backs, and wounded the pursuers; while the Hellenes must fall back fighting every step of the way they had measured in the pursuit; so that by the end of that day they had not gone much more than three miles; but in the late afternoon they reached the villages. Here there was a return of the old despondency. Cheirisophus and the eldest of the generals blamed Xenophon for leaving the main body to give chase and endangering himself thereby, while he could not damage the enemy one whit the more.

Xenophon admitted that they were right in blaming him: no better proof of that was wanted than the result. "The fact is," he added, "I was driven to pursue; it was too trying to look on and see our men suffer so badly, and be unable to retaliate. However, when we did charge, there is no denying the truth of what you say; we were not a whit more able to injure the enemy, while we had considerable difficulty in beating a retreat ourselves. Thank heaven they did not come upon us in any great force, but were only a handful of men; so that the injury they did us was not large, as it might have been; and at least it has served to show us what we need. At present the enemy shoot and sling beyond our range, so that our Cretan archers are no match for them; our hand-throwers cannot reach as far; and when we pursue, it is not possible to push the pursuit to any great distance from the main body, and within the short distance no foot-soldier, however fleet of foot, could overtake another foot-soldier who has a bow-shot the start of him. If, then, we are to exclude them from all possibility of injuring us as we march, we must get slingers as soon as possible and cavalry. I am told there are in the army some Rhodians, most of whom, they say, know how to sling, and their missile will reach even twice as far as the Persian slings (which, on account of their being loaded with stones as big as one's fist, have a comparatively short range; but the Rhodians are skilled in the use of leaden bullets (47)). Suppose, then, we investigate and find out first of all who among them possess slings, and for these slings offer the owner the money value; and to another, who will plait some more, hand over the money price; and for a third, who will volunteer to be enrolled as a slinger, invent some other sort of privilege, I think we shall soon find people to come forward capable of helping us. There are horses in the army I know; some few with myself, others belonging to Clearchus's stud, and a good many others captured from the enemy, used for carrying baggage. Let us take the pick of these, supplying their places by ordinary baggage animals, and equipping the horses for cavalry. I should not wonder if our troopers gave some annoyance to these fugitives."

These proposals were carried, and that night two hundred slingers were enrolled,

January 14, Tuesday

and next day as many as fifty horse and horsemen passed muster as duly qualified; buff jackets and cuirasses were provided for them, and a commandant of cavalry appointed to command--Lycius, the son of Polystratus, by name, an Athenian.

IV

That day they remained inactive,

January 15, Wednesday
Arrival at Larissa (likely Nimrud, ancient Kalhu, 30km south of Mosul)

but the next they rose earlier than usual, and set out betimes, for they had a ravine to cross, where they feared the enemy might attack them in the act of crossing. When they were across, Mithridates appeared again with one thousand horse, and archers and slingers to the number of four thousand. This whole body he had got by request from Tissaphernes, and in return he undertook to deliver up the Hellenes to Tissaphernes. He had grown contemptuous since his late attack, when, with so small a detachment, he had done, as he thought, a good deal of mischief, without the slightest loss to himself. When the Hellenes were not only right across, but had got about a mile from the ravine, Mithridates also crossed with his forces. An order had been passed down the lines, what light infantry and what heavy infantry were to take part in the pursuit; and the cavalry were instructed to follow up the pursuit with confidence, as a considerable support was in their rear. So, when Mithridates had come up with them, and they were well within arrow and sling shot, the bugle sounded the signal to the Hellenes; and immediately the detachment under orders rushed to close quarters, and the cavalry charged. There the enemy preferred not to wait, but fled towards the ravine. In this pursuit the Asiatics lost several of their infantry killed, and of their cavalry as many as eighteen were taken prisoners in the ravine. As to those who were slain the Hellenes, acting upon impulse, mutilated their bodies, by way of impressing their enemy with as frightful an image as possible. So fared the foe and so fell back; but the Hellenes, continuing their march in safety for the rest of that day, reached the river Tigris. Here they came upon a large deserted city, the name of which was Larissa (48): a place inhabited by the Medes in days of old; the breadth of its walls was twenty-five feet, and the height of them a hundred, and the circuit of the whole two parasangs. It was built of clay-bricks, supported on a stone basis twenty feet high. This city the king of the Persians (49) besieged, what time the Persians strove to snatch their empire from the Medes, but he could in no wise take it; then a cloud hid the face of the sun and blotted out the light thereof, until the inhabitants were gone out of the city, and so it was taken. By the side of this city there was a stone pyramid in breadth a hundred feet, and in height two hundred feet; in it were many of the barbarians who had fled for refuge from the neighbouring villages.

January 16, Thursday
Arrival at Mespila (ancient Nineveh, just north of Mosul)

From this place they marched one stage of six parasangs to a great deserted fortress (which lay over against the city), and the name of that city was Mespila (50). The Medes once dwelt in it. The basement was made of polished stone full of shells; fifty feet was the breadth of it, and fifty feet the height; and on this basement was reared a wall of brick, the breadth whereof was fifty feet and the height thereof four hundred; and the circuit of the wall was six parasangs. Hither, as the story goes, Medea (51), the king's wife, betook herself in flight what time the Medes lost their empire at the hands of the Persians. To this city also the king of the Pesians laid siege, but could not take it either by length of days or strength of hand. But Zeus sent amazement on the inhabitants thereof, and so it was taken.

January 17, Friday

From this place they marched one stage--four parasangs. But, while still on this stage, Tissaphernes made his appearance. He had with him his own cavalry and a force belonging to Orontas, who had the king's daughter to wife; and there were, moreover, with them the Asiatics whom Cyrus had taken with him on his march up; together with those whom the king's brother had brought as a reinforcement to the king; besides those whom Tissaphernes himself had received as a gift from the king, so that the armament appeared to be very great. When they were close, he halted some of his regiments at the rear and wheeled others into position on either flank, but hesitated to attack, having no mind apparently to run any risks, and contenting himself with an order to his slingers to sling and his archers to shoot. But when the Rhodian slingers and the bowmen (52), posted at intervals, retaliated, and every shot told (for with the utmost pains to miss it would have been hard to do so under the circumstanecs), then Tissaphernes with all speed retired out of range, the other regiments following suit; and for the rest of the day the one party advanced and the other followed. But now the Asiatics had ceased to be dangerous with their sharpshooting. For the Rhodians could reach further than the Persian slingers, or, indeed, than most of the bowmen. The Persian bows are of great size, so that the Cretans found the arrows which were picked up serviceable, and persevered in using their enemies' arrows, and practised shooting with them, letting them fly upwards to a great height (53). There were also plenty of bowstrings found in the villages--and lead, which they turned to account for their slings. As a result of this day, then, the Hellenes chancing upon some villages had no sooner encamped than the barbarians fell back, having had distinctly the worst of it in the skirmishing.

January 18, Saturday

The next day was a day of inaction: they halted and took in supplies, as there was much corn in the villages; but on the day following, the march was continued through the plain (of the Tigris), and Tissaphernes still hung on their skirts with his skirmishers. And now it was that the Hellenes discovered the defect of marching in a square with an enemy following. As a matter of necessity, whenever the wings of an army so disposed draw together, either where a road narrows, or hills close in, or a bridge has to be crossed, the heavy infantry cannot help being squeezed out of their ranks, and march with difficulty, partly from actual pressure, and partly from the general confusion that ensues. Or, supposing the wings are again extended, the troops have hardly recovered from their former distress before they are pulled asunder, and there is a wide space between the wings, and the men concerned lose confidence in themselves, especially with an enemy close behind. What happened, when a bridge had to be crossed or other passage effected, was, that each unit of the force pressed on in anxiety to get over first, and at these moments it was easy for the enemy to make an attack. The generals accordingly, having recognised the defect, set about curing it. To do so, they made six lochi, or divisions of a hundred men apiece, each of which had its own set of captains and under-officers in command of half and quarter companies. It was the duty of these new companies, during a march, whenever the flanks needed to close in, to fall back to the rear, so as to disencumber the wings. This they did by wheeling clear of them. When the sides of the oblong again extended, they filled up the interstices, if the gap were narrow, by columns of companies, if broader, by columns of half-companies, or, if broader still, by columns of quarter-companies, so that the space between was always filled up. If again it were necessary to effect a passage by bridge or otherwise, there was no confusion, the several companies crossing in turns; or, if the occasion arose to form in line of battle, these companies came up to the front and fell in (54).

January 19, Sunday

In this way they advanced four stages,

January 24, Friday

but ere the fifth was completed, they came in sight of a palace of some sort, with villages clustered round it; they could further see that the road leading to this place pursued its course over high undulating hillocks, the spur of the mountain range, under which lay the village. These knolls were a welcome sight to the Hellenes, naturally enough, as the enemy were cavalry. However, when they had issued from the plain and ascended the first crest, and were in the act of descending it so as to mount the next, at this juncture the barbarians came upon them. From the high ground down the sheer steep they poured a volley of darts, slingstones, and arrows, which they discharged "under the lash (55)," wounding many, until they got the better of the Hellenic light troops, and drove them for shelter behind the heavy infantry, so that this day that arm was altogether useless, huddling in the mob of sutlers, both slingers and archers alike.

But when the Hellenes, being so pressed, made an attempt to pursue, they could barely scale to the summit, being heavy-armed troops, while the enemy as lightly sprung away; and they suffered similarly in retiring to join the rest of the army. And then, on the second hill, the whole had to be gone through again; so that when it came to the third hillock, they determined not to move the main body of troops from their position until they had brought up a squadron of light infantry from the right flank of the square to a point on the mountain range. When this detachment were once posted above their pursuers, the latter desisted from attacking the main body in its descent, for fear of being cut off and finding themselves between two assailants. Thus the rest of the day they moved on in two divisions: one set keeping to the road by the hillocks, the other marching parallel on the higher level along the mountains; and thus they reached the villages and appointed eight surgeons to attend to the many wounded.

January 25, Saturday

Here they halted three days for the sake of the wounded chiefly, while a further inducement was the plentiful supply of provisions which they found, wheat and wine, and large stores of barley laid up for horses. These supplies had been collected by the ruling satrap of the country.

January 28, Tuesday

On the fourth day they began their descent into the plain; but when Tissaphernes overtook them, necessity taught them to camp in the first village they caught sight of, and give over the attempt of marching and fighting simultaneously, as so many were hors de combat, being either on the list of wounded themselves, or else engaged in carrying the wounded, or laden with the heavy arms of those so occupied. But when they were once encamped, and the barbarians, advancing upon the village, made an attempt to harass them with their sharp-shooters, the superiority of the Hellenes was pronounced. To sustain a running fight with an enemy constantly attacking was one thing; to keep him at arm's length from a fixed base of action another: and the difference was much in their favour. But when it was late afternoon, the time had come for the enemy to withdraw, since the habit of the barbarian was never to encamp within seven or eight miles of the Hellenic camp. This he did in apprehension of a night attack, for a Persian army is good for nothing at night. Their horses are haltered, and, as a rule, hobbled as well, to prevent their escaping, as they might if loose; so that, if any alarm occurs, the trooper has to saddle and bridle his horse, and then he must put on his own cuirass, and then mount--all which performances are difficult at night and in the midst of confusion. For this reason they always encamped at a distance from the Hellenes. When the Hellenes perceived that they were preparing to retire, and that the order was being given, the herald's cry, "Pack up for starting," might be heard before the enemy was fairly out of earshot. For a while the Asiatics paused, as if unwilling to be gone; but as night closed in, off they went, for it did not suit their notions of expediency to set off on a march and arrive by night. And now, when the Hellenes saw that they were really and clearly gone, they too broke up their camp and pursued their march till they had traversed seven and a half miles. Thus the distance between the two armies grew to be so great, that

January 29, Wednesday

the next day the enemy did not appear at all,

January 31, Friday

nor yet on the third day;

February 01, Saturday

but on the fourth the barbarians had pushed on by a forced night march and occupied a commanding position on the right, where the Hellenes had to pass. It was a narrow mountain spur (56) overhanging the descent into the plain.

But when Cheirisophus saw that this ridge was occupied, he summoned Xenophon from the rear, bidding him at the same time to bring up peltasts to the front. That Xenophon hesitated to do, for Tissaphernes and his whole army were coming up and were well within sight. Galloping up to the front himself, he asked: "Why do you summon me?" The other answered him: "The reason is plain; look yonder; this crest which overhangs our descent has been occupied. There is no passing, until we have dislodged these fellows; why have you not brought up the light infantry?" Xenophon explained: he had not thought it desirable to leave the rear unprotected, with an enemy appearing in the field of view. "However, it is time," he added, "to decide how we are to dislodge these fellows from the crest." At this moment his eye fell on the peak of the mountain, rising immediately above their army, and he could see an approach leading from it to the crest in question where the enemy lay. He exclaimed: "The best thing we can do, Cheirisophus, is to make a dash at the height itself, and with what speed we may. If we take it, the party in command of the road will never be able to stop. If you like, stay in command of the army, and I will go; or, if you prefer, do you go to the mountain, and I will stay here."--"I leave it to you," Cheirisophus answered, "to choose which you like best." Xenophon remarking, "I am the younger," elected to go; but he stipulated for a detachment from the front to accompany him, since it was a long way to fetch up troops from the rear. Accordingly Cheirisophus furnished him with the light infantry from the front, reoccupying their place by those from the centre. He also gave him, to form part of the detachment, the three hundred of the picked corps (57) under his own command at the head of the square.

They set out from the low ground with all the haste imaginable. But the enemy in position on the crest no sooner perceived their advance upon the summit of the pass than they themselves set off full tilt in a rival race for the summit too. Hoarse were the shouts of the Hellenic troops as the men cheered their companions forwards, and hoarse the answering shouts from the troops of Tissaphernes, urging on theirs. Xenophon, mounted on his charger, rode beside his men, and roused their ardour the while. "Now for it, brave sirs; bethink you that this race is for Hellas!--now or never!--to find your boys, your wives; one small effort, and the rest of the march we shall pursue in peace, without ever a blow to strike; now for it." But Soteridas the Sicyonian said: "We are not on equal terms, Xenophon; you are mounted on a horse; I can hardly get along with my shield to carry;" and he, on hearing the reproach, leapt from his horse. In another instant he had pushed Soteridas from the ranks, snatched from him his shield, and begun marching as quickly as he might under the circumstances, having his horseman's cuirass to carry as well, so that he was sore pressed; but he continued to cheer on the troops: exhorting those in front to lead on and the men toiling behind to follow up (58). Soteridas was not spared by the rest of the men. They gave him blows, they pelted him, they showered him with abuse, till they compelled him to take back his shield and march on; and the other, remounting, led them on horseback as long as the footing held; but when the ground became too steep, he left his horse and pressed forward on foot, and so they found themselves on the summit before the enemy.

V

There and then the barbarians turned and fled as best they might, and the Hellenes held the summit, while the troops with Tissaphernes and Ariaeus turned aside and disappeared by another road. The main body with Cheirisophus made its way down into the plain and encamped in a village filled with good things of divers sorts. Nor did this village stand alone; there were others not a few in this plain of the Tigris equally overflowing with plenty. It was now afternoon; and all of a sudden the enemy came in sight on the plain, and succeeded in cutting down some of the Hellenes belonging to parties who were scattered over the flat land in quest of spoil. Indeed, many herds of cattle had been caught whilst being conveyed across to the other side of the river. And now Tissaphernes and his troops made an attempt to burn the villages, and some of the Hellenes were disposed to take the matter deeply to heart, being apprehensive that they might not know where to get provisions if the enemy burnt the villages. Cheirisophus and his men were returning from their sally of defence when Xenophon and his party descended, and the latter rode along the ranks as the rescuing party came up, and greeted them thus: "Do you not see, men of Hellas, they admit that the country is now ours; what they stipulated against our doing when they made the treaty, viz. that we were not to fire the king's country, they are now themselves doing--setting fire to it as if it were not their own. But we will be even with them; if they leave provisions for themselves anywhere, there also shall they see us marching;" and, turning to Cheirisophus, he added: "But it strikes me, we should sally forth against these incendiaries and protect our country." Cheirisophus retorted: "That is not quite my view; I say, let us do a little burning ourselves, and they will cease all the quicker." When they had got back to the villages, while the rest were busy about provisions, the generals and officers met: and here there was deep despondency. For on the one side were exceedingly high mountains; on the other a river of such depth that they failed to reach the bottom with their spears. In the midst of their perplexities, a Rhodian came up with a proposal, as follows: "I am ready, sirs to carry you across, four thousand heavy infantry at a time; if you will furnish me with what I need and give me a talent into the bargain for my pains." When asked, "What shall you need?" he replied: "Two thousand wine-skins. I see there are plenty of sheep and goats and asses. They have only to be flayed, and their skins inflated, and they will readily give us a passage. I shall want also the straps which you use for the baggage animals. With these I shall couple the skins to one another; then I shall moor each skin by attaching stones and letting them down like anchors into the water. Then I shall carry them across, and when I have fastened the links at both ends, I shall place layers of wood on them and a coating of earth on the top of that. You will see in a minute that there's no danger of your drowning, for every skin will be able to support a couple of men without sinking, and the wood and earth will prevent your slipping off." The generals thought it a pretty invention enough, but its realisation impracticable, for on the other side were masses of cavalry posted and ready to bar the passage; who, to begin with, would not suffer the first detachment of crossers to carry out any item of the programme.

February 02, Sunday

Under these circumstances, the next day they turned right about face, and began retracing their steps in the direction of Babylon to the unburnt villages, having previously set fire to those they left, so that the enemy did not ride up to them, but stood and stared, all agape to see in what direction the Hellenes would betake themselves and what they were minded to do. Here, again, while the rest of the soldiers were busy about provisions, the generals and officers met in council, and after collecting the prisoners together, submitted them to a cross-examination touching the whole country round, the names, and so forth, of each district. The prisoners informed them that the regions south, through which they had come, belonged to the district towards Babylon and Media; the road east led to Susa and Ecbatana, where the king is said to spend summer and spring; crossing the river, the road west led to Lydia and Ionia; and the part through the mountains facing towards the Great Bear, led, they said, to the Carduchians (59). They were a people, so said the prisoners, dwelling up on the hills, addicted to war, and not subject to the king; so much so that once, when a royal army one hundred and twenty thousand strong had invaded them, not a man came back, owing to the intricacies of the country. Occasionally, however, they made truce or treaty with the satrap in the plain, and, for the nonce, there would be intercourse: "they will come in and out amongst us," "and we will go in and out amongst them," said the captives.

After hearing these statements, the generals seated apart those who claimed to have any special knowledge of the country in any direction; they put them to sit apart without making it clear which particular route they intended to take. Finally the resolution to which they came was that they must force a passage through the hills into the territory of the Kurds; since, according to what their informants told them, when they had once passed these, they would find themselves in Armenia--the rich and large territory governed by Orontas; and from Armenia, it would be easy to proceed in any direction whatever. Thereupon they offered sacrifice, so as to be ready to start on the march as soon as the right moment appeared to have arrived. Their chief fear was that the high pass over the mountains must be occupied in advance: and a general order was issued, that after supper every one should get his kit together for starting, and repose, in readiness to follow as soon as the word of command was given.

BOOK IV (In the preceding portion of the narrative a full account is given of the incidents of the march up to the battle, and of the occurrences after the battle during the truce which was established between the king and the Hellenes, who marched up with Cyrus, and thirdly, of the fighting to which the Hellenes were exposed, after the king and Tissaphernes had broken the treaty, while a Persian army hung on their rear. Having finally reached a point at which the Tigris was absolutely impassable owing to its depth and breadth, while there was no passage along the bank itself, and the Carduchian hills hung sheer over the river, the generals took the resolution above mentioned of forcing a passage through the mountains. The information derived from the prisoners taken along the way led them to believe that once across the Carduchian mountains they would have the choice either of crossing the Tigris--if they liked to do so--at its sources in Armenia, or of going round them, if so they preferred. Report further said that the sources of the Euphrates also were not far from those of the Tigris, and this is actually the case. The advance into the country of the Carduchians was conducted with a view partly to secrecy, and partly to speed, so as to effect their entry before the enemy could occupy the passes.)

I

It was now about the last watch, and enough of the night remained to allow them to cross the valley under cover of darkness; when, at the word of command, they rose and set off on their march,

February 03, Monday
Arrival at the Carduchian Mountains (possibly the İkiyaka Mountains (also known as Samdi Dağ) near the village of Dağlıca in the district of Yüksekova, modern Turkey)

reaching the mountains at daybreak. At this stage of the march Cheirisophus, at the head of his own division, with the whole of the light troops, led the van, while Xenophon followed behind with the heavy infantry of the rearguard, but without any light troops, since there seemed to be no danger of pursuit or attack from the rear, while they were making their way up hill. Cheirisophus reached the summit without any of the enemy perceiving him. Then he led on slowly, and the rest of the army followed, wave upon wave, cresting the summit and descending into the villages which nestled in the hollows and recesses of the hills. Thereupon the Carduchians abandoned their dwelling places, and with their wives and children fled to the mountains; so there was plenty of provisions to be got for the mere trouble of taking, and the homesteads too were well supplied with a copious store of bronze vessels and utensils which the Hellenes kept their hands off, abstaining at the same time from all pursuit of the folk themselves, gently handling them, in hopes that the Carduchians might be willing to give them friendly passage through their country, since they too were enemies of the king: only they helped themselves to such provisions as fell in their way, which indeed was a sheer necessity. But the Carduchians neither gave ear, when they called to them, nor showed any other friendly sign; and now, as the last of the Hellenes descended into the villages from the pass, they were already in the dark, since, owing to the narrowness of the road, the whole day had been spent in the ascent and descent. At that instant a party of the Carduchians, who had collected, made an attack on the hindmost men, killing some and wounding others with stones and arrows--though it was quite a small body who attacked. The fact was, the approach of the Hellenic army had taken them by surprise; if, however, they had mustered in larger force at this time, the chances are that a large portion of the army would have been annihilated. As it was, they got into quarters, and bivouacked in the villages that night, while the Carduchians kept many watch-fires blazing in a circle on the mountains, and kept each other in sight all round. But with the dawn the generals and officers of the Hellenes met and resolved to proceed, taking only the necessary number of stout baggage animals, and leaving the weaklings behind. They resolved further to let go free all the lately-captured slaves in the host; for the pace of the march was necessarily rendered slow by the quantity of animals and prisoners, and the number of non-combatants in attendance on these was excessive, while, with such a crowd of human beings to satisfy, twice the amount of provisions had to be procured and carried. These resolutions passed, they caused a proclamation by herald to be made for their enforcement.

February 04, Tuesday

When they had breakfasted and the march recommenced, the generals planted themselves a little to one side in a narrow place, and when they found any of the aforesaid slaves or other property still retained, they confiscated them. The soldiers yielded obedience, except where some smuggler, prompted by desire of a good-looking boy or woman, managed to make off with his prize. During this day they contrived to get along after a fashion, now fighting and now resting. But on the next day they were visited by a great storm, in spite of which they were obliged to continue the march, owing to insufficiency of provisions. Cheirisophus was as usual leading in front, while Xenophon headed the rearguard, when the enemy began a violent and sustained attack. At one narrow place after another they came up quite close, pouring in volleys of arrows and slingstones, so that the Hellenes had no choice but to make sallies in pursuit and then again recoil, making but very little progress. Over and over again Xenophon would send an order to the front to slacken pace, when the enemy were pressing their attack severely. As a rule, when the word was so passed up, Cheirisophus slackened; but sometimes instead of slackening, Cheirisophus quickened, sending down a counter-order to the rear to follow on quickly. It was clear that there was something or other happening, but there was no time to go to the front and discover the cause of the hurry. Under the circumstances the march, at any rate in the rear, became very like a rout, and here a brave man lost his life, Cleonymus the Laconian, shot with an arrow in the ribs right through shield and corselet, as also Basias, an

Arcadian, shot clean through the head. As soon as they reached a halting-place, Xenophon, without more ado, came up to Cheirisophus, and took him to task for not having waited, "whereby," he said, "we were forced to fight and flee at the same moment; and now it has cost us the lives of two fine fellows; they are dead, and we were not able to pick up their bodies or bury them." Cheirisophus answered: "Look up there," pointing as he spoke to the mountain, "do you see how inaccessible it all is? only this one road, which you see, going straight up, and on it all that crowd of men who have seized and are guarding the single exit. That is why I hastened on, and why I could not wait for you, hoping to be beforehand with them yonder in seizing the pass: the guides we have got say there is no other way." And Xenophon replied: "But I have got two prisoners also; the enemy annoyed us so much that we laid an ambuscade for them, which also gave us time to recover our breaths; we killed some of them, and did our best to catch one or two alive--for this very reason--that we might have guides who knew the country, to depend upon." The two were brought up at once and questioned separately: "Did they know of any other road than the one visible?" The first said no; and in spite of all sorts of terrors applied to extract a better answer--"no," he persisted. When nothing could be got out of him, he was killed before the eyes of his fellow. This latter then explained: "Yonder man said, he did not know, because he has got a daughter married to a husband in those parts. I can take you," he added, "by a good road, practicable even for beasts." And when asked whether there was any point on it difficult to pass, he replied that there was a col which it would be impossible to pass unless it were occupied in advance. Then it was resolved to summon the officers of the light infantry and some of those of the heavy infantry, and to acquaint them with the state of affairs, and ask them whether any of them were minded to distinguish themselves, and would step forward as volunteers on an expedition. Two or three heavy infantry soldiers stepped forward at once--two Arcadians, Aristonymus of Methydrium, and Agasias of Stymphalus--and in emulation of these, a third, also an Arcadian, Callimachus from Parrhasia, who said he was ready to go, and would get volunteers from the whole army to join him. "I know," he added, "there will be no lack of youngsters to follow where I lead." After that they asked, "Were there any captains of light infantry willing to accompany the expedition?" Aristeas, a Chian, who on several occasions proved his usefulness to the army on such service, volunteered.

II

It was already late afternoon, when they ordered the storming party to take a snatch of food and set off; then they bound the guide and handed him over to them. The agreement was, that if they succeeded in taking the summit they were to guard the position that night, and at daybreak to give a signal by bugle. At this signal the party on the summit were to attack the enemy in occupation of the visible pass, while the generals with the main body would bring up their succours; making their way up with what speed they might. With this understanding, off they set, two thousand strong; and there was a heavy downpour of rain, but Xenophon, with his rearguard, began advancing to the visible pass, so that the enemy might fix his attention on this road, and the party creeping round might, as much as possible, elude observation. Now when the rearguard, so advancing, had reached a ravine which they must cross in order to strike up the steep, at that instant the barbarians began rolling down great boulders, each a wagon load (60), some larger, some smaller; against the rocks they crashed and splintered flying like slingstones in every direction--so that it was absolutely out of the question even to approach the entrance of the pass. Some of the officers finding themselves baulked at this point, kept trying other ways, nor did they desist till darkness set in; and then, when they thought they would not be seen retiring, they returned to supper. Some of them who had been on duty in the rearguard had had no breakfast (it so happened). However, the enemy never ceased rolling down their stones all through the night, as was easy to infer from the booming sound.

The party with the guide made a circuit and surprised the enemy's guards seated round their fire, and after killing some, and driving out the rest, took their places, thinking that they were in possession of the height. As a matter of fact they were not, for above them lay a breast-like hill (61) skirted by the narrow road on which they had found the guards seated. Still, from the spot in question there was an approach to the enemy, who were seated on the pass before mentioned.

Here then they passed the night,

February 05, Wednesday

but at the first glimpse of dawn they marched stealthily and in battle order against the enemy. There was a mist, so that they could get quite close without being observed. But as soon as they caught sight of one another, the trumpet sounded, and with a loud cheer they rushed upon the fellows, who did not wait their coming, but left the road and made off; with the loss of only a few lives however, so nimble were they. Cheirisophus and his men, catching the sound of the bugle, charged up by the well-marked road, while others of the generals pushed their way up by pathless routes, where each division chanced to be; the men mounting as they were best able, and hoisting one another up by means of their spears; and these were the first to unite with the party who had already taken the position by storm. Xenophon, with the rearguard, followed the path which the party with the guide had taken, since it was easiest for the beasts of burthen; one half of his men he had posted in rear of the baggage animals; the other half he had with himself. In their course they encountered a crest above the road, occupied by the enemy, whom they must either dislodge or be themselves cut off from the rest of the Hellenes. The men by themselves could have taken the same route as the rest, but the baggage animals could not mount by any other way than this. Here then, with shouts of encouragement to each other, they dashed at the hill with their storming columns, not from all sides, but leaving an avenue of escape for the enemy, if he chose to avail himself of it. For a while, as the men scrambled up where each best could, the natives kept up a fire of arrows and darts, yet did not receive them at close quarters, but presently left the position in flight. No sooner, however, were the Hellenes safely past this crest, than they came in sight of another in front of them, also occupied, and deemed it advisable to storm it also. But now it struck Xenophon that if they left the ridge just taken unprotected in their rear, the enemy might re-occupy it and attack the baggage animals as they filed past, presenting a long extended line owing to the narrowness of the road by which they made their way. To obviate this, he left some officers in charge of the ridge--Cephisodorus, son of Cephisophon, an Athenian; Amphicrates, the son of Amphidemus, an Athenian; and Archagoras, an Argive exile--while he in person with the rest of the men attacked the second ridge; this they took in the same fashion, only to find that they had still a third knoll left, far the steepest of the three. This was none other than the mamelon mentioned as above the outpost, which had been captured over their fire by the volunteer storming party in the night. But when the Hellenes were close, the natives, to the astonishment of all, without a struggle deserted the knoll. It was conjectured that they had left their position from fear of being encircled and besieged, but the fact was that they, from their higher ground, had been able to see what was going on in the rear, and had all made off in this fashion to attack the rearguard. So then Xenophon, with the youngest men, scaled up to the top, leaving orders to the rest to march on slowly, so as to allow the hindmost companies to unite with them; they were to advance by the road, and when they reached the level to ground arms (62). Meanwhile the Argive Archagoras arrived, in full flight, with the announcement that they had been dislodged from the first ridge, and that Cephisodorus and Amphicrates were slain, with a number of others besides, all in fact who had not jumped down the crags and so reached the rearguard. After this achievement the barbarians came to a crest facing the mamelon, and

Xenophon held a colloquy with them by means of an interpreter, to negotiate a truce, and demanded back the dead bodies. These they agreed to restore if he would not burn their houses, and to these terms Xenophon agreed. Meanwhile, as the rest of the army filed past, and the colloquy was proceeding, all the people of the place had time to gather gradually, and the enemy formed; and as soon as the Hellenes began to descend from the mamelon to join the others where the troops were halted, on rushed the foe, in full force, with hue and cry. They reached the summit of the mamelon from which Xenophon was descending, and began rolling down crags. One man's leg was crushed to pieces. Xenophon was left by his shield-bearer, who carried off his shield, but Eurylochus of Lusia (63), an Arcadian hoplite, ran up to him, and threw his shield in front to protect both of them; so the two together beat a retreat, and so too the rest, and joined the serried ranks of the main body.

After this the whole Hellenic force united, and took up their quarters there in numerous beautiful dwellings, with an ample store of provisions, for there was wine so plentiful that they had it in cemented cisterns. Xenophon and Cheirisophus arranged to recover the dead, and in return restored the guide; afterwards they did everything for the dead, according to the means at their disposal, with the customary honours paid to good men.

February 06, Thursday

Next day they set off without a guide; and the enemy, by keeping up a continuous battle and occupying in advance every narrow place, obstructed passage after passage. Accordingly, whenever the van was obstructed, Xenophon, from behind, made a dash up the hills and broke the barricade, and freed the vanguard by endeavouring to get above the obstructing enemy. Whenever the rear was the point attacked, Cheirisophus, in the same way, made a detour, and by endeavouring to mount higher than the barricaders, freed the passage for the rear rank; and in this way, turn and turn about, they rescued each other, and paid unflinching attention to their mutual needs. At times it happened that, the relief party having mounted, encountered considerable annoyance in their descent from the barbarians, who were so agile that they allowed them to come up quite close, before they turned back, and still escaped, partly no doubt because the only weapons they had to carry were bows and slings. They were, moreover, excellent archers, using bows nearly three cubits long and arrows more than two cubits. When discharging the arrow, they draw the string by getting a purchase with the left foot planted forward on the lower end of the bow.

The arrows pierced through shield and cuirass, and the Hellenes, when they got hold of them, used them as javelins, fitting them to their thongs. In these districts the Cretans were highly serviceable. They were under the command of Stratocles, a Cretan.

III

During this day they bivouacked in the villages which lie above the plain of the river Centrites (64), which is about two hundred feet broad. It is the frontier river between Armenia and the country of the Carduchians. Here the Hellenes recruited themselves, and the sight of the plain filled them with joy, for the river was but six or seven furlongs distant from the mountains of the Carduchians.

{river Centrites was also called Nicephorius and now as the Aras/ Araxes River – likely somewhere near the modern Iran-Turkey border and northwest of lake Urmia}

February 09, Sunday

For the moment then they bivouacked right happily; they had their provisions, they had also many memories of the labours that were now passed; seeing that the last seven days spent in traversing the country of the Carduchians had been one long continuous battle, which had cost them more suffering than the whole of their troubles at the hands of the king and Tissaphernes put together. As though they were truly quit of them for ever, they laid their heads to rest in sweet content.

February 10, Monday

But with the morrow's dawn they espied horsemen at a certain point across the river, armed cap-a-pie, as if they meant to dispute the passage. Infantry, too, drawn up in line upon the banks above the cavalry, threatened to prevent them debouching into Armenia. These troops were Armenian and Mardian and Chaldaean mercenaries belonging to Orontas and Artuchas. The last of the three, the Chaldaeans, were said to be a free and brave set of people. They were armed with long wicker shields and lances. The banks before named on which they were drawn up were a hundred yards or more distant from the river, and the single road which was visible was one leading upwards and looking like a regular artificially constructed highway. At this point the Hellenes endeavoured to cross, but on their making the attempt the water proved to be more than breast-deep, and the river bed was rough with great slippery stones, and as to holding their arms in the water, it was out of the question--the stream swept them away--or if they tried to carry them over the head, the body was left exposed to the arrows and other missiles; accordingly they turned back and encamped there by the bank of the river. At the point where they had themselves been last night, up on the mountains, they could see the Carduchians collected in large numbers and under arms. A shadow of deep despair again descended on their souls, whichever way they turned their eyes--in front lay the river so difficult to ford; over, on the other side, a new enemy threatening to bar the passage; on the hills behind, the Carduchians ready to fall upon their rear should they once again attempt to cross. Thus for this day and night they halted, sunk in perplexity. But Xenophon had a dream. In his sleep he thought that he was bound in fetters, but these, of their own accord, fell from off him, so that he was loosed, and could stretch his legs as freely as he wished (65).

February 11, Tuesday

So at the first glimpse of daylight he came to Cheirisophus and told him that he had hopes that all things would go well, and related to him his dream.

The other was well pleased, and with the first faint gleam of dawn the generals all were present and did sacrifice; and the victims were favourable in the first essay. Retiring from the sacrifice, the generals and officers issued an order to the troops to take their breakfasts; and while Xenophon was taking his, two young men came running up to him, for every one knew that, breakfasting or supping, he was always accessible, or that even if asleep any one was welcome to awaken him who had anything to say bearing on the business of war. What the two young men had at this time to say was that they had been collecting brushwood for fire, and had presently espied on the opposite side, in among some rocks which came down to the river's brink, an old man and some women and little girls depositing, as it would appear, bags of clothes in a cavernous rock. When they saw them, it struck them that it was safe to cross; in any case the enemy's cavalry could not approach at this point. So they stripped naked, expecting to have to swim for it, and with their long knives in their hands began crossing, but going forward crossed without being wet up to the fork. Once across they captured the clothes, and came back again. Accordingly Xenophon at once poured out a libation himself, and bade the two young fellows fill the cup and pray to the gods, who showed to him this vision and to them a passage, to bring all other blessings for them to accomplishment. When he had poured out the libation, he at once led the two young men to Cheirisophus, and they repeated to him their story. Cheirisophus, on hearing it, offered libations also, and when they had performed them, they sent a general order to the troops to pack up ready for starting, while they themselves called a meeting of the generals and took counsel how they might best effect a passage, so as to overpower the enemy in front without suffering any loss from the men behind. And they resolved that Cheirisophus should lead the van and cross with half the army, the other half still remaining behind under Xenophon, while the baggage animals and the mob of sutlers were to cross between the two divisions. When all was duly ordered the move began, the young men pioneering them, and keeping the river on their left. It was about four furlongs' march to the crossing, and as they moved along the bank, the squadrons of cavalry kept pace with them on the opposite side. But when they had reached a point in a line with the ford, and the cliff-like banks of the river, they grounded arms, and first Cheirisophus himself placed a wreath upon his brows, and throwing off his cloak (66), resumed his arms, passing the order to all the rest to do the same, and bade the captains form their companies in open order in deep columns, some to left and some to right of himself. Meanwhile the soothsayers were slaying a victim over the river, and the enemy were letting fly their arrows and slingstones; but as yet they were out of range. As soon as the victims were favourable, all the soldiers began singing the battle hymn, and with the notes of the paean mingled the shouting of the men accompanied by the shriller chant of the women, for there were many women (67) in the camp.

So Cheirisophus with his detachment stepped in. But Xenophon, taking the most active-bodied of the rearguard, began running back at full speed to the passage facing the egress into the hills of Armenia, making a feint of crossing at that point to intercept their cavalry on the river bank. The enemy, seeing Cheirisophus's detachment easily crossing the stream, and Xenophon's men racing back, were seized with the fear of being intercepted, and fled at full speed in the direction of the road which emerges from the stream. But when they were come opposite to it they raced up hill towards their mountains. Then Lycius, who commanded the cavalry, and Aeschines, who was in command of the division of light infantry attached to Cheirisophus, no sooner saw them fleeing so lustily than they were after them, and the soldiers shouted not to fall behind (68), but to follow them right up to the mountains. Cheirisophus, on getting across, forbore to pursue the cavalry, but advanced by the bluffs which reached to the river to attack the enemy overhead. And these, seeing their own cavalry fleeing, seeing also the heavy infantry advancing upon them, abandoned the heights above the river.

Xenophon, as soon as he saw that things were going well on the other side, fell back with all speed to join the troops engaged in crossing, for by this time the Carduchians were well in sight, descending into the plain to attack their rear. Cheirisophus was in possession of the higher ground, and Lycius, with his little squadron, in an attempt to follow up the pursuit, had captured some stragglers of their baggage-bearers, and with them some handsome apparel and drinking-cups. The baggage animals of the Hellenes and the mob of non-combatants were just about to cross, when Xenonphon turned his troops right about to face the Carduchians. Vis-a-vis he formed his line, passing the order to the captains each to form his company into sections, and to deploy them into line by the left, the captains of companies and lieutenants in command of sections to advance to meet the Carduchians, while the rear leaders would keep their position facing the river. But when the Carduchians saw the rearguard so stript of the mass, and looking now like a mere handful of men, they advanced all the more quickly, singing certain songs the while. Then, as matters were safe with him, Cheirisophus sent back the peltasts and slingers and archers to join Xenophon, with orders to carry out his instructions. They were in the act of recrossing, when Xenophon, who saw their intention, sent a messenger across, bidding them wait there at the river's brink without crossing; but as soon as he and his detachment began to cross they were to step in facing him in two flanking divisions right and left of them, as if in the act of crossing; the javelin men with their javelins on the thong, and the bowmen with their arrows on the string; but they were not to advance far into the stream. The order passed to his own men was: "Wait till you are within sling-shot, and the shield rattles, then sound the paean and charge the enemy. As soon as he turns, and the bugle from the river sounds for 'the attack,' you will face about to the right, the rear rank leading, and the whole detachment falling back and crossing the river as quickly as possible, every one preserving his original rank, so as to avoid tramelling one another: the bravest man is he who gets to the other side first." The Carduchians, seeing that the remnant left was the merest handful (for many even of those whose duty it was to remain had gone off in their anxiety to protect their beasts of burden, or their personal kit, or their mistresses), bore down upon them valorously, and opened fire with slingstones and arrows. But the Hellenes, raising the battle hymn, dashed at them at a run, and they did not await them; armed well enough for mountain warfare, and with a view to sudden attack followed by speedy flight, they were not by any means sufficiently equipped for an engagement at close quarters. At this instant the signal of the bugle was heard. Its notes added wings to the flight of the barbarians, but the

Hellenes turned right about in the opposite direction, and betook themselves to the river with what speed they might. Some of the enemy, here a man and there another, perceived, and running back to the river, let fly their arrows and wounded a few; but the majority, even when the Hellenes were well across, were still to be seen pursuing their flight. The detachment which came to meet Xenophon's men, carried away by their valour, advanced further than they had need to, and had to cross back again in the rear of Xenophon's men, and of these too a few were wounded.

IV

The passage effected, they fell into line about mid-day, and marched through Armenian territory, one long plain with smooth rolling hillocks, not less than five parasangs in distance; for owing to the wars of this people with the Carduchians there were no villages near the river. The village eventually reached was large, and possessed a palace belonging to the satrap, and most of the houses were crowned with turrets; provisions were plentiful.

February 12, Wednesday

From this village they marched two stages--ten parasangs--

February 14, Friday

until they had surmounted the sources of the river Tigris; and from this point they marched three stages--fifteen parasangs—

February 17, Monday
Arrival at Teleboas river (possibly North of modern day Diyarabakir and unlikely the Botan river, Botan Çayı,)

to the river Teleboas. This was a fine stream, though not large, and there were many villages about it. The district was named Western Armenia. The lieutenant-governor of it was Tiribazus, the king's friend, and whenever the latter paid a visit, he alone had the privilege of mounting the king upon his horse. This officer rode up to the Hellenes with a body of cavalry, and sending forward an interpreter, stated that he desired a colloquy with the leaders. The generals resolved to hear what he had to say; and advancing on their side to within speaking distance, they demanded what he wanted. He replied that he wished to make a treaty with them, in accordance with which he on his side would abstain from injuring the Hellenes, if they would not burn his houses, but merely take such provisions as they needed. This proposal satisfied the generals, and a treaty was made on the terms suggested. From this place they marched three stages--fifteen parasangs--through plain country, Tiribazus the while keeping close behind with his own forces more than a mile off.

February 20, Thursday
Arrival at Palace in Tiribazus (In the mountainous area North of modern day Diyarabakir, Turkey)

Presently they reached a palace with villages clustered round about it, which were full of supplies in great variety. But while they were encamping in the night, there was a heavy fall of snow, and

February 21, Friday

in the morning it was resolved to billet out the different regiments, with their generals, throughout the villages. There was no enemy in sight, and the proceeding seemed prudent, owing to the quantity of snow. In these quarters they had for provisions all the good things there are--sacrificial beasts, corn, old wines with an exquisite bouquet, dried grapes, and vegetables of all sorts. But some of the stragglers from the camp reported having seen an army, and the blaze of many watchfires in the night. Accordingly the generals concluded that it was not prudent to separate their quarters in this way, and a resolution was passed to bring the troops together again. After that they reunited, the more so that the weather promised to be fine with a clear sky; but while they lay there in open quarters, during the night down came so thick a fall of snow that it completely covered up the stacks of arms and the men themselves lying down. It cramped and crippled the baggage animals; and there was great unreadiness to get up, so gently fell the snow as they lay there warm and comfortable, and formed a blanket, except where it slipped off the sleepers' shoulders; and it was not until Xenophon roused himself to get up, and, without his cloak on (69), began to split wood, that quickly first one and then another got up, and taking the log away from him, fell to splitting.

Thereat the rest followed suit, got up, and began kindling fire and oiling their bodies, for there was a scented unguent to be found there in abundance, which they used instead of oil. It was made from pig's fat, sesame, bitter almonds, and turpentine. There was a sweet oil also to be found, made of the same ingredients.

After this it was resolved that they must again separate their quarters and get under cover in the villages. At this news the soldiers, with much joy and shouting, rushed upon the covered houses and the provisions; but all who in their blind folly had set fire to the houses when they left them before, now paid the penalty in the poor quarters they got.

February 22, Saturday

From this place one night they sent off a party under Democrates, a Temenite (70), up into the mountains, where the stragglers reported having seen watchfires. The leader selected was a man whose judgement might be depended upon to verify the truth of the matter. With a happy gift to distinguish between fact and fiction, he had often been successfully appealed to. He went and reported that he had seen no watchfires, but he had got a man, whom he brought back with him, carrying a Persian bow and quiver, and a sagaris or battleaxe like those worn by the Amazons. When asked "from what country he came," the prisoner answered that he was "a Persian, and was going from the army of Tiribazus to get provisions." They next asked him "how large the army was, and for what object it had been collected." His answer was that "it consisted of Tiribazus at the head of his own forces, and aided by some Chalybian and Taochian mercenaries. Tiribazus had got it together," he added, "meaning to attack the Hellenes on the high mountain pass, in a defile which was the sole passage."

February 23, Sunday

When the generals heard this news, they resolved to collect the troops, and they set off at once, taking the prisoner to act as guide, and leaving a garrison behind with Sophaenetus the Stymphalian in command of those who remained in the camp. As soon as they had begun to cross the hills, the light infantry, advancing in front and catching sight of the camp, did not wait for the heavy infantry, but with a loud shout rushed upon the enemy's entrenchment. The natives, hearing the din and clatter, did not care to stop, but took rapidly to their heels. But, for all their expedition, some of them were killed, and as many as twenty horses were captured, with the tent of Tiribazus, and its contents, silver-footed couches and goblets, besides certain persons styling themselves the butlers and bakers. As soon as the generals of the heavy infantry division had learnt the news, they resolved to return to the camp with all speed, for fear of an attack being made on the remnant left behind. The recall was sounded and the retreat commenced; the camp was reached the same day.

February 24, Monday

V

The next day it was resolved that they should set off with all possible speed, before the enemy had time to collect and occupy the defile. Having got their kit and baggage together, they at once began their march through deep snow with several guides, and, crossing the high pass the same day on which Tiribazus was to have attacked them, got safely into cantonments. From this point they marched three desert stages--fifteen parassangs--

February 27, Thursday

to the river Euphrates, and crossed it in water up to the waist. The sources of the river were reported to be at no great distance. From this place they marched through deep snow over a flat country three stages--fifteen parasangs (71). The last of these marches was trying, with the north wind blowing in their teeth, drying up everything and benumbing the men. Here one of the seers suggested to them to do sacrifice to Boreas, and sacrifice was done. The effect was obvious to all in the diminished fierceness of the blast. But there was six feet of snow, so that many of the baggage animals and slaves were lost, and about thirty of the men themselves.

March 01, Saturday

They spent the whole night in kindling fire; for there was fortunately no dearth of wood at the halting-place; only those who came late into camp had no wood. Accordingly those who had arrived a good while and had kindled fires were not for allowing these late-comers near the fires, unless they would in return give a share of their corn or of any other victuals they might have. Here then a general exchange of goods was set up. Where the fire was kindled the snow melted, and great trenches formed themselves down to the bare earth, and here it was possible to measure the depth of the snow.

March 02, Sunday

Leaving these quarters, they marched the whole of the next day over snow, and many of the men were afflicted with "boulimia" (or hunger-faintness). Xenophon, who was guarding the rear, came upon some men who had dropt down, and he did not know what ailed them; but some one who was experienced in such matters suggested to him that they had evidently got boulimia; and if they got something to eat, they would revive. Then he went the round of the baggage train, and laying an embargo on any eatables he could see, doled out with his own hands, or sent off other able-bodied agents to distribute to the sufferers, who as soon as they had taken a mouthful got on their legs again and continued the march. On and on they marched, and about dusk Cheirisophus reached a village, and surprised some women and girls who had come from the village to fetch water at the fountain outside the stockade. These asked them who they were. The interpreters answered for them in Persian: "They were on their way from the king to the satrap;" in reply to which the women gave them to understand that the satrap was not at home, but was away a parasang farther on. As it was late they entered with the water-carriers within the stockade to visit the headman of the village. Accordingly Cheirisophus and as many of the troops as were able got into cantonments there, while the rest of the soldiers--those namely who were unable to complete the march-- had to spend the night out, without food and without fire; under the circumstances some of the men perished. On the heels of the army hung perpetually bands of the enemy, snatching away disabled baggage animals and fighting with each other over the carcases. And in its track not seldom were left to their fate disabled soldiers, struck down with snow-blindness or with toes mortified by frostbite. As to the eyes, it was some alleviation against the snow to march with something black before them; for the feet, the only remedy was to keep in motion without stopping for an instant, and to loose the sandal at night. If they went to sleep with the sandals on, the thong worked into the feet, and the sandals were frozen fast to them. This was partly due to the fact that, since their old sandals had failed, they wore untanned brogues made of newly-flayed ox-hides. It was owing to some such dire necessity that a party of men fell out and were left behind, and seeing a black-looking patch of ground where the snow had evidently disappeared, they conjectured it must have been melted; and this was actually so, owing to a spring of some sort which was to be seen steaming up in a dell close by. To this they had turned aside and sat down, and were loth to go a step further. But Xenophon, with his rearguard, perceived them, and begged and implored them by all manner of means not to be left behind, telling them that the enemy were after them in large packs pursuing; and he ended by growing angry. They merely bade him put a knife to their throats; not one step farther would they stir. Then it seemed best to frighten the pursuing enemy if possible, and prevent their falling upon the invalids. It was already dusk, and the pursuers were advancing with much noise and hubbub, wrangling and disputing over their spoils. Then all of a sudden the rearguard, in the plenitude of health and strength (72), sprang up out of their lair and run upon the enemy, whilst those weary wights (73) bawled out as loud as their sick throats could sound, and clashed their spears against their shields; and the enemy in terror hurled themselves through the snow into the dell, and not one of them ever uttered a sound again.

Xenophon and his party, telling the sick folk that next day people would come for them, set off, and before they had gone half a mile they fell in with some soldiers who had laid down to rest on the snow with their cloaks wrapped round them, but never a guard was established, and they made them get up. Their explanation was that those in front would not move on. Passing by this group he sent forward the strongest of his light infantry in advance, with orders to find out what the stoppage was. They reported that the whole army lay reposing in such fashion. That being so, Xenophon's men had nothing for it but to bivouac in the open air also, without fire and supperless, merely posting what pickets they could under the circumstances.

March 03, Monday

But as soon as it drew towards day, Xenophon despatched the youngest of his men to the sick folk behind, with orders to make them get up and force them to proceed. Meanwhile Cheirisophus had sent some of his men quartered in the village to enquire how they fared in the rear; they were overjoyed to see them, and handed over the sick folk to them to carry into camp, while they themselves continued their march forward, and ere twenty furlongs were past reached the village in which Cheirisophus was quartered.

As soon as the two divisions were met, the resolution was come to that it would be safe to billet the regiments throughout the villages; Cheirisophus remained where he was, while the rest drew lots for the villages in sight, and then, with their several detachments, marched off to their respective destinations. It was here that Polycrates, an Athenian and captain of a company, asked for leave of absence--he wished to be off on a quest of his own; and putting himself at the head of the active men of the division, he ran to the village which had been allotted to Xenophon. He surprised within it the villagers with their headman, and seventeen young horses which were being reared as a tribute for the king, and, last of all, the headman's own daughter, a young bride only eight days wed. Her husband had gone off to chase hares, and so he escaped being taken with the other villagers. The houses were underground structures with an aperture like the mouth of a well by which to enter, but they were broad and spacious below. The entrance for the beasts of burden was dug out, but the human occupants descended by a ladder. In these dwellings were to be found goats and sheep and cattle, and cocks and hens, with their various progeny. The flocks and herds were all reared under cover upon green food. There were stores within of wheat and barley and vegetables, and wine made from barley in great big bowls; the grains of barley malt lay floating in the beverage up to the lip of the vessel, and reeds lay in them, some longer, some shorter, without joints; when you were thirsty you must take one of these into your mouth, and suck. The beverage without admixture of water was very strong, and of a delicious flavour to certain palates, but the taste must be acquired. Xenophon made the headman of the village his guest at supper, and bade him keep a good heart; so far from robbing him of his children, they would fill his house full of good things in return for what they took before they went away; only he must set them an example, and discover some blessing or other for the army, until they found themselves with another tribe. To this he readily assented, and with the utmost cordiality showed them the cellar where the wine was buried. For this night then, having taken up their several quarters as described, they slumbered in the midst of plenty, one and all, with the headman under watch and ward, and his children with him safe in sight.

March 04, Tuesday

But on the following day Xenophon took the headman and set off to Cheirisophus, making a round of the villages, and at each place turning in to visit the different parties. Everywhere alike he found them faring sumptuously and merry-making. There was not a single village where they did not insist on setting a breakfast before them, and on the same table were spread half a dozen dishes at least, lamb, kid, pork, veal, fowls, with various sorts of bread, some of wheat and some of barley. When, as an act of courtesy, any one wished to drink his neighbour's health, he would drag him to the big bowl, and when there, he must duck his head and take a long pull, drinking like an ox. The headman, they insisted everywhere, must accept as a present whatever he liked to have. But he would accept nothing, except where he espied any of his relations, when he made a point of taking them off, him or her, with himself. When they reached Cheirisophus they found a similar scene. There too the men were feasting in their quarters, garlanded with whisps of hay and dry grass, and Armenian boys were playing the part of waiters in barbaric costumes, only they had to point out by gesture to the boys what they were to do, like deaf and dumb. After the first formalities, when Cheirisophus and Xenophon had greeted one another like bosom friends, they interrogated the headman in common by means of the Persian-speaking interpreter. "What was the country?" they asked: he replied, "Armenia." And again, "For whom are the horses being bred?" "They are tribute for the king," he replied. "And the neighbouring country?" "Is the land of the Chalybes," he said; and he described the road which led to it. So for the present Xenophon went off, taking the headman back with him to his household and friends. He also made him a present of an oldish horse which he had got; he had heard that the headman was a priest of the sun, and so he could fatten up the beast and sacrifice him; otherwise he was afraid it might die outright, for it had been injured by the long marching. For himself he took his pick of the colts, and gave a colt apiece to each of his fellow-generals and officers. The horses here were smaller than the Persian horses, but much more spirited. It was here too that their friend the headman explained to them, how they should wrap small bags or sacks around the feet of the horses and other cattle when marching through the snow, for without such precautions the creatures sank up to their bellies.

March 12, Wednesday

VI

When a week had passed, on the eighth day Xenophon delivered over the guide (that is to say, the village headman) to Cheirisophus. He left the headman's household safe behind in the village, with the exception of his son, a lad in the bloom of youth. This boy was entrusted to Episthenes of Amphipolis to guard; if the headman proved himself a good guide, he was to take away his son also at his departure. They finally made his house the repository of all the good things they could contrive to get together; then they broke up their camp and commenced to march, the headman guiding them through the snow unfettered.

March 15, Saturday

When they had reached the third stage Cheirisophus flew into a rage with him, because he had not brought them to any villages. The headman pleaded that there were none in this part. Cheirisophus struck him, but forgot to bind him, and the end of it was that the headman ran away in the night and was gone, leaving his son behind him. This was the sole ground of difference between Cheirisophus and Xenophon during the march, this combination of ill-treatment and neglect in the case of the guide. As to the boy, Episthenes conceived a passion for him, and took him home with him, and found in him the most faithful of friends. After this they marched seven stages at the rate of five parasangs a day,

March 22, Saturday
Arrival at The River Phasis (In the north of Eastern Anatolia)
(The river here is unlikely the Phasis/ Rioni next to the Black Sea)

to the banks of the river Phasis (74), which is a hundred feet broad: and thence they marched another couple of stages, ten parasangs; but at the pass leading down into the plain there appeared in front of them a mixed body of Chalybes and Taochians and Phasianians. When Cheirisophus caught sight of the enemy on the pass at a distance of about three or four miles, he ceased marching, not caring to approach the enemy with his troops in column, and he passed down the order to the others: to deploy their companies to the front, that the troops might form into line. As soon as the rearguard had come up, he assembled the generals and officers, and addressed them: "The enemy, as you see, are in occupation of the mountain pass, it is time we should consider how we are to make the best fight to win it. My opinion is, that we should give orders to the troops to take their morning meal, whilst we deliberate whether we should cross the mountains to-day or to-morrow." "My opinion," said Cleanor, "is, that as soon as we have breakfasted, we should arm for the fight and attack the enemy, without loss of time, for if we fritter away to-day, the enemy who are now content to look at us, will grow bolder, and with their growing courage, depend upon it, others more numerous will join them."

After him Xenophon spoke: "This," he said, "is how I see the matter; if fight we must, let us make preparation to sell our lives dearly, but if we desire to cross with the greatest ease, the point to consider is, how we may get the fewest wounds and throw away the smallest number of good men. Well then, that part of the mountain which is visible stretches nearly seven miles. Where are the men posted to intercept us? except at the road itself, they are nowhere to be seen. It is much better to try if possible to steal a point of this desert mountain unobserved, and before they know where we are, secure the prize, than to fly at a strong position and an enemy thoroughly prepared. Since it is much easier to march up a mountain without fighting than to tramp along a level when assailants are at either hand; and provided he has not to fight, a man will see what lies at his feet much more plainly even at night than in broad daylight in the midst of battle; and a rough road to feet that roam in peace may be pleasanter than a smooth surface with the bullets whistling about your ears (75). Nor is it so impossible, I take it, to steal a march, since it is open to us to go by night, when we cannot be seen, and to fall back so far that they will never notice us. In my opinion, however, if we make a feint of attacking here, we shall find the mountain chain all the more deserted elsewhere, since the enemy will be waiting for us here in thicker swarm.

"But what right have I to be drawing conclusions about stealing in your presence, Cheirisophus? for you Lacedaemonians, as I have often been told, you who belong to the 'peers,' practise stealing from your boyhood up; and it is no disgrace but honourable rather to steal, except such things as the law forbids; and in order, I presume, to stimulate your sense of secretiveness, and to make you master thieves, it is lawful for you further to get a whipping if you are caught. Now then you have a fine opportunity of displaying your training. But take care we are not caught stealing over the mountain, or we shall catch it ourselves." "For all that," retorted Cheirisophus, "I have heard that you Athenians are clever hands at stealing the public moneys; and that too though there is a fearful risk for the person so employed; but, I am told, it is your best men who are addicted to it; if it is your best men who are thought worthy to rule. So it is a fine opportunity for yourself also, Xenophon, to exhibit your education." "And I," replied Xenophon, "am ready to take the rear division, as soon as we have supped, and seize the mountain chain. I have already got guides, for the light troops laid an ambuscade, and seized some of the cut-purse vagabonds who hung on our rear. I am further informed by them that the mountain is not inaccessible, but is grazed by goats and cattle, so that if we can once get hold of any portion of it, there will be no difficulty as regards our animals--

they can cross. As to the enemy, I expect they will not even wait for us any longer, when they once see us on a level with themselves on the heights, for they do not even at present care to come down and meet us on fair ground." Cheirisophus answered: "But why should you go and leave your command in the rear? Send others rather, unless a band of volunteers will present themselves." Thereupon Aristonymus the Methydrian came forward with some heavy infantry, and Nicomachus the Oetean with another body of light troops, and they made an agreement to kindle several watch-fires as soon as they held the heights. The arrangements made, they breakfasted; and after breakfast Cheirisophus advanced the whole army ten furlongs closer towards the enemy, so as to strengthen the impression that he intended to attack them at that point. But as soon as they had supped and night had fallen, the party under orders set off and occupied the mountain, while the main body rested where they were. Now as soon as the enemy perceived that the mountain was taken, they banished all thought of sleep, and kept many watch-fires blazing throughout the night.

March 23, Sunday   <Diodorus March 27, Thursday>

But at break of day Cheirisophus offered sacrifice, and began advancing along the road, while the detachment which held the mountain advanced pari passu by the high ground. The larger mass of the enemy, on his side, remained still on the mountain-pass, but a section of them turned to confront the detachment on the heights. Before the main bodies had time to draw together, the detachment on the height came to close quarters, and the Hellenes were victorious and gave chase. Meanwhile the light division of the Hellenes, issuing from the plain, were rapidly advancing against the serried lines of the enemy, whilst Cheirisophus followed up with his heavy infantry at quick march. But the enemy on the road no sooner saw their higher division being worsted than they fled, and some few of them were slain, and a vast number of wicker shields were taken, which the Hellenes hacked to pieces with their short swords and rendered useless. So when they had reached the summit of the pass, they sacrificed and set up a trophy, and descending into the plain, reached villages abounding in good things of every kind.

March 24, Monday   **<Diodorus March 28, Friday>**

VII

After this they marched

March 29, Saturday   **<Diodorus April 02, Wednesday>**
Arrival in the land of the Taochians

into the country of the Taochians five stages--thirty parasangs--and provisions failed; for the Taochians lived in strong places, into which they had carried up all their stores. Now when the army arrived before one of these strong places--a mere fortress, without city or houses, into which a motley crowd of men and women and numerous flocks and herds were gathered--Cheirisophus attacked at once. When the first regiment fell back tired, a second advanced, and again a third, for it was impossible to surround the place in full force, as it was encircled by a river. Presently Xenophon came up with the rearguard, consisting of both light and heavy infantry, whereupon Cheirisophus halted him with the words: "In the nick of time you have come; we must take this place, for the troops have no provisions, unless we take it." Thereupon they consulted together, and to Xenophon's inquiry, "What it was which hindered their simply walking in?" Cheirisophus replied, "There is just this one narrow approach which you see, but when we attempt to pass it by they roll down volleys of stones from yonder overhanging crag," pointing up, "and this is the state in which you find yourself, if you chance to be caught;" and he pointed to some poor fellows with their legs or ribs crushed to bits. "But when they have expended their ammunition," said Xenophon, "there is nothing else, is there, to hinder our passing? Certainly, except yonder handful of fellows, there is no one in front of us that we can see; and of them, only two or three apparently are armed, and the distance to be traversed under fire is, as your eyes will tell you, about one hundred and fifty feet as near as can be, and of this space the first hundred is thickly covered with great pines at intervals; under cover of these, what harm can come to our men from a pelt of stones, flying or rolling? So then, there is only fifty feet left to cross, during a lull of stones." "Ay," said Cheirisophus, "but with our first attempt to approach the bush a galling fire of stones commences." "The very thing we want," said the other, "for they will use up their ammunition all the quicker; but let us select a point from which we shall have only a brief space to run across, if we can, and from which it will be easier to get back, if we wish." Thereupon Cheirisophus and Xenophon set out with Callimachus the Parrhasian, the captain in command of the officers of the rearguard that day; the rest of the captains remained out of danger. That done, the next step was for a party of about seventy men to get away under the trees, not in a body, but one by one, every one using his best precaution; and Agasis the Stymphalian, and Aristonymous the Methydrian, who were also officers of the rearguard, were posted as supports outside the trees; for it was not possible for more than a single company to stand safely within the trees. Here Callimachus hit upon a pretty contrivance--he ran forward from the tree under which he was posted two or three paces, and as soon as the stones came whizzing, he retired easily, but at each excursion more than ten wagon-loads of rocks were expended. Agasias, seeing how Callimachus was amusing himself, and the whole army looking on as spectators, was seized with the fear that he might miss his chance of being first to run the gauntlet of the enemy's fire and get into the place. So, without a word of summons to his neighbour, Aristonymous, or to Eurylochus of Lusia, both comrades of his, or to any one else, off he set on his own account, and passed the whole detachment. But Callimachus, seeing him tearing past, caught hold of his shield by the rim, and in the meantime Aristonymous the Methydrian ran past both, and after him Eurylochus of Lusia; for they were one and all aspirants to valour, and in that high pursuit, each was the eager rival of the rest. So in this strife of honour, the three of them took the fortress, and when they had once rushed in, not a stone more was hurled from overhead. And here a terrible spectacle displayed itself: the women first cast their infants down the cliff, and then they cast themselves after their fallen little ones, and the men likewise. In such a scene, Aeneas the Stymphalian, an officer, caught sight of a man with a fine dress about to throw himself over, and seized hold of him to stop him; but the other caught him to his arms, and both were gone in an instant headlong down the crags, and were killed. Out of this place the merest handful of human beings were taken prisoners, but cattle and asses in abundance and flocks of sheep. From this place they marched through the Chalybes (76) seven stages, fifty parasangs.

April 05, Saturday <Diodorus April 24, Thursday>
Arrival at the River Harpasus

These were the bravest men whom they encountered on the whole march, coming cheerily to close quarters with them. They wore linen cuirasses reaching to the groin, and instead of the ordinary "wings" or basques, a thickly-plaited fringe of cords. They were also provided with greaves and helmets, and at the girdle a short sabre, about as long as the Laconian dagger, with which they cut the throats of those they mastered, and after severing the head from the trunk they would march along carrying it, singing and dancing, when they drew within their enemy's field of view. They carried also a spear fifteen cubits long, lanced at one end (77). This folk stayed in regular townships, and whenever the Hellenes passed by they invariably hung close on their heels fighting. They had dwelling-places in their fortresses, and into them they had carried up their supplies, sot hat the Hellenes could get nothing from this district, but supported themselves on the flocks and herds they had taken from the Taochians. After this the Hellenes reached the river Harpasus, which was four hundred feet broad. Hence they marched through the Scythenians four stages--twenty parasangs--

April 09, Wednesday   <Diodorus April 28, Monday>
In the land of Scythenians

through a long level country to more villages, among which they halted three days, and got in supplies.

April 12, Saturday   <Diodorus May 01, Thursday>

Passing on from thence in four stages of twenty parasangs,

April 16, Wednesday   <Diodorus May 05, Monday>
Arrival at Gymnias

they reached a large and prosperous well-populated city, which went by the name of Gymnias (78), from which the governor of the country sent them a guide to lead them through a district hostile to his own. This guide told them that within five days he would lead them to a place from which they would see the sea, "and," he added, "if I fail of my word, you are free to take my life." Accordingly he put himself at their head; but he no sooner set foot in the country hostile to himself than he fell to encouraging them to burn and harry the land; indeed his exhortations were so earnest, it was plain that it was for this he had come, and not out of the good-will he bore the Hellenes.

April 17, Thursday   **<Diodorus May 6, Tuesday>**
Leave Gymnias

April 22, Tuesday   **<Diodorus May 21, Wednesday >**
Arrival at Theches

On the fifth day they reached the mountain, the name of which was Theches (79). No sooner had the men in front ascended it and caught sight of the sea than a great cry arose, and Xenophon, in the rearguard, catching the sound of it, conjectured that another set of enemies must surely be attacking in front; for they were followed by the inhabitants of the country, which was all aflame; indeed the rearguard had killed some and captured others alive by laying an ambuscade; they had taken also about twenty wicker shields, covered with the raw hides of shaggy oxen.

But as the shout became louder and nearer, and those who from time to time came up, began racing at the top of their speed towards the shouters, and the shouting continually recommenced with yet greater volume as the numbers increased, Xenophon settled in his mind that something extraordinary must have happened, so he mounted his horse, and taking with him Lycius and the cavalry, he galloped to the rescue. Presently they could hear the soldiers shouting and passing on the joyful word, "The sea! the sea!" Thereupon they began running, rearguard and all, and the baggage animals and horses came galloping up. But when they had reached the summit, then indeed they fell to embracing one another--generals and officers and all--and the tears trickled down their cheeks. And on a sudden, some one, whoever it was, having passed down the order, the soldiers began bringing stones and erecting a great cairn, whereon they dedicated a host of untanned skins, and staves, and captured wicker shields, and with his own hand the guide hacked the shields to pieces, inviting the rest to follow his example. After this the Hellenes dismissed the guide with a present raised from the common store, to wit, a horse, a silver bowl, a Persian dress, and ten darics; but what he most begged to have were their rings, and of these he got several from the soldiers. So, after pointing out to them a village where they would find quarters, and the road by which they would proceed towards the land of the Macrones, as evening fell, he turned his back upon them in the night and was gone.

4 RETURN EXPEDITION HOME

April 23, Wednesday   **<Diodorus May 22, Thursday>**
Through the land of Macrones (Northern Black Sea Region, modern Turkey)

VIII

From this point the Hellenes marched through the country of the Macrones three stages--ten parasangs, and on the first day they reached the river, which formed the boundary between the land of the Macrones and the land of the Scythenians. Above them, on their right, they had a country of the sternest and ruggedest character, and on their left another river, into which the frontier river discharges itself, and which they must cross. This was thickly fringed with trees which, though not of any great bulk, were closely packed. As soon as they came up to them, the Hellenes proceeded to cut them down in their haste to get out of the place as soon as possible. But the Macrones, armed with wicker shields and lances and hair tunics, were already drawn up to receive them opposite the crossing. They were cheering one another on, and kept up a steady pelt of stones into the river, though they failed to reach the other side or do any harm. At this juncture one of the light infantry came up to Xenophon; he had been, he said, a slave at Athens, and he wished to tell him that he recognised the speech of these people. "I think," said he, "that this must be my native country, and if there is no objection I will have a talk with them." "No objection at all," replied Xenophon, "pray talk to them, and ask them first, who they are." In answer to this question they said, "they were Macrones." "Well, then," said he, "ask them why they are drawn up in battle and want to fight with us." They answered, "Because you are invading our country." The generals bade him say: "If so, it is with not intention certainly of doing it or you any harm: but

104

we have been at war with the king, and are now returning to Hellas, and all we want is to reach the sea." The others asked, "Were they willing to give them pledges to that effect?" They replied: "Yes, they were ready to give and receive pledges to that effect." Then the Macrones gave a barbaric lance to the Hellenes, and the Hellenes a Hellenic lance to them: "for these," they said, "would serve as pledges," and both sides called upon the gods to witness. After the pledges were exchanged, the Macrones fell to vigorously hewing down trees and constructing a road to help them across, mingling freely with the Hellenes and fraternising in their midst, and they afforded them as good as market as they could, and for three days conducted them on their march, until they had brought them safely to the confines of the Colchians.

April 26, Saturday   <Diodorus May 25, Sunday>
Arrival in the land of Colchians and Honey Sickness

At this point they were confronted by a great mountain chain, which however was accessible, and on it the Colchians were drawn up for battle. In the first instance, the Hellenes drew up opposite in line of battle, as though they were minded to assault the hill in that order; but afterwards the generals determined to hold a council of war, and consider how to make the fairest fight. Accordingly Xenophon said: "I am not for advancing in line, but advise to form companies by columns. To begin with, the line," he urged, "would be scattered and thrown into disorder at once; for we shall find the mountain full of inequalities, it will be pathless here and easy to traverse there. The mere fact of first having formed in line, and then seeing the line thrown into disorder, must exercise a disheartening effect. Again, if we advance several deep, the enemy will none the less overlap us, and turn their superfluous numbers to account as best they like; while, if we march in shallow order, we may fully expect our line to be cut through and through by the thick rain of missiles and rush of men, and if this happen anywhere along the line, the whole line will equally suffer. No; my notion is to form columns by companies, covering ground sufficient with spaces between the companies to allow the last companies of each flank to be outside the enemy's flanks. Thus we shall with our extreme companies be outside the enemy's line, and the best men at the head of their columns will lead the attack, and every company will pick its way where the ground is easy; also it will be difficult for the enemy to force his way into the intervening spaces, when there are companies on both sides; nor will it be easy for him to cut in twain any individual company marching in column. If, too, any particular company should be pressed, the neighbouring company will come to the rescue, or if at any point any single company succeed in reaching the height, from that moment not one man of the enemy will stand his ground." This proposal was carried, and they formed into columns by companies (80). Then Xenophon, returning from the right wing to the left, addressed the soldiers. "Men," he said, "these men whom you see in front of you are the sole obstacles still interposed between us and the haven of our hopes so long deferred. We will swallow them up whole, without cooking (81), if we can."

The several divisions fell into position, the companies were formed into columns, and the result was a total of something like eighty companies of heavy infantry, each company consisting on an average of a hundred men. The light infantry and bowmen were arranged in three divisions--two outside to support the left and the right respectively, and the third in the centre--each division consisting of about six hundred men (82).

Before starting, the generals passed the order to offer prayer; and with the prayer and battle hymn rising from their lips they commenced their advance. Cheirisophus and Xenophon, and the light infantry with them, advanced outside the enemy's line to right and left, and the enemy, seeing their advance, made an effort to keep parallel and confront them, but in order to do so, as he extended partly to right and partly to left, he was pulled to pieces, and there was a large space or hollow left in the centre of his line. Seeing them separate thus, the light infantry attached to the Arcadian battalion, under command of Aeschines, an Arcarnanian, mistook the movement for flight, and with a loud shout rushed on, and these were the first to scale the mountain summit; but they were closely followed up by the Arcadian heavy infantry, under command of Cleanor of Orchomenus. When they began running in that way, the enemy stood their ground no longer, but betook themselves to flight, one in one direction, one in another, and the Hellenes scaled the hill and found quarters in numerous villages which contained supplies in abundance. Here, generally speaking, there was nothing to excite their wonderment, but the numbers of bee-hives were indeed astonishing, and so were certain properties of the honey (83). The effect upon the soldiers who tasted the combs was, that they all went for the nonce quite off their heads, and suffered from vomiting and diarrhoea, with a total inability to stand steady on their legs. A small dose produced a condition not unlike violent drunkenness, a large one an attack very like a fit of madness, and some dropped down, apparently at death's door. So they lay, hundreds of them, as if there had been a great defeat, a prey to the cruellest despondency.

April 27, Sunday   **<Diodorus May 26, Monday>**

But the next day, none had died; and almost at the same hour of the day at which they had eaten they recovered their senses,

April 30, Wednesday   **<Diodorus May 29, Thursday>**

and on the third or fourth day got on their legs again like convalescents after a severe course of medical treatment.

From this place they marched on two stages--seven parasangs--

May 2, Friday   **<Diodorus May 31, Saturday>**
Arrival at Trapezus

and reached the sea at Trapezus (84), a populous Hellenic city on the Euxine Sea, a colony of the Sinopeans, in the territory of the Colchians. Here they halted about thirty days in the villages of the Colchians, which they used as a base of operations to ravage the whole territory of Colchis. The men of Trapezus supplied the army with a market, entertained them, and gave them, as gifts of hospitality, oxen and wheat and wine. Further, they negotiated with them in behalf of their neighbours the Colchians, who dwelt in the plain for the most part, and from this folk also came gifts of hospitality in the shape of cattle.

And now the Hellenes made preparation for the sacrifice which they had vowed,

June 2, Monday   **<Diodorus July 1, Tuesday>**
Sacrifices and Games of Thanks

and a sufficient number of cattle came in for them to offer thank-offerings for safe guidance to Zeus the Saviour, and to Heracles (85), and to the other gods, according to their vows. They instituted also a gymnastic contest on the mountain side, just where they were quartered, and chose Dracontius, a Spartan (who had been banished from home when a lad, having unintentionally slain another boy with a blow of his dagger), to superintend the course, and be president of the games.

June 4, Wednesday   **<Diodorus July 3, Thursday>**

As soon as the sacrifices were over, they handed over the hides of the beasts to Dracontius, and bade him lead the way to his racecourse. He merely waved his hand and pointed to where they were standing, and said, "There, this ridge is just the place for running, anywhere, everywhere." "But how," it was asked, "will they manage to wrestle on the hard scrubby ground?" "Oh! worse knocks for those who are thrown," the president replied. There was a mile race for boys, the majority being captive lads; and for the long race more than sixty Cretans competed; there was wrestling, boxing, and the pankration (86). Altogether it was a beautiful spectacle. There was a large number of entries, and the emulation, with their companions, male and female, standing as spectators, was immense. There was horse-racing also; the riders had to gallop down a steep incline to the sea, and then turn and come up again to the altar, and on the descent more than half rolled head over heels, and then back they came toiling up the tremendous steep, scarcely out of a walking pace. Loud were the shouts, the laughter, and the cheers.

BOOK V (In the preceding portion of the narrative a detailed account is given of all that the Hellenes did, and how they fared on the march up with Cyrus; and also of all that befell them on their march subsequently, until they reached the seaboard of the Euxine Sea, or Pontus, and the Hellenic city of Trapezus, where they duly offered the sacrifice for safe deliverance which they had vowed to offer as soon as they set foot on a friendly soil.)

June 7, Saturday   **<Diodorus July 6, Sunday>**
Counsel for the Remainder of the march

I

After this they met and took counsel concerning the remainder of the march. The first speaker was Antileon of Thurii. He rose and said: "For my part, sirs, I am weary by this time of getting kit together and packing up for a start, of walking and running and carrying heavy arms, and of tramping along in line, or mounting guard, and doing battle. The sole desire I now have is to cease from all these pains, and for the future, since here we have the sea before us, to sail on and on, 'stretched out in sleep,' like Odysseus, and so to find myself in Hellas." When they heard these remarks, the soldiers showed their approval with loud cries of "well said," and then another spoke to the same effect, and then another, and indeed all present. Then Cheirisophus got up and said: "I have a friend, sirs, who, as good hap will have it, is now high admiral, Anaxibius. If you like to send me to him, I think I can safely promise to return with some men-of-war and other vessels which will carry us. All you have to do, if you are really minded to go home by sea, is to wait here till I come. I will be back ere long." The soldiers were delighted at these words, and voted that Cheirisophus should set sail on his mission without delay. After him, Xenophon got up, and spoke as follows: "Cheirisophus, it is agreed, sets out in search of vessels, and we are going to await him. Let me tell you what, in my opinion, it is reasonable to do while we are waiting. First of all, we must provide ourselves with necessaries from hostile territory, for there is not a sufficient market, nor, if there were, have we, with a few solitary exceptions, the means of purchase. Now, the district is hostile, so that if you set off in search of provisions without care and precaution, the chances are that many of us will be lost. To meet this risk, I propose that we should organise foraging parties to capture provisions, and, for the rest, not roam about the country at random. The organisation of the matter should be left to us." (The resolution was passed.) "Please listen to another proposal;" he continued: "Some of you, no doubt, will be going out to pillage. It will be best, I think, that whoever does so should in each case before starting inform us of his intent, and in what direction he means to go, so that we may know the exact number of those who are out and of those who stop behind. Thus we shall be able to help in preparing and starting the expedition where necessary; and in case of aid or reinforcements being called for, we shall know in what direction to proceed; or, again, if the attempt is to be undertaken by raw or less expert hands, we may throw in the weight of our experience and advice by endeavouring to discover the strength of those whom they design to attack." This proposal was also carried. "Here is another point," he continued, "to which I would draw your attention. Our enemies will not lack leisure to make raids upon us: nor is it unnatural, that they should lay plots for us; for we have appropriated what is theirs; they are seated over us ever on the watch. I propose then that we should have regular outposts round the camp. If we take it in succession to do picket and outlook duty, the enemy will be less able to harry us. And here is another point for your observation; supposing we knew for certain that Cheirisophus must return with a sufficient number of vessels, there would be no need of the remark, but as that is still problematical, I propose that we should try to get together vessels on the spot also. If he comes and finds us already provided for here, we shall have more ships than we need, that is all; while, if he fails to bring them, we shall have the local supply to fall back upon. I see ships sailing past perpetually, so we have only to ask the loan of some war-ships from the men of Trapezus, and we can bring them into port, and safeguard them with their rudders unshipped, until we have enough to carry us. By this course I think we shall not fail of finding the means of transport requisite." That resolution was also passed. He proceeded: "Consider whether you think it equitable to support by means of a general fund the ships' companies which we so impress, while they wait here for our benefit, and to agree upon a fare, on the principle of repaying kindnesses in kind." That too was passed. "Well then," said he, "in case, after all, our endeavours should not be crowned with success, and we find that we have not vessels enough, I propose that we should enjoin on the cities along the seaboard the duty of constructing and putting in order the roads, which we hear are impassable. They will be only too glad to obey, no doubt, out of mere terror and their desire to be rid of us." This last proposal was met by loud cries and protestations against the idea of going by land at all. So, perceiving their infatuation, he did not put the question to the vote, but eventually persuaded the cities voluntarily to construct roads by the suggestion, "If you get your roads in good order, we shall all the sooner be gone." They further got a fifty-oared galley from the Trapezuntines, and gave the command of it to Dexippus, a Laconian, one of the perioeci (87). This man altogether neglected to collect vessels on the offing, but slunk off himself, and vanished, ship and all, out of Pontus. Later on, however, he paid the penalty of his misdeeds. He became involved in some meddling and making in Thrace at the court of Seuthes, and was put to death by the Laconian Nicander. They also got a thirty-oared galley, the command of which was entrusted to Polycrates, an Athenian, and that officer brought into harbour to the camp all the vessels he could lay his hands on. If these were laden, they took out the freights and appointed guards to keep an eye on their preservation, whilst they used the ships themselves for transport service on the coast. While matters stood at this point, the Hellenes used to make forays with varying success; sometimes they captured prey and sometimes they failed. On one occasion Cleanetus led his own and another company against a strong position, and was killed himself, with many others of his party.

June 16, Monday   **<Diodorus July 15, Tuesday>**

II

The time came when it was no longer possible to capture provisions, going and returning to the camp in one day. In consequence of this, Xenophon took some guides from the Trapezuntines and led half the army out against the Drilae, leaving the other half to guard the camp. That was necessary, since the Colchians, who had been ousted from their houses, were assembled thickly, and sat eyeing them from the heights above; on the other hand the Trapezuntines, being friendly to the native inhabitants, were not for leading the Hellenes to places where it was easy to capture provisions. But against the Drilae, from whom they personally suffered, they would lead them with enthusiasm, up into mountainous and scarcely accessible fortresses, and against the most warlike people of any in the Pontus.

June 18, Wednesday   **<Diodorus July 17, Thursday>**
Battle against the Drilae

But when the Hellenes had reached the uplands, the Drilae set fire to all their fastnesses which they thought could be taken easily, and beat a retreat; and except here and there a stray pig or bullock or other animal which had escaped the fire there was nothing to capture; but there was one fastness which served as their metropolis: into this the different streams of people collected; round it ran a tremendously deep ravine, and the approaches to the place were difficult. So the light infantry ran forward five or six furlongs in advance of the heavy infantry, and crossed the ravine; and seeing quantities of sheep and other things, proceeded to attack the place. Close at their heels followed a number of those who had set out on the foray armed with spears, so that the storming party across the ravine amounted to more than two thousand. But, finding that they could not take the place by a coup-de-main, as there was a trench running round it, mounded up some breadth, with a stockade on the top of the earthwork and a close-packed row of wooden bastions, they made an attempt to run back, but the enemy fell upon them from the rear. To get away by a sudden rush was out of the question, since the descent from the fortress into the ravine only admitted of moving in single file. Under the circumstances they sent to Xenophon, who was in command of the heavy infantry. The messenger came and delivered his message: "There is a fastness choke full of all sorts of stores, but we cannot take it, it is too strong; nor can we easily get away; the enemy rush out and deliver battle, and the return is difficult." On hearing this,

Xenophon pushed forward his heavy infantry to the edge of the ravine, and there ordered them to take up a position, while he himself with the officers crossed over to determine whether it were better to withdraw the party already across, or to bring over the heavy infantry also, on the supposition that the fortress might be taken. In favour of the latter opinion it was agreed that the retreat must cost many lives, and the officers were further disposed to think, they could take the place. Xenophon consented, relying on the victims, for the seers had announced, that there would be a battle, but that the result of the expedition would be good. So he sent the officers to bring the heavy troops across, while he himself remained, having drawn off all the light infantry and forbidden all sharp-shooting at long range. As soon as the heavy infantry had arrived, he ordered each captain to form his company, in whatever way he hoped to make it most effective in the coming struggle. Side by side together they stood, these captains, not for the first time to-day competitors for the award of manly virtue. While they were thus employed, he--the general--was engaged in passing down his order along the ranks of the light infantry and archers respectively to march with the javelin on its thong and the arrow to the string, ready at the word "shoot" to discharge their missiles, while the light troops were to have their wallets well stocked with slingstones; lastly, he despatched his adjutants to see to the proper carrying out of these orders. And now the preparations were complete: the officers and lieutenants and all others claiming to be peers of these, were drawn up in their several places. With a glance each was able to command the rest in the crescent-like disposition which the ground invited. Presently the notes of the battle hymn arose, the clarion spoke, and with a thrilling cry in honour of the warrior-god, commenced a rush of the heavy infantry at full speed under cover of a storm of missiles, lances, arrows, bullets, but most of all stones hurled from the hand with ceaseless pelt, while there were some who brought firebrands to bear. Overwhelmed by this crowd of missiles, the enemy left their stockades and their bastion towers, which gave Agasias the Stymphalian and Philoxenus of Pellene a chance not to be missed; laying aside their heavy arms, up they went in bare tunics only, and one hauled another up, and meantime another had mounted, and the place was taken, as they thought. Then the peltasts and light troops rushed in and began snatching what each man could. Xenophon the while, posted at the gates, kept back as many of the hoplites as he could, for there were other enemies now visible on certain strong citadel heights; and after a lapse of no long time a shout arose within, and the men came running back, some still clutching what they had seized; and presently here and there a wounded man; and mighty was the jostling about the portals. To the questions which were put to them the outpouring fugitives repeated the same story: there was a citadel within and enemies in crowds were making savage sallies and beating the fellows inside. At that

Xenophon ordered Tolmides the herald to proclaim: "Enter all who are minded to capture aught." In poured the surging multitude, and the counter-current of persons elbowing their passage in prevailed over the stream of those who issued forth, until they beat back and cooped up the enemy within the citadel again. So outside the citadel everything was sacked and pillaged by the Hellenes, and the heavy infantry took up their position, some about the stockades, others along the road leading up to the citadel. Xenophon and the officers meantime considered the possibility of taking the citadel, for if so, their safety was assured; but if otherwise, it would be very difficult to get away. As the result of their deliberations they agreed that the place was impregnable. Then they began making preparations for the retreat. Each set of men proceeded to pull down the palisading which faced themselves; further, they sent away all who were useless or who had enough to do to carry their burdens, with the mass of the heavy infantry accompanying them; the officers in each case leaving behind men whom they could severally depend on. But as soon as they began to retreat, out rushed upon them from within a host of fellows, armed with wicker shields and lances, greaves and Paphlagonian helmets. Others might be seen scaling the houses on this side and that of the road leading into the citadel. Even pursuit in the direction of the citadel was dangerous, since the enemy kept hurling down on them great beams from above, so that to stop and to make off were alike dangerous, and night approaching was full of terrors. But in the midst of their fighting and their despair some god gave them a means of safety. All of a sudden, by whatsoever hand ignited, a flame shot up; it came from a house on the right hand, and as this gradually fell in, the people from the other houses on the right took to their heels and fled. Xenophon, laying this lesson of fortune to heart, gave orders to set fire to the left-hand houses also, which being of wood burned quickly, with the result that the occupants of these also took to flight. The men immediately at their front were the sole annoyance now, and these were safe to fall upon them as they made their exit and in their descent. Here then the word was passed for all who were out of range to bring up logs of wood and pile them between themselves and the enemy, and when there was enough of these they set them on fire; they also fired the houses along the trench-work itself, so as to occupy the attention of the enemy. Thus they got off, though with difficulty, and escaped from the place by putting a fire between them and the enemy; and the whole city was burnt down, houses, turrets, stockading, and everything belonging to it except the citadel.

June 19, Thursday   **\<Diodorus July 18, Friday\>**

Next day the Hellenes were bent on getting back with the provisions; but as they dreaded the descent to Trapezus, which was precipitous and narrow, they laid a false ambuscade, and a Mysian, called after the name of his nation (Mysus) (88), took ten of the Cretans and halted in some thick brushy ground, where he made a feint of endeavouring to escape the notice of the enemy. The glint of their light shields, which were of brass, now and again gleamed through the brushwood. The enemy, seeing it all through the thicket, were confirmed in their fears of an ambuscade. But the army meanwhile was quietly making its descent; and when it appeared that they had crept down far enough, the signal was given to the Mysian to flee as fast as he could, and he, springing up, fled with his men. The rest of the party, that is the Cretans, saying, "We are caught if we race," left the road and plunged into a wood, and tumbling and rolling down the gullies were saved. The Mysian, fleeing along the road, kept crying for assistance, which they sent him, and picked him up wounded. The party of rescue now beat a retreat themselves with their face to the foe, exposed to a shower of missiles, to which some of the Cretan bowmen responded with their arrows.

June 20, Friday   **\<Diodorus July 19, Saturday\>**

In this way they all reached the camp in safety

June 28, Saturday   **\<Diodorus July 27, Sunday\>**

III

Now when Cheirisophus did not arrive, and the supply of ships was insufficient, and to get provisions longer was impossible, they resolved to depart. On board the vessels they embarked the sick, and those above forty years of age, with the boys and women, and all the baggage which the solders were not absolutely forced to take for their own use.

July 1, Tuesday   **<Diodorus July 30, Wednesday>**

The two eldest generals, Philesius and Sophaenetus, were put in charge, and so the party embarked, while the rest resumed their march, for the road was now completely constructed.

Continuing their march that day and the next,

July 3, Thursday   **<Diodorus August 1, Friday>**
Arrival at Cerasus (modern Giresun in Turkey)

on the third they reached Cerasus, a Hellenic city on the sea, and a colony of Sinope, in the country of the Colchians. Here they halted ten days, and there was a review and numbering of the troops under arms, when there were found to be eight thousand six hundred men. So many had escaped; the rest had perished at the hands of the enemy, or by reason of the snow, or else disease. At this time and place they divided the money accruing from the captives sold, and a tithe selected for Apollo and Artemis of the Ephesians was divided between the generals, each of whom took a portion to guard for the gods, Neon the Asinaean (89) taking on behalf of Cheirisophus.

Out of the portion which fell to Xenophon he caused a dedicatory offering to Apollo to be made and dedicated among the treasures of the Athenians at Delphi (90). It was inscribed with his own name and that of Proxenus, his friend, who was killed with Clearchus. The gift for Artemis of the Ephesians was, in the first instance, left behind by him in Asia at the time when he left that part of the world himself with Agesilaus on the march into Boeotia (91). He left it behind in charge of Megabyzus, the sacristan of the goddess, thinking that the voyage on which he was starting was fraught with danger. In the event of his coming out of it alive, he charged Megabyzus to restore to him the deposit; but should any evil happen to him, then he was to cause to be made and to dedicate on his behalf to Artemis, whatsoever thing he thought would be pleasing to the goddess.

In the days of his banishment, when Xenophon was now established by the Lacedaemonians as a colonist in Scillus (92), a place which lies on the main road to Olympia, Megabyzus arrived on his way to Olympia as a spectator to attend the games, and restored to him the deposit. Xenophon took the money and bought for the goddess a plot of ground at a point indicated to him by the oracle. The plot, it so happened, had its own Selinus river flowing through it, just as at Ephesus the river Selinus flows past the temple of Artemis, and in both streams fish and mussels are to be found. On the estate at Scillus there is hunting and shooting of all the beasts of the chase that are.

Here with the sacred money he built an altar and a temple, and ever after, year by year, tithed the fruits of the land in their season and did sacrifice to the goddess, while all the citizens and neighbours, men and women, shared in the festival. The goddess herself provided for the banqueters meat and loaves and wine and sweetmeats, with portions of the victims sacrificed from the sacred pasture, as also of those which were slain in the chase; for Xenophon's own lads, with the lads of the other citizens, always made a hunting excursion against the festival day, in which any grown men who liked might join. The game was captured partly from the sacred district itself, partly from Pholoe (93), pigs and gazelles and stags. The place lies on the direct road from Lacedaemon to Olympia, about twenty furlongs from the temple of Zeus in Olympia, and within the sacred enclosure there is meadow-land and wood-covered hills, suited to the breeding of pigs and goats and cattle and horses, so that even the sumpter animals of the pilgrims passing to the feast fare sumptuously. The shrine is girdled by a grove of cultivated trees, yielding dessert fruits in their season. The temple itself is a facsimile on a small scale of the great temple at Ephesus, and the image of the goddess is like the golden statue at Ephesus, save only that it is made, not of gold, but of cypress wood. Beside the temple stands a column bearing this inscription:--*The place is sacred to artemis. He who holds it and enjoys the fruits of it is bound to sacrifice yearly a tithe of the produce. And from the residue thereof to keep in repair the shrine. If any man fail in aught of this the goddess herself will look to it that the matter shall not sleep.*

July 14, Monday   <Diodorus August 12, Tuesday>
Leave Cerasus (modern Giresun in Turkey)

IV

From Cerasus they continued the march, the same portion of the troops being conveyed by sea as before, and the rest marching by land.

July 15, Tuesday   <Diodorus August 13, Wednesday>
Arrival at the borders of the Mossynoecians 'wood tower livers'
(possibly near Piraziz in Turkey, the wood coming from hazelnut
trees Corylus colurna)

When they had reached the frontiers of the Mossynoecians (94) they sent to
him Timesitheus the Trapezuntine, who was the proxenos (95) of the
Mossynoecians, to inquire whether they were to pass through their territory
as friends or foes. They, trusting in their strongholds, replied that they
would not give them passage. It was then that Timesitheus informed them
that the Mossynoecians on the farther side of the country were hostile to
these members of the tribe; and it was resolved to invite the former to
make an alliance, if they wished it.

July 16, Wednesday   <Diodorus August 14, Thursday>
Conference with the Mossynoecians

So Timesitheus was sent, and came back with their chiefs. On their arrival
there was a conference of the Mossynoecian chiefs and the generals of the
Hellenes, and Xenophon made a speech which Timesitheus interpreted. He
said: "Men of the Mossynoecians, our desire is to reach Hellas in safety; and
since we have no vessels we must needs go by foot, but these people who,
as we hear, are your enemies, prevent us. Will you take us for your allies?
Now is your chance to exact vengeance for any wrong, which they at any
time may have put upon you, and for the future they will be your subjects;
but if you send us about our business, consider and ask yourselves from
what quarter will you ever again obtain so strong a force to help you?" To
this the chief of the Mossynoecians made answer:--that the proposal was in
accordance with their wishes and they welcomed the alliance. "Good," said
Xenophon, "but to what use do you propose to put us, if we become your
allies? And what will you in turn be able to do to assist our passage?" They
replied: "We can make an incursion into this country hostile to yourselves
and us, from the opposite side, and also send you ships and men to this
place, who will aid you in fighting and conduct you on the road."

On this understanding, they exchanged pledges and were gone.

July 17, Thursday   **<Diodorus August 15, Friday>**

The next day they returned, bringing three hundred canoes, each hollowed out of a single trunk. There were three men in each, two of whom disembarked and fell into rank, whilst the third remained. Then the one set took the boats and sailed back again, whilst the other two-thirds who remained marshalled themselves in the following way. They stood in rows of about a hundred each, like the rows of dancers in a chorus, standing vis-a-vis to one another, and all bearing wicker shields, made of white oxhide, shaggy, and shaped like an ivy leaf; in the right hand they brandished a javelin about six cubits long, with a lance in front, and rounded like a ball at the butt end of the shaft. Their bodies were clad in short frocks, scarcely reaching to the knees and in texture closely resembling that of a linen bedclothes' bag; on their heads they wore leathern helmets just like the Paphlagonian helmet, with a tuft of hair in the middle, as like a tiara in shape as possible. They carried moreover iron battle-axes. Then one of them gave, as it were, the key-note and started, while the rest, taking up the strain and the step, followed singing and marking time. Passing through the various corps and heavy armed battalions of the Hellenes, they marched straight against the enemy, to what appeared the most assailable of his fortresses. It was situated in front of the city, or mother city, as it is called, which latter contains the high citadel of the Mossynoecians. This citadel was the real bone of contention, the occupants at any time being acknowledged as the masters of all the other Mossynoecians. The present holders (so it was explained) had no right to its possession; for the sake of self-aggrandisement they had seized what was really common property. Some of the Hellenes followed the attacking party, not under the orders of the generals, but for the sake of plunder. As they advanced, the enemy for a while kept quiet; but as they got near the place, they made a sortie and routed them, killing several of the barbarians as well as some of the Hellenes who had gone up with them; and so pursued them until they saw the Hellenes advancing to the rescue. Then they turned round and made off, first cutting off the heads of the dead men and flaunting them in the face of the Hellenes and of their own private foes, dancing the while and singing in a measured strain. But the Hellenes were much vexed to think that their foes had only been rendered bolder, while the Hellenes who had formed part of the expedition had turned tail and fled, in spite of their numbers; a thing which had not happened previously during the whole expedition.

July 18, Friday   **<Diodorus August 16, Saturday>**

So Xenophon called a meeting of the Hellenes and spoke as follows:
"Soldiers, do not in any wise be cast down by what has happened, be sure
that good no less than evil will be the result; for to begin with, you now
know certainly that those who are going to guide us are in very deed hostile
to those with whom necessity drives us to quarrel; and, in the next place,
some of our own body, these Hellenes who have made so light of orderly
array and conjoint action with ourselves, as though they must needs achieve
in the company of barbarians all they could with ourselves, have paid the
penalty and been taught a lesson, so that another time they will be less
prone to leave our ranks. But you must be prepared to show these friendly
barbarians that you are of a better sort, and prove to the enemy that battle
with the undisciplined is one thing, but with men like yourselves another."
Accordingly they halted, as they were, that day.

July 19, Saturday   **<Diodorus August 17, Sunday>**

Next day they sacrificed and finding the victims favourable, they
breakfasted, formed the companies into columns, and with their barbarians
arranged in similar order on their left, began their march. Between the
companies were the archers only slightly retired behind the front of the
heavy infantry, on account of the enemy's active light troops, who ran down
and kept up volleys of stones. These were held in check by the archers and
peltasts; and steadily step by step the mass marched on, first to the position
from which the barbarians and those with them had been driven two days
back, and where the enemy were now drawn up to meet them. Thus it came
to pass that the barbarians first grappled with the peltasts and maintained
the battle until the heavy infantry were close, when they turned and fled.
The peltasts followed without delay, and pursued them right up to their city,
while the heavy troops in unbroken order followed. As soon as they were
up at the houses of the capital, there and then the enemy, collecting all
together in one strong body, fought valiantly, and hurled their javelins, or
else clenched their long stout spears, almost too heavy for a man to wield,
and did their best to ward off the attack at close quarters. But when the
Hellenes, instead of giving way, kept massing together more thickly, the
barbarians fled from this place also, and in a body deserted the fortress.
Their king, who sat in his wooden tower or mossyn, built on the citadel
(there he sits and there they maintain him, all at the common cost, and
guard him narrowly), refused to come forth, as did also those in the fortress
first taken, and so were burnt to a cinder where they were, their mossyns,

themselves, and all. The Hellenes, pillaging and ransacking these places, discovered in the different houses treasures and magazines of loaves, pile upon pile, "the ancestral stores," as the Mossynoecians told them; but the new corn was laid up apart with the straw-stalk and ear together, and this was for the most part spelt. Slices of dolphin were another discovery, in narrow-necked jars, all properly salted and pickled; and there was blubber of dolphin in vessels, which the Mossynoecians used precisely as the Hellenes use oil. Then there were large stores of nuts on the upper floor, the broad kind without a division (96). This was also a chief article of food with them--boiled nuts and baked loaves. Wine was also discovered. This, from its rough, dry quality, tasted sharp when drunk pure, but mixed with water was sweet and fragrant.

July 20, Sunday   <Diodorus August 18, Monday>

The Hellenes breakfasted and then started forward on their march, having first delivered the stronghold to their allies among the Mossynoecians. As for the other strongholds belonging to tribes allied with their foes, which they passed en route, the most accessible were either deserted by their inhabitants or gave in their adhesion voluntarily. The following description will apply to the majority of them: the cities were on an average ten miles apart, some more, some less; but so elevated is the country and intersected by such deep clefts that if they chose to shout across to one another, their cries would be heard from one city to another. When, in the course of their march, they came upon a friendly population, these would entertain them with exhibitions of fatted children belonging to the wealthy classes, fed up on boiled chestnuts until they were as white as white can be, of skin plump and delicate, and very nearly as broad as they were long, with their backs variegated and their breasts tattooed with patterns of all sorts of flowers. They sought after the women in the Hellenic army, and would fain have laid with them openly in broad daylight, for that was their custom. The whole community, male and female alike, were fair-complexioned and white-skinned. It was agreed that this was the most barbaric and outlandish people that they had passed through on the whole expedition, and the furthest removed from the Hellenic customs, doing in a crowd precisely what other people would prefer to do in solitude, and when alone behaving exactly as others would behave in company, talking to themselves and laughing at their own expense, standing still and then again capering about, wherever they might chance to be, without rhyme or reason, as if their sole business were to show off to the rest of the world.

July 27, Sunday   **<Diodorus August 25, Monday>**
Arrival at the Chalybes

V

Through this country, friendly or hostile as the chance might be, the Hellenes marched, eight stages in all, and reached the Chalybes. These were a people few in number, and subject to the Mossynoecians. Their livelihood was for the most part derived from mining and forging iron. Thence they came to the Tibarenians. The country of the Tibarenians was far more level, and their fortresses lay on the seaboard and were less strong, whether by art or nature. The generals wanted to attack these places, so that the army might get some pickings, and they would not accept the gifts of hospitality which came in from the Tibarenians, but bidding them wait till they had taken counsel, they proceeded to offer sacrifice. After several abortive attempts, the seers at last pronounced an opinion that the gods in no wise countenanced war. Then they accepted the gifts of hospitality, and marching through what was now recognised as a friendly country,

July 29, Tuesday   **<Diodorus August 27, Wednesday>**
Arrival at Cotyora (Ordu in Turkey)

in two days reached Cotyora, a Hellenic city, and a colony of Sinope, albeit situated in the territory of the Tibarenians (97).

Here they halted forty-five days,

August 3, Sunday   **<Diodorus September 1, Monday>**

during which they first of all sacrificed to the gods, and instituted processions, each set of the Hellenes according to their several tribes, with gymnastic contests. Provisions they got in meanwhile, partly from Paphlagonia, partly from the estates of the Cotyorites, for the latter would neither provide them a market nor receive their sick within their walls.

August 8, Friday   **<Diodorus September 6, Saturday>**

Meanwhile ambassadors arrived from Sinope, full of fears, not only for the Cotyorites and their city, which belonged to Sinope, and brought in tribute, but also for the territory which, as they had heard, was being pillaged. Accordingly they came to the camp and made a speech. Hecatonymus, who was reported to be a clever orator, acted as their spokesman: "Soldiers," he said, "the city of the Sinopeans has sent us to offer you, as Hellenes, our compliments and congratulations on your victories over the barbarians; and next, to express our joyful satisfaction that you have surmounted all those terrible sufferings of which we have heard, and have reached this place in safety. As Hellenes we claim to receive at your hands, as fellow-Hellenes, kindness and not harm. We have certainly not ourselves set you an example heretofore of evil treatment. Now the Cotyorites are our colonists. It was we who gave them this country to dwell in, having taken it from the barbarians; for which reason also they, with the men of Cerasus and Trapezus, pay us an appointed tribute. So that, whatever mischief you inflict on the men of Cotyora, the city of Sinope takes as personal to herself. At the present time we hear that you have made forcible entry into their city, some of you, and are quartered in the houses, besides taking forcibly from the Cotyorite estates whatever you need, by hook and by crook. Now against these things we enter protest. If you mean to go on so doing, you will drive us to make friends with Corylas and the Paphlagonians, or any one else we can find." To meet these charges Xenophon, on behalf of the soldiers, rose and said: "As to ourselves, men of Sinope, having got so far, we are well content to have saved our bodies and our arms. Indeed it was impossible at one and the same moment to keep our enemies at bay and to despoil them of their goods and chattels. And now, since we have reached Hellenic cities, how has it fared with us? At Trapezus they gave us a market, and we paid for our provisions at a fair market price. In return for the honour they did us, and the gifts of hospitality they gave the army, we requited them with honour. Where the barbarian was friendly to them, we stayed our hands from injury; or under their escort, we did damage to their enemies to the utmost of our power. Ask them, what sort of people they found us. They are here, some of them, to answer for themselves. Their fellow-citizens and the state of Trapezus, for friendship's sake, have sent them with us to act as our guides. "But wherever we come, be it foreign or Hellenic soil, and find no market for provisions, we are wont to help ourselves, not out of insolence but from necessity. There have been tribes like the Carduchians, the Taochians, the Chaldaeans, which, albeit they were not subject to the great king, yet were no less formidable than independent. These we had to bring over by our arms. The necessity of getting provisions forced us; since they refused to offer us a market. Whereas some other folk, like the Macrones, in spite of their being barbarians, we regarded as our friends, simply because they did provide us with the best market in their power, and we took no single thing of theirs by force. But, to come to these Cotyorites, whom you claim to be your people, if we have taken aught from them, they have themselves to blame, for they did not deal with us as friends, but shut their gates in our faces. They would neither welcome us within nor furnish us with a market without. The only justification they alleged was that your governor (98) had authorised this conduct.

"As to your assertion," he continued, turning to Hecatonymus, "that we have got in by force and have taken up quarters, this is what we did. We requested them to receive our sick and wounded under cover; and when they refused to open their gates, we walked in where the place itself invited us. All the violence we have committed amounts to this, that our sick folk are quartered under cover, paying for their expenses, and we keep a sentry at the gates, so that our sick and wounded may not lie at the mercy of your governor, but we may have it in our power to remove them whenever we like. The rest of us, you observe, are camping under the canopy of heaven, in regular rank and file, and we are ready to requite kindness with kindness, but to repel evil vigorously. And as for your threat," he said, once again turning to the spokesman, "that you will, if it suits you, make alliance with Corylas and the Paphlagonians to attack us, for our part, we have no objection to fighting both sets of you, if so be we must; we have already fought others many times more numerous than you. Besides, 'if it suits us,' as you put it, to make the Paphlagonian our friend (report says that he has a hankering after your city and some other places on the seaboard), we can enhance the value of our friendship by helping to win for him what he covets." Thereupon the ambassadors showed very plainly their annoyance with Hecatonymus, on account of the style of his remarks, and one of them stept forward to explain that their intention in coming was not at all to raise a war, but on the contrary to demonstrate their friendliness. "And if you come to Sinope itself," the speaker continued, "we will welcome you there with gifts of hospitality. Meanwhile we will enjoin upon the citizens of this place to give you what they can; for we can see that every word of what you say is true." Thereupon the Cotyorites sent gifts of hospitality, and the generals of the Hellenes entertained the ambassadors of the Sinopeans. Many and friendly were the topics of conversation; freely flowed the talk on things in general; and, in particular, both parties were able to make inquiries and satisfy their curiosity concerning the remaining portion of the march.

VI

Such was the conclusion of that day.

August 9, Saturday   **<Diodorus September 7, Sunday>**

On the following day the generals summoned an assembly of the soldiers, when it was resolved to invite the men of Sinope, and to take advice with them touching the remainder of the journey. In the event of their having to continue it on foot, the Sinopeans through their acquaintance with Paphlagonia would be useful to them; while, if they had to go by sea, the services of the same people would be at a premium; for who but they could furnish ships sufficient for the army? Accordingly, they summoned their ambassadors, and took counsel with them, begging them, on the strength of the sacred ties which bind Hellenes to Hellenes, to inaugurate the good reception they had spoken of, by present kindliness and their best advice. Hecatonymus rose and wished at once to offer an apology with regard to what he had said about the possibility of making friends with the Paphlagonians. "The words were not intended," he said, "to convey a threat, as though they were minded to go to war with the Hellenes, but as meaning rather: albeit we have it in our power to be friendly with the barbarians, we will choose the Hellenes." Then, being urged to aid them by some advice, with a pious ejaculation, he commenced: "If I bestow upon you the best counsel I am able, God grant that blessings in abundance may descend on me; but if the contrary, may evil betide me! 'Sacred counsel (99),' as the saying goes--well, sirs, if ever the saying held, it should hold I think to-day; when, if I be proved to have given you good counsel, I shall not lack panegyrists, or if evil, your imprecations will be many-tongued.

"As to trouble, I am quite aware, we shall have much more trouble if you are conveyed by sea, for we must provide the vessels; whereas, if you go by land, all the fighting will evolve on you. Still, let come what may, it behoves me to state my views. I have an intimate acquaintance with the country of the Paphlagonians and their power. The country possesses the two features of hill and vale, that is to say, the fairest plains and the highest mountains. To begin with the mountains, I know the exact point at which you must make your entry. It is precisely where the horns of a mountain tower over both sides of the road. Let the merest handful of men occupy these and they can hold the pass with ease; for when that is done not all the enemies in the world could effect a passage. I could point out the whole with my finger, if you like to send any one with me to the scene. "So much for the mountain barrier. But the next thing I know is that there are plains and a cavalry which the barbarians themselves hold to be superior to the entire cavalry of the great king. Why, only the other day these people refused to present themselves to the summons of the king; their chief is too proud for that. "But now, supposing you were able to seize the mountain barrier, by stealth, or expedition, before the enemy could stop you; supposing further,

124

you were able to win an engagement in the plain against not only their cavalry but their more than one hundred and twenty thousand infantry--you will only find yourself face to face with rivers, a series of them. First the Thermodon, three hundred feet broad, which I take it will be difficult to pass, especially with a host of foes in front and another following behind. Next comes the Iris river, three hundred feet broad; and thirdly, the Halys, at least two furlongs broad, which you could not possibly cross without vessels, and who is going to supply you with vessels? In the same way too the Parthenius is impassable, which you will reach if you cross the Halys. For my part, then, I consider the land-journey, I will not say difficult, but absolutely impossible for you. Whereas if you go by sea, you can coast along from here to Sinope, and from Sinope to Heraclea. From Heraclea onwards there is no difficulty, whether by land or by sea; for there are plenty of vessels at Heraclea." After he had finished his remarks, some of his hearers thought they detected a certain bias in them. He would not have spoken so, but for his friendship with Corylas, whose official representative he was. Others guessed he had an itching palm, and that he was hoping to receive a present for his "sacred advice." Others again suspected that his object was to prevent their going by foot and doing some mischief to the country of the Sinopeans. However that might be, the Hellenes voted in favour of continuing the journey by sea. After this Xenophon said: "Sinopeans, the army has chosen that method of procedure which you advise, and thus the matter stands. If there are sure to be vessels enough to make it impossible for a single man to be left behind, go by sea we will; but if part of us are to be left while part go by sea, we will not set foot on board the vessels. One fact we plainly recognise, strength is everything to us. So long as we have the mastery, we shall be able to protect ourselves and get provisions; but if we are once caught at the mercy of our foes, it is plain, we shall be reduced to slavery." On hearing this the ambassadors bade them send an embassy, which they did, to wit,

August 11, Monday   <Diodorus September 9, Tuesday>
Ambassadors sent to the Sinopeans

Callimachus the Arcadian, and Ariston the Athenian, and Samolas the Achaean. So these set off,

August 13, Wednesday   <Diodorus September 11, Thursday>
Xenophon considers the possibility of setting up a colony

but meanwhile a thought shaped itself in the mind of Xenophon, as there before his eyes lay that vast army of Hellene hoplites, and that other array of peltasts, archers, and slingers, with cavalry to boot, and all in a state of thorough efficiency from long practice, hardened veterans, and all collected in Pontus, where to raise so large a force would cost a mint of money. Then the idea dawned upon him: how noble an opportunity to acquire new territory and power for Hellas, by the founding of a colony--a city of no mean size, moreover, said he to himself, as he reckoned up their own numbers--and besides themselves a population planted on the shores of Pontus. Thereupon he summoned Silanus the Ambraciot, the soothsayer of Cyrus above mentioned, and before breathing a syllable to any of the soldiers, he consulted the victims by sacrifice.

August 14, Thursday   <Diodorus September 12, Friday>

But Silanus, in apprehension lest these ideas might embody themselves, and the army be permanently halted at some point or other, set a tale going among the men, to the effect that Xenophon was minded to detain the army and found a city in order to win himself a name and acquire power, Silanus himself being minded to reach Hellas with all possible speed, for the simple reason that he had still got the three thousand darics presented to him by Cyrus on the occasion of the sacrifice when he hit the truth so happily about the ten days. Silanus's story was variously received, some few of the soldiers thinking it would be an excellent thing to stay in that country; but the majority were strongly averse.

August 16, Saturday   <Diodorus September 14, Sunday>
Timasion and Thorax make deal with a Heracleot and the Sinopeans

The next incident was that Timasion the Dardanian, with Thorax the Boeotian, addressed themselves to some Heracleot and Sinopean traders who had come to Cotyora, and told them that if they did not find means to furnish the army with pay sufficient to keep them in provisions on the homeward voyage, all that great force would most likely settle down permanently in Pontus. "Xenophon has a pet idea," they continued, "which he urges upon us. We are to wait until the ships come, and then we are suddenly to turn round to the army and say: 'Soldiers, we now see the straits we are in, unable to keep ourselves in provisions on the return voyage, or to make our friends at home a little present at the end of our journey. But if you like to select some place on the inhabited seaboard of the Black Sea which may take your fancy and there put in, this is open to you to do. Those who like to go home, go; those who care to stay here, stay. You have got vessels now, so that you can make a sudden pounce upon any point you choose.'" The merchants went off with this tale and reported it to every city they came to in turn, nor did they go alone, but Timasion the Dardanian sent a fellow-citizen of his own, Eurymachus, with the Boeotian Thorax, to repeat the same story.

August 18, Monday　　　　　**<Diodorus September 16, Tuesday>**

So when it reached the ears of the men of Sinope and the Heracleots,

August 20, Wednesday　　　　**<Diodorus September 18, Thursday>**

they sent to Timasion and pressed him to accept of a gratuity, in return for which he was to arrange for the departure of the troops.

August 21, Thursday　　　　　**<Diodorus September 19, Friday>**

Timasion was only too glad to hear this, and he took the opportunity when the soldiers were convened in meeting to make the following remarks: "Soldiers," he said, "do not set your thoughts on staying here; let Hellas, and Hellas only, be the object of your affection, for I am told that certain persons have been sacrificing on this very question, without saying a word to you. Now I can promise you, if you once leave these waters, to furnish you with regular monthly pay, dating from the first of the month, at the rate of one cyzicene (100) a head per month. I will bring you to the Troad, from which part I am an exile, and my own state is at your service. They will receive me with open arms. I will be your guide personally, and I will take you to places where you will get plenty of money. I know every corner of the Aeolid, and Phrygia, and the Troad, and indeed the whole satrapy of Pharnabazus, partly because it is my birthplace, partly from campaigns in that region with Clearchus and Dercylidas (101)."

No sooner had he ceased than up got Thorax the Boeotian. This was a man who had a standing battle with Xenophon about the generalship of the army. What he said was that, if they once got fairly out of the Euxine, there was the Chersonese, a beautiful and prosperous country, where they could settle or not, as they chose. Those who liked could stay; and those who liked could return to their homes; how ridiculous then, when there was so much territory in Hellas and to spare, to be poking about (102) in the land of the barbarian. "But until you find yourselves there," he added, "I, no less than Timasion, can guarantee you regular pay." This he said, knowing what promises had been made Timasion by the men of Heraclea and Sinope to induce them to set sail.

Meanwhile Xenophon held his peace. Then up got Philesius and Lycon, two Achaeans: "It was monstrous," they said, "that Xenophon should be privately persuading people to stop there, and consulting the victims for that end, without letting the army into the secret, or breathing a syllable in public about the matter." When it came to this, Xenophon was forced to get up, and speak as follows: "Sirs, you are well aware that my habit is to sacrifice at all times; whether in your own behalf or my own, I strive in every thought, word, and deed to be directed as is best for yourselves and for me. And in the present instance my sole object was to learn whether it were better even so much as to broach the subject, and so take action, or to have absolutely nothing to do with the project. Now Silanus the soothsayer assured me by his answer of what was the main point: 'the victims were favourable.' No doubt Silanus knew that I was not unversed myself in his lore, as I have so often assisted at the sacrifice; but he added that there were symptoms in the victims of some guile or conspiracy against me. That was a happy discovery on his part, seeing that he was himself conspiring at the moment to traduce me before you; since it was he who set the tale going that I had actually made up my mind to carry out these projects without procuring your consent. Now, for my part, if I saw that you were in any difficulties, I should set myself to discover how you might capture a city, on the understanding of course that all who wished might sail away at once, leaving those who did not wish, to follow at a later date, with something perhaps in their pockets to benefit their friends at home. Now, however, as I see that the men of Heraclea and Sinope are to send you ships to assist you to sail away, and more than one person guarantees to give you regular monthly pay, it is, I admit, a rare chance to be safely piloted to the haven of our hopes, and at the same time to receive pay for our preservation. For myself I have done with that dream, and to those, who came to me to urge these projects, my advice is to have done with them. In fact, this is my view. As long as you stay together united as to-day, you will command respect and procure provisions; for might certainly exercises a right over what belongs to the weaker. But once broken up, with your force split into bits, you will neither be able to get subsistence, nor indeed will you get off without paying dearly for it. In fact, my resolution coincides precisely with yours. It is that we should set off for Hellas, and if any one stops behind, or is caught deserting before the whole army is in safety, let him be judged as an evil-doer. Pray let all who are in favour of this proposition hold up their hands." They all held them up; only Silanus began shouting and vainly striving to maintain the right of departure for all who liked to depart. But the soldiers would not suffer him, threatening him that if he were himself caught attempting to run away they would inflict the aforesaid penalty.

August 23, Saturday   **<Diodorus September 21, Sunday>**

After this, when the Heracleots learned that the departure by sea was resolved upon, and that the measure itself emanated from Xenophon, they sent the vessels indeed; but as to the money which they had promised to Timasion and Thorax as pay for the soldiers, they were not as good as their word, in fact they cheated them both. Thus the two who had guaranteed regular monthly pay were utterly confounded, and stood in terror of the soldiers.

August 25, Monday   **<Diodorus September 23, Tuesday>**

What they did then, was to take to them the other generals to whom they had communicated their former transactions (that is to say, all except Neon the Asniaean, who, as lieutenant-general, was acting for Cheirisophus during his continued absence). This done they came in a body to Xenophon and said that their views were changed. As they had now got the ships, they thought it best to sail to the Phasis, and seize the territory of the Phasians (whose present king was a descendant of Aeetes (103)). Xenophon's reply was curt:--Not one syllable would he have to say himself to the army in this matter, "But," he added, "if you like, you can summon an assembly and have your say." Thereupon Timasion the Dardanian set forth as his opinion:--It were best to hold no parliament at present, but first to go and conciliate, each of them, his own officers. Thus they went away and proceeded to execute their plans.

August 26, Tuesday   <Diodorus September 24, Wednesday>

VII

Presently the soldiers came to learn what was in course of agitation, and Neon gave out that Xenophon had persuaded the other generals to adopt his views, and had a plan to cheat the soldiers and take them back to the Phasis.

August 27, Wednesday   <Diodorus September 25, Thursday>

The soldiers were highly indignant; meetings were held; little groups gathered ominously; and there seemed an alarming probability that they would repeat the violence with which they had lately treated the heralds of the Colchians and the clerks of the market; when all who did not save themselves by jumping into the sea were stoned to death.

August 28, Thursday   <Diodorus September 26, Friday>

So Xenophon, seeing what a storm was brewing, resolved to anticipate matters so far as to summon a meeting of the men without delay, and thus prevent their collecting of their own accord, and he ordered the herald to announce an assembly. The voice of the herald was no sooner heard than they rushed with great readiness to the place of meeting. Then Xenophon, without accusing the generals of having come to him, made the following speech: "I hear that a charge is brought against me. It is I apparently who am going to cheat you and carry you off to Phasis. I beg you by all that is holy to listen to me; and if there be found any guilt in me, let me not leave this place till I have paid the penalty of my misdoing; but if my accusers are found guilty, treat them as they deserve. I presume, sirs, you know where the sun rises and where he sets, and that he who would go to Hellas must needs journey towards the sunset; whereas he who seeks the land of the barbarian must contrariwise fix his face towards the dawn. Now is that a point in which a man might hope to cheat you? Could any one make you believe that the sun rises here and sets there, or that he sets here and rises there? And doubtless you know this too, that it is Boreas, the north wind, who bears the mariner out of Pontus towards Hellas, and the south wind inwards towards the Phasis, whence the saying-- "'When the North wind doth blow Home to Hellas we will go (104).'

130

"He would be a clever fellow who could befool you into embarking with a south wind blowing. That sounds all very well, you think, only I may get you on board during a calm. Granted, but I shall be on board my one ship, and you on board another hundred at least, and how am I to constrain you to voyage with me against your will, or by what cajolery shall I carry you off? But I will imagine you so far befooled and bewitched by me, that I have got you to the Phasis; we proceed to disembark on dry land. At last it will come out, that wherever you are, you are not in Hellas, and the inventor of the trick will be one sole man, and you who have been caught by it will number something like ten thousand with swords in your hands. I do not know how a man could better ensure his own punishment than by embarking on such a policy with regards to himself and you. "Nay, these tales are the invention of silly fellows who are jealous of the honour you bestow on me. A most uncalled-for jealousy! Do I hinder any of them from speaking any word of import in his power? of striking a blow in your behalf and his own, if that is his choice? or, finally, of keeping his eyes and ears open to secure your safety? What is it? In your choice of leaders do I stand in the way of any one, is that it? Let him step forward, I yield him place; he shall be your general; only he must prove that he has your good at heart. "For myself, I have done; but for yourselves, if any of you conceive either that he himself could be the victim of a fraud, or that he could victimise any one else in such a thing as this, let him open his lips and explain to us how. Take your time, but when you have sifted the matter to your hearts' content, do not go away without suffering me to tell you of something which I see looming. If it should burst upon us and prove in fact anything like what it gives signs of being now, it is time for us to take counsel for ourselves and see that we do not prove ourselves to be the worst and basest of men in the sight of gods and men, be they friends or be they foes." The words moved the curiosity of the soldiers. They marvelled what this matter might be, and bade him explain. Thereupon he began again: "You will not have forgotten certain places in the hills--barbaric fastnesses, but friendly to the Cerasuntines--from which people used to come down and sell us large cattle and other things which they possessed, and if I mistake not, some of you went to the nearest of these places and made purchases in the market and came back again. Clearetus the captain learnt of this place, that it was but a little one and unguarded. Why should it be guarded since it was friendly? so the folk thought. Thus he stole upon it in the dead of night, and meant to sack it without saying a word to any of us. His design was, if he took the place, not to return again to the army, but to mount a vessel which, with his messmates on board her, was sailing past at the time, and stowing away what he had seized, to set sail and begone beyond the Euxine. All this had been agreed upon and arranged with his comrades on board the vessel, as I now discover. Accordingly, he summoned to his side all whom he could persuade, and set off at their head against the little place. But dawn overtook him on his march. The men collected out of their strongholds, and whether from a distance or close quarters, made such a fight that they killed Clearetus and a good many of the rest, and only a few of them got safe back to Cerasus. "These things took place on the day on which we started to come hither on foot; while some of those who were to go by sea were still at Cerasus, not having as yet weighed anchor. After this, according to what the Cerasuntines state, there arrived three inhabitants of the place which had been attacked; three elderly men, seeking an interview with our public assembly. Not finding us, they addressed themselves to the men of Cerasus, and told them, they were astonished that we should have thought it right to attack them; however, when, as the Cerasuntines assert, they had assured them that the occurrence was not authorised by public consent, they were pleased, and proposed to sail here, not only to state to us what had occurred, but to offer that those who were interested should take up and bury the bodies of the slain. "But among the Hellenes still at Cerasus were some of those who had escaped. They found out in which direction the barbarians were minded to go, and not only had the face themselves to pelt them with stones, but vociferously encouraged their neighbours to do the same. The three men--ambassadors, mark you--were slain, stoned to death. After this occurrence, the men of Cerasus came to us and reported the affair, and we generals, on being informed, were annoyed at what had taken place, and took counsel with the Cerasuntines how the dead bodies of the Hellenes might be buried. While seated in conclave outside the camp, we suddenly were aware of a great hubbub. We heard cries: 'Cut them down!' 'Shoot them!' 'Stone them!' and presently we caught sight of a mass of people racing towards us with stones in their hands, and others picking them up. The Cerasuntines, naturally enough, considering the incident they had lately witnessed, retired in terror to their vessels, and, upon my word, some of us did not feel too comfortable. All I could do was to go to them and inquire what it all meant. Some of them had not the slightest notion, although they had stones in their hands, but chancing on some one who was better informed, I was told by him that 'the clerks of the market were treating the army most scandalously.' Just then some one got sight of the market clerk, Zelarchus, making his way off towards the sea, and lifted up his voice aloud, and the rest responding to the cry as if a wild boar or a stag had been started, they rushed upon him. "The Cerasuntines, seeing a rush in their direction, thought that, without a doubt, it was directed against themselves, and fled with all speed and threw themselves into the sea, in which proceeding they were imitated by some few of our own men, and all who did not know how to swim were drowned. But now, what do you think of their case, these men of Cerasus? They had done no wrong. They were simply afraid that some madness had seized us, like that to which dogs are liable. "I say then, if proceedings like this are to be the order of the day, you had better consider what the ultimate condition of the army is like to be. As a body you will not have it in your power to undertake war against whom you like, or to conclude peace. But in private any one who chooses will conduct the army on any quest which takes his fancy. And when ambassadors come to you to demand peace, or whatever it may be, officious people will put them to death and prevent your hearing the proposals which brought them to you. The next step will be that those whom you as a body may choose as generals will be of no account; but any one who likes to elect himself general, and will adopt the formula 'Shoot him! shoot him!' will be competent to cut down whomsoever he pleases untried, be it general or private soldier, if only he have sufficient followers, as was the case just now. But just consider what these self-appointed generals have achieved for you. Zelarchus, the clerk of the market, may possibly have done you a wrong; if so, he has sailed off and is gone without paying you any penalty; or he may be guiltless, in which case we have driven him from the army in terror of perishing unjustly without a trial. While those who stoned the ambassadors have contrived so cleverly that we alone of all Hellenes cannot approach Cerasus safely without a strong force, and the corpses which the very men who slew them themselves invited us to bury, we cannot now pick up with safety even under a flag of truce. Who indeed would care to carry a flag of truce, or go as a herald with the blood of heralds upon his hands? All we could do was to implore the Cerasuntines to bury them. "If then you approve of such doings, have a resolution passed to that effect, so that, with a prospect of like occurrences in the future, a man may privately set up a guard and do his best to fix his tent where he can find a strong position with a commanding site. If, however, these seem to you to be the deeds rather of wild beasts than of human beings, bethink you of some means by which to stay them; or else, in heaven's name, how shall we do sacrifice to the gods gladly, with impious deeds to answer for? or how shall we, who lay the knife to each other's throats, give battle to our enemies? What friendly city will receive us when they see rampant lawlessness in our midst? Who will have the courage to afford us a market, when we prove our worthlessness in these weightiest concerns? and what becomes of the praise we expect to win from the mouths of men? who will vouchsafe it to us, if this is our behaviour? Should we not ourselves bestow the worst of names on the perpetrators of like deeds?" After this they rose, and, as one man, proposed that the ringleaders in these matters should be punished; and that for the future, to set an example of lawlessness should be forbidden. Every such ringleader was to be prosecuted on the capital charge; the generals were to bring all offenders to the bar of justice; prosecutions for all other misdemeanours committed since the death of Cyrus were to be instituted; and they ended by constituting the officers into a board of dicasts (105); and upon the strong representation of Xenophon, with the concurrence of the soothsayers, it was resolved to purify the army, and this purification was made.

VIII

It was further resolved that the generals themselves should undergo a judicial examination in reference to their conduct in past time.

August 29, Friday   <Diodorus September 27, Saturday>
Commencement of Judicial Examination of the Army

In course of investigation, Philesius and Xanthicles respectively were condemned to pay a sum of twenty minae, to meet a deficiency to that amount incurred during the guardianship of the cargoes of the merchantmen. Sophaenetus was fined ten minae for inadequate performance of his duty as one of the chief officers selected.

August 30, Saturday   <Diodorus September 28, Sunday>
Charges against Xenophon and his defence

Against Xenophon a charge was brought by certain people, who asserted that they had been beaten by him, and framed the indictment as one of personal outrage with violence (106). Xenophon got up and demanded that the first speaker should state "where and when it was he had received these blows." The other, so challenged, answered, "When we were perishing of cold and there was a great depth of snow." Xenophon said: "Upon my word, with weather such as you describe, when our provisions had run out, when the wine could not even be smelt, when numbers were dropping down dead beat, so acute was the suffering, with the enemy close on our heels; certainly, if at such a season as that I was guilty of outrage, I plead guilty to being a more outrageous brute than the ass, which is too wanton, they say, to feel fatigue. Still, I wish you would tell us," said he, "what led to my striking you. Did I ask you for something and, on your refusing it to me, did I proceed to beat you? Was it a debt, for which I demanded payment? or a quarrel about some boy or other? Was I the worse for liquor, and behaving like a drunkard?" When the man met each of these questions with a negative, he questioned him further: "Are you a heavy infantry soldier?" "No," said he. "A peltast, then?" "No, nor yet a peltast"; but he had been ordered by his messmates to drive a mule, although he was a free man. Then at last he recognised him, and inquired: "Are you the fellow who carried home the sick man?" "Yes, I am," said he, "thanks to your driving; and you made havoc of my messmates' kit." "Havoc!" said Xenophon: "Nay, I distributed it; some to one man, some to another to carry, and bade them bring the things safely to me; and when I got them back I delivered them all safely to you, and you, on your side, had rendered an account to me of the man. Let me tell you," he continued, turning to the court, "what the circumstances were; it is worth hearing:--

"A man was left behind from inability to proceed farther; I recognised the poor fellow sufficiently to see that he was one of ours, and I forced you, sir, to carry him to save his life. For if I am not much mistaken, the enemy were close at our heels?" The fellow assented to this. "Well then," said Xenophon, "after I had sent you forward, I overtook you again, as I came up with the rearguard; you were digging a trench with intent to bury the man; I pulled up and said something in commendation; as we stood by the poor fellow twitched his leg, and the bystanders all cried out, 'Why, the man's alive!' Your remark was: 'Alive or not as he likes, I am not going to carry him' Then I struck you. Yes! you are right, for it looked very much as if you knew him to be alive." "Well," said he, "was he any the less dead when I reported him to you?" "Nay," retorted Xenophon, "by the same token we shall all one day be dead, but that is no reason why meantime we should all be buried alive?" Then there was a general shout: "If Xenophon had given the fellow a few more blows, it might have been better." The others were now called upon to state the grounds on which they had been beaten in each case; but when they refused to get up, he proceeded to state them himself. "I confess, sirs, to having struck certain men for failure in discipline. These were men who were quite content to owe their safety to us. Whilst the rest of the world marched on in rank and did whatever fighting had to be done, they preferred to leave the ranks, and rush forward to loot and enrich themselves at our expense. Now, if this conduct were to be the rule, general ruin would be the result. I do not deny that I have given blows to this man or the other who played the poltroon and refused to get up, helplessly abandoning himself to the enemy; and so I forced them to march on. For once in the severe wintry weather I myself happened to sit down for a long time, whilst waiting for a party who were getting their kit together, and I discovered how difficult it was to get up again and stretch one's legs. After this personal experience, whenever I saw any one else seated in slack and lazy mood, I tried to spur him on. The mere movement and effort to play the man caused warmth and moisture, whereas it was plain that sitting down and keeping quiet helped the blood to freeze and the toes to mortify, calamities which really befell several of the men, as you yourselves are aware. "I can imagine a third case, that of some straggler stopping behind, merely to rest for rest's sake, and hindering you in front and us behind alike from pressing on the march. If he got a blow with the fist from me it saved him a thrust with the lance from the enemy. In fact, the opportunity they enjoy to-day of taking vengeance on me for any treatment which I put upon them wrongfully, is derived from their salvation then; whereas, if they had fallen into the enemy's hands, let them ask themselves for what outrage, however great, they could expect to get satisfaction now. My defence," he continued, "is simple: if I chastised any one for his own good, I claim to suffer the same penalties as parents pay their children or masters their boys. Does not the surgeon also cauterise and cut us for our good? But if you really believe that these acts are the outcome of wanton insolence, I beg you to observe that although to-day, thank God! I am heartier than formerly, I wear a bolder front now than then, and I drink more wine, yet I never strike a soul; no, for I see that you have reached smooth water. When storm arises, and a great sea strikes the vessel amidships, a mere shake of the head will make the look-out man furious with the crew in the forecastle, or the helmsman with the men in the stern sheets, for at such a crisis even a slight slip may ruin everything. But I appeal to your own verdict, already recorded, in proof that I was justified in striking these men. You stood by, sirs, with swords, not voting tablets, in your hands, and it was in your power to aid the fellows if you liked; but, to speak the honest truth, you neither aided them nor did you join me in striking the disorderly. In other words, you enabled any evilly-disposed person among them to give rein to his wantonness by your passivity. For if you will be at pains to investigate, you will find that those who were then most cowardly are the ringleaders to-day in brutality and outrage. "There is Boiscus the boxer, a Thessalian, what a battle he fought then to escape carrying his shield! so tired was he, and to-day I am told he has stripped several citizens of Cotyora of the clothes on their backs. If then you are wise, you will treat this personage in a way the contrary to that in which men treat dogs. A savage dog is tied up on the day and loosed at night, but if you are wise you will tie this fellow up at night and only let him loose in the day. "But really," he added, "it does surprise me with what keenness you remember and recount the times when I incurred the hatred of some one; but some other occasions when I eased the burden of winter and storm for any of you, or beat off an enemy, or helped to minister to you in sickness and want, not a soul of you remembers these. Or when for any noble deed done by any of you I praised the doer, and according to my ability did honour to this brave man or that; these things have slipped from your memories, and are clean forgotten. Yet it were surely more noble, just, and holy, sweeter and kindlier to treasure the memory of good rather than of evil." He ended, and then one after another of the assembly got up and began recalling incidents of the kind suggested, and things ended not so unpleasantly after all.

September 1, Monday   <Diodorus September 30, Tuesday>
Food raids into Paphlagonia (corresponding to an area in the region of Karaoluk in modern-day Turkey)

BOOK VI

I

After this, whilst waiting, they lived partly on supplies from the market, partly on the fruit of raids into Paphlagonia. The Paphlagonians, on their side, showed much skill in kidnapping stragglers, wherever they could lay hands on them, and in the night time tried to do mischief to those whose quarters were at a distance from the camp.

September 4, Thursday   <Diodorus October 3, Friday>
Arrival of Paphlagonian Ambassadors

The result was that their relations to one another were exceedingly hostile, so much so that Corylas, who was the chief of Paphlagonia at that date, sent ambassadors to the Hellenes, bearing horses and fine apparel, and charged with a proposal on the part of Corylas to make terms with the Hellenes on the principle of mutual forbearance from injuries. The generals replied that they would consult with the army about the matter. Meanwhile they gave them a hospitable reception, to which they invited certain members of the army whose claims were obvious. They sacrificed some of the captive cattle and other sacrificial beasts, and with these they furnished forth a sufficiently festal entertainment, and reclining on their truckle beds, fell to eating and drinking out of beakers made of horn which they happened to find in the country. But as soon as the libation was ended and they had sung the hymn, up got first some Thracians, who performed a dance under arms to the sound of a pipe, leaping high into the air with much nimbleness, and brandishing their swords, till at last one man struck his fellow, and every one thought he was really wounded, so skilfully and artistically did he fall, and the Paphlagonians screamed out. Then he that gave the blow stripped the other of his arms, and marched off chanting the "Sitalcas (107)," whilst others of the Thracians bore off the other, who lay as if dead, though he had not received even a scratch.

After this some Aenianians (108) and Magnesians got up and fell to dancing the Carpaea, as it is called, under arms. This was the manner of the dance: one man lays aside his arms and proceeds to drive a yoke of oxen, and while he drives he sows, turning him about frequently, as though he were afraid of something; up comes a cattle-lifter, and no sooner does the ploughman catch sight of him afar, than he snatches up his arms and confronts him. They fight in front of his team, and all in rhythm to the sound of the pipe. At last the robber binds the countryman and drives off the team. Or sometimes the cattle-driver binds the robber, and then he puts him under the yoke beside the oxen, with his two hands tied behind his back, and off he drives.

After this a Mysian came in with a light shield in either hand and danced, at one time going through a pantomime, as if he were dealing with two assailants at once; at another plying his shields as if to face a single foe, and then again he would whirl about and throw somersaults, keeping the shields in his hands, so that it was a beautiful spectacle. Last of all he danced the Persian dance, clashing the shields together, crouching down on one knee and springing up again from earth; and all this he did in measured time to the sound of the flute. After him the Mantineans stepped upon the stage, and some other Arcadians also stood up; they had accoutred themselves in all their warlike finery. They marched with measured tread, pipes playing, to the tune of the 'warrior's march (109)'; the notes of the paean rose, lightly their limbs moved in dance, as in solemn procession to the holy gods. The Paphlagonians looked upon it as something truly strange that all these dances should be under arms; and the Mysians, seeing their astonishment persuaded one of the Arcadians who had got a dancing girl to let him introduce her, which he did after dressing her up magnificently and giving her a light shield. When, lithe of limb, she danced the Pyrrhic (110), loud clapping followed; and the Paphlagonians asked, "If these women fought by their side in battle?" to which they answered, "To be sure, it was the women who routed the great King, and drove him out of camp." So ended the night.

September 5, Friday   **<Diodorus October 4, Saturday>**

But next day the generals introduced the embassy to the army, and the soldiers passed a resolution in the sense proposed: between themselves and the Paphlagonians there was to be a mutual abstinence from injuries. After this the ambassadors went on their way,

September 13, Saturday   \<Diodorus October 12, Sunday\>
Left Cotyora (Ordu in Turkey)

and the Hellenes, as soon as it was thought that sufficient vessels had arrived, went on board ship, and voyaged a day and a night with a fair breeze, keeping Paphlagonia on their left.

September 14, Thursday   \<Diodorus October 26, Monday\>
Arrival at Sinope (Sinop in modern day Turkey)

And on the following day, arriving at Sinope, they came to moorings in the harbour of Harmene, near Sinope (111). The Sinopeans, though inhabitants of Paphlagonia, are really colonists of the Milesians. They sent gifts of hospitality to the Hellenes, three thousand measures of barley with fifteen hundred jars of wine. At this place Cheirisophus rejoined them with a man-of-war. The soldiers certainly expected that, having come, he would have brought them something, but he brought them nothing, except complimentary phrases, on the part of Anaxibius, the high admiral, and the rest, who sent them their congratulations, coupled with a promise on the part of Anaxibius that, as soon as they were outside the Euxine, pay would be forthcoming.

At Harmene the army halted five days; and now that they seemed to be so close to Hellas, the question how they were to reach home not empty-handed presented itself more forcibly to their minds than heretofore. The conclusion they came to was to appoint a single general, since one man would be better able to handle the troops, by night or by day, than was possible while the generalship was divided. If secrecy were desirable, it would be easier to keep matters dark, or if again expedition were an object, there would be less risk of arriving a day too late, since mutual explanations would be avoided, and whatever approved itself to the single judgement would at once be carried into effect, whereas previously the generals had done everything in obedience to the opinion of the majority. With these ideas working in their minds, they turned to Xenophon, and the officers came to him and told him that this was how the soldiers viewed matters; and each of them, displaying a warmth of kindly feeling, pressed him to accept the office. Xenophon partly would have liked to do so, in the belief that by so doing he would win to himself a higher repute in the esteem of his friends, and that his name would be reported to the city written large; and by some stroke of fortune he might even be the discoverer of some blessing to the army collectively. These and the like considerations elated him; he had a strong desire to hold the supreme command. But then again, as he turned the matter over, the conviction deepened in his mind that the issue of the future is to every man uncertain; and hence there was the risk of perhaps losing such reputation has he had already acquired. He was in sore straights, and, not knowing how to decide, it seemed best to him to lay the matter before heaven. Accordingly, he led two victims to the altar and made sacrifice to Zeus the King, for it was he and no other who had been named by the oracle at Delphi, and his belief was that the vision which he had beheld when he first essayed to undertake the joint administration of the army was sent to him by that god. He also recalled to mind a circumstance which befell him still earlier, when setting out from Ephesus to associate himself with Cyrus (112);--how an eagle screamed on his right hand from the east, and still remained perched, and the soothsayer who was escorting him said that it was a great and royal omen (113); indicating glory and yet suffering; for the punier race of birds only attack the eagle when seated. "Yet," added he, "it bodes not gain in money; for the eagle seizes his food, not when seated, but on the wing."

Thus Xenophon sacrificed, and the god as plainly as might be gave him a sign, neither to demand the generalship, nor, if chosen, to accept the office. And that was how the matter stood when the army met, and the proposal to elect a single leader was unanimous.

September 19, Friday　　　　　**<Diodorus October 18, Saturday>**

After this resolution was passed, they proposed Xenophon for election, and when it seemed quite evident that they would elect him, if he put the question to the vote, he got up and spoke as follows:-- "Sirs, I am but mortal, and must needs be happy to be honoured by you. I thank you, and am grateful, and my prayer is that the gods may grant me to be an instrument of blessing to you. Still, when I consider it closer, thus, in the presence of a Lacedaemonian, to be preferred by you as general, seems to me but ill conducive either to your interests or to mine, since you will the less readily obtain from them hereafter anything you may need, while for myself I look upon acceptance as even somewhat dangerous. Do I not see and know with what persistence these Lacedaemonians prosecuted the war till finally they forced our State to acknowledge the leadership of

Lacedaemon? This confession once extorted from their antagonists, they ceased warring at once, and the siege of the city was at an end. If, with these facts before my eyes, I seem to be doing all I can to neutralise their high self-esteem, I cannot escape the reflection that personally I may be taught wisdom by a painful process. But with your own idea that under a single general there will be less factiousness than when there were many, be assured that in choosing some other than me you will not find me factious. I hold that whosoever sets up factious opposition to his leader factiously opposes his own safety. While if you determine to choose me, I should not be surprised were that choice to entail upon you and me the resentment of other people." After those remarks on Xenophon's part, many more got up, one after another, insisting on the propriety of his undertaking the command. One of them, Agasias the Stymphalian, said: It was really ridiculous, if things had come to this pass that the Lacedeamonians are to fly into a rage because a number of friends have met together to dinner, and omitted to choose a Lacedaemonian to sit at the head of the table. "Really, if that is how matters stand," said he, "I do not see what right we have to be officers even, we who are only Arcadians." That sally brought down the plaudits of the assembly; and Xenophon, seeing that something more was needed, stepped forward again and spoke, "Pardon, sirs," he said, "let me make a clean breast of it. I swear to you by all the gods and goddesses; verily and indeed, I no sooner perceived your purpose, than I consulted the victims, whether it was better for you to entrust this leadership to me, and for me to undertake it, or the reverse. And the gods vouchsafed a sign to me so plain that even a common man might understand it, and perceive that from such sovereignty I must needs hold myself aloof." Under these circumstances they chose Cheirisophus, who, after his election, stepped forward and said: "Nay, sirs, be well assured of this, that had you chosen some one else, I for my part should not have set up factious opposition. As to Xenophon, I believe you have done him a good turn by not appointing him; for even now Dexippus has gone some way in traducing him to Anaxibius, as far as it lay in his power to do so, and that, in spite of my attempts to silence him. What he said was that he believed Xenophon would rather share the command of Clearchus's army with Timasion, a Dardanian, than with himself, a Laconian. But," continued Cheirisophus, "since your choice has fallen upon me, I will make it my endeavour to do you all the good in my power; so make your preparations to weigh anchor to-morrow; wind and weather permitting, we will voyage to Heraclea; every one must endeavour, therefore, to put in at that port; and for the rest we will consult, when we are come thither."

September 20, Saturday   <Diodorus October 19, Sunday>
Leave at Sinope (Sinop in modern day Turkey)

II

The next day they weighed anchor and set sail from Harmene with a fair
breeze, two days' voyage along the coast. (As they coasted along they came
in sight of Jason's beach (114), where, as the story says, the ship Argo came
to moorings; and then the mouths of the rivers, first the Thermodon, then
the Iris, then the Halys, and next to it the Parthenius.)

September 22, Monday   <Diodorus October 21, Tuesday>
Arrival at Heraclea (Heraclea Pontica, Karadeniz Ereğli in modern
day Turkey)

Coasting past (the latter), they reached Heraclea (115), a Hellenic city and a
colony of the Megarians, situated in the territory of the Mariandynians. So
they came to anchorage off the Acherusian Chersonese, where Heracles
(116) is said to have descended to bring up the dog Cerberus, at a point
where they still show the marks of his descent, a deep cleft more than two
furlongs down. Here the Heracleots sent the Hellenes, as gifts of
hospitality, three thousand measures of barley and two thousand jars of
wine, twenty beeves and one hundred sheep. Through the flat country here
flows the Lycus river, as it is called, about two hundred feet in breadth.

September 23, Tuesday   <Diodorus October 22, Wednesday>
Decision to split the army into three arms for the final stages of the
return

The soldiers held a meeting, and took counsel about the remainder of the
journey: should they make their exit from the Pontus by sea or by land? and
Lycon the Achaean got up and said: "I am astonished, sirs, that the generals
do not endeavour to provide us more efficiently with provisions. These
gifts of hospitality will not afford three days' victuals for the army; nor do I
see from what region we are to provide ourselves as we march. My
proposal, therefore, is to demand of the Heracleots at least three thousand
cyzicenes." Another speaker suggested, "not less than ten thousand. Let us
at once, before we break up this meeting, send ambassadors to the city and
ascertain their answer to the demand and take counsel accordingly."

Thereupon they proceeded to put up as ambassadors, first and foremost Cheirisophus, as he had been chosen general-in-chief; others also named Xenophon. But both Cheirisophus and Xenophon stoutly declined, maintaining both alike that they could not compel a Hellenic city, actually friendly, to give anything which they did not spontaneously offer. So, since these two appeared to be backward, the soldiers sent Lycon the Achaean, Callimachus the Parrhasian, and Agasias the Stymphalian. These three went and announced the resolutions passed by the army. Lycon, it was said, even went so far as to threaten certain consequences in case they refused to comply. The Heracleots said they would deliberate; and, without more ado, they got together their goods and chattels from their farms and fields outside, and dismantled the market outside and transferred it within, after which the gates were closed, and arms appeared at the battlements of the walls. At that check, the authors of these tumultuary measures fell to accusing the generals, as if they had marred the proceeding; and the Arcadians and Archaeans banded together, chiefly under the auspices of the two ringleaders, Callimachus the Parrhasian and Lycon the Achaean. The language they held was to this effect: It was outrageous that a single Athenian and a Lacedaemonian, who had not contributed a soldier to the expedition, should rule Peloponnesians; scandalous that they themselves should bear the toils whilst others pocketed the spoils, and that too though the preservation of the army was due to themselves; for, as every one must admit, to the Arcadians and Achaeans the credit of that achievement was due, and the rest of the army went for nothing (which was indeed so far true that the Arcadians and Achaeans did form numerically the larger half of the whole army). What then did common sense suggest? Why, that they, the Arcadians and Achaeans, should make common cause, choose generals for themselves independently, continue the march, and try somewhat to better their condition. This proposal was carried. All the Arcadians and Achaeans who chanced to be with Cheirisophus left him and Xenophon, setting up for themselves and choosing ten generals of their own. These ten, it was decreed, were to put into effect such measures as approved themselves to the majority. Thus the absolute authority vested in Cheirisophus was terminated there and then, within less than a week of his appointment. Xenophon, however was minded to prosecute the journey in their company, thinking that this would be a safer plan than for each to start on his own account. But Neon threw in his weight in favour of separate action. "Every one for himself," he said, for he had heard from Cheirisophus that Cleander, the Spartan governor-general at Byzantium, talked of coming to Calpe Haven with some war vessels. Neon's advice was due to his desire to secure a passage home in these war vessels for themselves and their soldiers, without allowing any one else to share in their good-fortune. As for Cheirisophus, he was at once so out of heart at the turn things had taken, and soured with the whole army, that he left it to his subordinate, Neon, to do just what he liked. Xenophon, on his side, would still have been glad to be quit of the expedition and sail home; but on offering sacrifice to Heracles the Leader, and seeking advice, whether it were better and more desirable to continue the march in charge of the soldiers who had remained faithful, or to take his departure, the god indicated to him by the victims that he should adopt the former course. In this way the army was now split up into three divisions (117). First, the Arcadians and Achaeans, over four thousand five hundred men, all heavy infantry. Secondly, Cheirisophus and his men, viz. one thousand four hundred heavy infantry and the seven hundred peltasts, or Clearchus's Thracians. Thirdly, Xenophon's division of one thousand seven hundred heavy infantry, and three hundred peltasts; but then he alone had the cavalry--about forty troopers.

September 27, Saturday   <Diodorus October 26, Sunday>
The Arcadians leave

The Arcadians, who had bargained with the Heracleots and got some vessels from them, were the first to set sail; they hoped, by pouncing suddenly on the Bithynians, to make as large a haul as possible. With that object they disembarked at Calpe Haven (118), pretty nearly at the middle point in Thrace.

September 28, Sunday   <Diodorus October 27, Monday>
Cheirisophus and his troops leave

Cheirisophus setting off straight from Heraclea, commenced a land march through the country; but having entered into Thrace, he preferred to cling to the seaboard, health and strength failing him.

September 29, Monday   <Diodorus October 28, Tuesday>
Xenophon and his troops leave

Xenophon, lastly, took vessels, and disembarking on the confines of Thrace and the Heracleotid, pushed forward through the heart of the country (119).

III

The Arcadians, disembarking under cover of night at Calpe Haven, marched against the nearest villages about thirty furlongs from the sea; and as soon as it was light, each of the ten generals led his company to attack one village, or if the village were large, a couple of companies advanced under their combined generals. They further agreed upon a certain knoll, where they were all eventually to assemble. So sudden was their attack that they seized a number of captives and enclosed a multitude of small cattle.

September 30, Tuesday   <Diodorus October 29, Wednesday>
Thracian attack on the Arcadians

But the Thracians who escaped began to collect again; for being light-armed troops they had slipped in large numbers through the hands of the heavy infantry; and now that they were got together they first attacked the company of the Arcadian general, Smicres, who had done his work and was retiring to the appointed meeting-place, driving along a large train of captives and cattle. For a good while the Hellenes maintained a running fight (120); but at the passage of a gorge the enemy routed them, slaying Smicres himself and those with him to a man. The fate of another company under command of Hegesander, another of the ten, was nearly as bad; only eight men escaped, Hegesander being one of them. The remaining captains eventually met, some with somewhat to show for their pains, others empty-handed.

The Thracians, having achieved this success, kept up a continual shouting and clatter of conversation to one another during the night;

October 1, Wednesday   <Diodorus October 30, Thursday>

but with day-dawn they marshalled themselves right round the knoll on which the Hellenes were encamped--both cavalry in large numbers and light-armed troops--while every minute the stream of new-comers grew greater. Then they commenced an attack on the heavy infantry in all security, for the Hellenes had not a single bowman, javelin-man, or mounted trooper amongst them; while the enemy rushed forward on foot or galloped up on horseback and let fly their javelins. It was vain to attempt to retaliate, so lightly did they spring back and escape; and ever the attack renewed itself from every point, so that on one side man after man was wounded, on the other not a soul was touched; the result being that they could not stir from their position, and the Thracians ended by cutting them off even from their water. In their despair they began to parley about a truce, and finally various concessions were made and terms agreed to between them; but the Thracians would not hear of giving hostages in answer to the demand of the Hellenes; at that point the matter rested. So fared it with the Arcadians. As to Cheirisophus, that general prosecuted his march along the seaboard, and without check reached Calpe Haven.

October 3, Thursday   \<Diodorus November 1, Saturday\>

Xenophon advanced through the heart of the country; and his cavalry pushing on in front, came upon some old men pursuing their road somewither, who were brought to him, and in answer to his question, whether they had caught sight of another Hellenic army anywhere, told him all that had already taken place, adding that at present they were being besieged upon a knoll with all the Thracians in close circle round them. Thereupon he kept the old men under strict guard to serve as guides in case of need; next, having appointed outposts, he called a meeting of the soldiers, and addressed them: "Soldiers, some of the Arcadians are dead and the rest are being besieged upon a certain knoll. Now my own belief is, that if they are to perish, with their deaths the seal is set to our own fate: since we must reckon with an enemy at once numerous and emboldened. Clearly our best course is to hasten to their rescue, if haply we may find them still alive, and do battle by their side rather than suffer isolation, confronting danger single-handed. "Let us then at once push forward as far as may seem opportune till supper-time, and then encamp. As long as we are marching, let Timasion, with the cavalry, gallop on in front, but without losing sight of us; and let him examine all closely in front, so that nothing may escape our observation." (At the same time too, he sent out some nimble fellows of the light-armed troops to the flanks and to the high tops, who were to give a signal if they espied anything anywhere; ordering them to burn everything inflammable which lay in their path.) "As for ourselves," he continued, "we need not look to find cover in any direction; for it is a long step back to Heraclea and a long leap across to Chrysopolis, and the enemy is at the door. The shortest road is to Calpe Haven, where we suppose Cheirisophus, if safe, to be; but then, when we get there, at Calpe Haven there are no vessels for us to sail away in; and if we stop here, we have not provisions for a single day. Suppose the beleaguered Arcadians left to their fate, we shall find it but a sorry alternative to run the gauntlet with

Cheirisophus's detachment alone; better to save them if we can, and with united forces work out our deliverance in common. But if so, we must set out with minds prepared, since to-day either a glorious death awaits us or the achievement of a deed of noblest emprise in the rescue of so many Hellene lives. Maybe it is God who leads us thus, God who chooses to humble the proud boaster, boasting as though he were exceedingly wise, but for us, the beginning of whose every act is by heaven's grace, that same God reserves a higher grade of honour. One duty I would recall to you, to apply your minds to the execution of the orders with promptitude." With these words he led the way. The cavalry, scattering as far in advance as was prudent, wherever they set foot, set fire. The peltasts moving parallel on the high ground were similarly employed, burning everything combustible they could discover. While the main army, wherever they came upon anything which had accidentally escaped, completed the work, so that the whole country looked as if it were ablaze; and the army might easily pass for a larger one. When the hour had come, they turned aside to a knoll and took up quarters; and there they espied the enemy's watch-fires. He was about forty furlongs distant. On their side also they kindled as many watch-fires as possible; but as soon as they had dined the order was passed to quench all the fires. So during the night they posted guards and slept.

October 4, Saturday   <Diodorus November 2, Sunday>
March back to aid the Arcadian s and arrival at Calpe Haven (likely Kerpe Limanı in Turkey)

But at daybreak they offered prayers to the gods, and drawing up in order of battle, began marching with what speed they might. Timasion and the cavalry, who had the guides with them, and were moving on briskly in front, found themselves without knowing it at the very knoll upon which the Hellenes had been beleaguered. But no army could they discover, whether of friend or foe; only some starveling old women and men, with a few sheep and oxen which had been left behind. This news they reported to Xenophon and the main body. At first the marvel was what had happened; but ere long they found out by inquiries from the folk who had been left behind, that the Thracians had set off immediately after sundown, and were gone; the Hellenes had waited till morning before they made off, but in what direction, they could not say. On hearing this, Xenophon's troops first breakfasted, and then getting their kit together began their march, desiring to unite with the rest at Calpe's Haven without loss of time. As they continued their march, they came across the track of the Arcadians and Achaeans along the road to Calpe, and both divisions arriving eventually at the same place, were overjoyed to see one another again, and they embraced each other like brothers. Then the Arcadians inquired of Xenophon's officers--why they had quenched the watch-fires?"At first," said they, "when we lost sight of your watch-fires, we expected you to attack the enemy in the night; and the enemy, so at least we imagined, must have been afraid of that and so set off. The time at any rate at which they set off would correspond. But when the requisite time had elapsed and you did not come, we concluded that you must have learnt what was happening to us, and in terror had made a bolt for it to the seaboard. We resolved not to be left behind by you; and that is how we also came to march hither."

IV

During this day they contented themselves with bivouacking there on the beach at the harbour. The place which goes by the name of Calpe Haven is in Asiatic Thrace, the name given to a region extending from the mouth of the Euxine all the way to Heraclea, which lies on the right hand as you sail into the Euxine. It is a long day's voyage for a war-ship, using her three banks of oars, from Byzantium to Heraclea, and between these two there is not a single Hellenic or friendly city, but only these Bithynian Thracians, who have a bad reputation for the savagery with which they treat any Hellenes cast ashore by shipwreck or otherwise thrown into their power. Now the haven of Calpe lies exactly midway, halving the voyage between Byzantium and Heraclea. It is a long promontory running out into the sea; the seaward portion being a rocky precipice, at no point less than twenty fathoms high; but on the landward side there is a neck about four hundred feet wide; and the space inside the neck is capable of accommodating ten thousand inhabitants, and there is a haven immediately under the crag with a beach facing the west. Then there is a copious spring of fresh water flowing on the very marge of the sea commanded by the stronghold. Again, there is plenty of wood of various sorts; but most plentiful of all, fine shipbuilding timber down to the very edge of the sea. The upland stretches into the heart of the country for twenty furlongs at least. It is good loamy soil, free from stones. For a still greater distance the seaboard is thickly grown with large timber trees of every description. The surrounding country is beautiful and spacious, containing numerous well populated villages. The soil produces barley and wheat, and pulse of all sorts, millet and sesame, figs in ample supply, with numerous vines producing sweet wines, and indeed everything else except olives. Such is the character of the country. The tents were pitched on the seaward-facing beach, the soldiers being altogether averse to camping on ground which might so easily be converted into a city. Indeed, their arrival at the place at all seemed very like the crafty design of some persons who were minded to form a city. The aversion was not unnatural, since the majority of the soldiers had not left their homes on so long a voyage from scantiness or subsistence, but attracted by the fame of Cyrus's virtues; some of them bringing followers, while others had expended money on the expedition. And amongst them was a third set who had run away from fathers and mothers; while a different class had left children behind, hoping to return to them with money or other gains. Other people with Cyrus won great success, they were told (121); why should it not be so with them? Being persons then of this description, the one longing of their hearts was to reach Hellas safely.

October 5, Sunday   **<Diodorus November 3, Monday>**

It was on the day after their meeting that Xenophon sacrificed as a preliminary to a military expedition; for it was needful to march out in search of provisions, besides which he designed burying the dead. As soon as the victims proved favourable they all setout, the Arcadians following with the rest. The majority of the dead, who had lain already five days, they buried just where they had fallen, in groups; to remove their bodies now would have been impossible. Some few, who lay off the roads, they got together and buried with what splendour they could, considering the means in their power. Others they could not find, and for these they erected a great cenotaph (122), and covered it with wreaths. When it was all done, they returned home to camp. At that time they supped, and went to rest.

October 6, Monday   **<Diodorus November 4, Tuesday>**

Next day there was a general meeting of the soldiers, collected chiefly by Agasias the Stymphalian, a captain, and Hieronymus, an Eleian, also a captain, and other seniors of the Arcadians; and they passed a resolution that, for the future, whoever revived the idea of breaking up the army should be punished by death. And the army, it was decided, would now resume its old position under the command of its former generals. Though Cheirisophus, indeed, had already died under medical treatment for fever (123); and Neon the Asinaean had taken his place.

After these resolutions Xenophon got up and said: "Soldiers, the journey must now, I presume, be conducted on foot; indeed, this is clear, since we have no vessels; and we are driven to commence it at once, for we have no provisions if we stop. We then," he continued, "will sacrifice, and you must prepare yourselves to fight now, if ever, for the spirit of the enemy has revived." Thereupon the generals sacrificed, in the presence of the Arcadian seer, Arexion; for Silanus the Ambraciot had chartered a vessel at Heraclea and made his escape ere this. Sacrificing with a view to departure, the victims proved unfavourable to them. Accordingly they waited that day. Certain people were bold enough to say that Xenophon, out of his desire to colonise the place, had persuaded the seer to say that the victims were unfavourable to departure.

October 7, Tuesday   <Diodorus November 5, Wednesday>

Consequently he proclaimed by herald next morning that any one who liked should be present at the sacrifice; or if he were a seer he was bidden to be present and help to inspect the victims. Then he sacrificed, and there were numbers present; but though the sacrifice on the question of departure was repeated as many as three times, the victims were persistently unfavourable. Thereat the soldiers were in high dudgeon, for the provisions they had brought with them had reached the lowest ebb, and there was no market to be had. Consequently there was another meeting, and Xenophon spoke again: "Men," said he, "the victims are, as you may see for yourselves, not yet favourable to the march; but meanwhile, I can see for myself that you are in need of provisions; accordingly we must narrow the sacrifice to the particular point." Some one got up and said: "Naturally enough the victims are unfavourable, for, as I learnt from some one on a vessel which arrived here yesterday by accident, Cleander, the governor at Byzantium, intends coming here with ships and men-of-war." Thereat they were all in favour of stopping; but they must needs go out for provisions, and with this object he again sacrificed three times, and the victims remained adverse. Things had now reached such a pass that the men actually came to Xenophon's tent to proclaim that they had no provisions. His sole answer was that he would not lead them out till the victims were favourable.

October 8, Wednesday   <Diodorus November 6, Thursday>
Attack by the cavalry of Pharnabazus

So again the next day he sacrificed; and nearly the whole army, so strong was the general anxiety, flocked round the victims; and now the very victims themselves failed. So the generals, instead of leading out the army, called the men together. Xenophon, as was incumbent on him, spoke: "It is quite possible that the enemy are collected in a body, and we shall have to fight. If we were to leave our baggage in the strong place" (pointing overhead) "and sally forth prepared for battle, the victims might favour us." But the soldiers, on hearing this proposal, cried out, "No need to take us inside that place; better sacrifice with all speed." Now sheep there were none any longer. So they purchased oxen from under a wagon and sacrificed; and Xenophon begged Cleanor the Arcadian to superintend the sacrifice on his behalf, in case there might be some change now. But even so there was no improvement. Now Neon was general in place of Cheirisophus, and seeing the men suffering so cruelly from want, he was willing to do them a good turn. So he got hold of some Heracleot or other who said he knew of villages close by from which they could get provisions, and proclaimed by herald: "If any one liked to come out and get provisions, be it known that he, Neon, would be their leader." So out came the men with spears, and wine skins and sacks and other vessels--two thousand strong in all. But when they had reached the villages and began to scatter for the purpose of foraging, Pharnabazus's cavalry were the first to fall upon them. They had come to the aid of the Bithynians, wishing, if possible, in conjunction with the latter, to hinder the Hellenes from entering Phrygia. These troopers killed no less than five hundred of the men; the rest fled for the lives up into the hill country. News of the catastrophe was presently brought into camp by one of those who had escaped, and Xenophon, seeing that the victims had not been favourable on that day, took a wagon bullock, in the absence of other sacrificial beasts, offered it up, and started for the rescue, he and the rest under thirty years of age to the last man. Thus they picked up the remnant of Neon's party and returned to camp. It was now about sunset; and the Hellenes in deep despondency were making their evening meal, when all of a sudden, through bush and brake, a party of Bithynians fell upon the pickets, cutting down some and chasing the rest into camp. In the midst of screams and shouts the Hellenes ran to their arms, one and all; yet to pursue or move the camp in the night seemed hardly safe, for the ground was thickly grown with bush; all they could do was to strengthen the outposts and keep watch under arms the livelong night.

October 9, Thursday   **<Diodorus November 7, Friday>**

V

And so they spent the night, but with day-dawn the generals led the way into the natural fastness, and the others picked up their arms and baggage and followed the lead. Before the breakfast-hour arrived, they had fenced off with a ditch the only side on which lay ingress into the place, and had palisaded off the whole, leaving only three gates. Anon a ship from Heraclea arrived bringing barleymeal, victim animals, and wine. Xenophon was up betimes, and made the usual offering before starting on an expedition, and at the first victim the sacrifice was favourable. Just as the sacrifice ended, the seer, Arexion the Parrhasian, caught sight of an eagle, which boded well, and bade Xenophon lead on. So they crossed the trench and grounded arms. Then proclamation was made by herald for the soldiers to breakfast and start on an expedition under arms; the mob of sutlers and the captured slaves would be left in camp. Accordingly the mass of the troops set out. Neon alone remained; for it seemed best to leave that general and his men to guard the contents of the camp. But when the officers and soldiers had left them in the lurch, they were so ashamed to stop in camp while the rest marched out, that they too set out, leaving only those above five-and-forty years of age. These then stayed, while the rest set out on the march. Before they had gone two miles, they stumbled upon dead bodies, and when they had brought up the rear of the column in a line with the first bodies to be seen, they began digging graves and burying all included in the column from end to end. After burying the first batch, they advanced, and again bringing the rear even with the first unburied bodies which appeared, they buried in the same way all which the line of troops included. Finally, reaching the road that led out of the villages where the bodies lay thick together, they collected them and laid them in a common grave. It was now about midday, when pushing forward the troops up to the villages without entering them, they proceeded to seize provisions, laying hands on everything they could set eyes on under cover of their lines; when suddenly they caught sight of the enemy cresting certain hillocks in front of them, duly marshalled in line--a large body of cavalry and infantry. It was Spithridates and Rhathines, sent by Pharnabazus with their force at their backs. As soon as the enemy caught sight of the Hellenes, they stood still, about two miles distant. Then Arexion the seer sacrificed, and at the first essay the victims were favourable. Whereupon Xenophon addressed the other generals: "I would advise, sirs, that we should detach one or more flying columns to support our main attack, so that in case of need at any point we may have reserves in readiness to assist our main body, and the enemy, in the confusion of battle, may find himself attacking the unbroken lines of troops not hitherto engaged." These views approved themselves to all. "Do you then," said he, "lead on the vanguard straight at the enemy. Do not let us stand parleying here, now that we have caught sight of him and he of us. I will detach the hindmost companies in the way we have decided upon and follow you." After that they quietly advanced, and he, withdrawing the rear-rank companies in three brigades consisting of a couple of hundred men apiece, commissioned the first on the right to follow the main body at the distance of a hundred feet. Samolas the Achaean was in command of this brigade. The duty of the second, under the command of Pyrrhias the Arcadian, was to follow in the centre. The last was posted on the left, with Phrasias, an Athenian, in command. As they advanced, the vanguard reached a large and difficult woody glen, and halted, not knowing whether the obstacle needed to be crossed or not. They passed down the word for the generals and officers to come forward to the front. Xenophon, wondering what it was that stopped the march, and presently hearing the above order passed along the ranks, rode up with all speed. As soon as they were met, Sophaenetus, as the eldest general, stated his opinion that the question, whether a gully of that kind ought to be crossed or not, was not worth discussing. Xenophon, with some ardour, retorted: "You know, sirs, I have not been in the habit hitherto of introducing you to danger which you might avoid. It is not your reputation for courage surely that is at stake, but your safe return home. But now the matter stands thus: It is impossible to retire from this point without a battle; if we do not advance against the enemy ourselves, he will follow us as soon as we have turned our backs and attack us. Consider, then; is it better to go and meet the foe with arms advanced, or with arms reversed to watch him as he assails us on our rear? You know this at any rate, that to retire before an enemy has nothing glorious about it, whereas attack engenders courage even in a coward. For my part, I would rather at any time attack with half my men than retreat with twice the number. As to these fellows, if we attack them, I am sure you do not really expect them to await us; though, if we retreat, we know for certain they will be emboldened to pursue us. Nay, if the result of crossing is to place a difficult gully behind us when we are on the point of engaging, surely that is an advantage worth seizing. At least, if it were left to me, I would choose that everything should appear smooth and passable to the enemy, which may invite retreat; but for ourselves we may bless the ground which teaches us that except in victory we have no deliverance. It astonishes me that any one should deem this particular gully a whit more terrible than any of the other barriers which we have successfully passed. How impassable was the plain, had we failed to conquer their cavalry! how insurmountable the mountains already traversed by us, with all their peltasts in hot pursuit at our heels! Nay, when we have safely reached the sea, the Pontus will present a somewhat formidable gully, when we have neither vessels to convey us away nor corn to keep us alive whilst we stop. But we shall no sooner be there than we must be off again to get provisions. Surely it is better to fight to-day after a good breakfast than to-morrow on an empty stomach. Sirs, the offerings are favourable to us, the omens are propitious, the victims more than promising; let us attack the enemy! Now that they have had a good look at us, these fellows must not be allowed to enjoy their dinners or choose a camp at their own sweet will." After that the officers bade him lead on. None gainsaid, and he led the way. His orders were to cross the gully, where each man chanced to find himself. By this method, as it seemed to him, the troops would more quickly mass themselves on the far side than was possible, if they defiled along (124) the bridge which spanned the gully. But once across he passed along the line and addressed the troops: "Sirs, call to mind what by help of the gods you have already done. Bethink you of the battles you have won at close quarters with the foe; of the fate which awaits those who flee before their foes. Forget not that we stand at the very doors of Hellas. Follow in the steps of Heracles, our guide, and cheer each the other onwards by name. Sweet were it surely by some brave and noble word or deed, spoken or done this day, to leave the memory of oneself in the hearts of those one loves."

These words were spoken as he rode past, and simultaneously he began leading on the troops in battle line; and, placing the peltasts on either flank of the main body, they moved against the enemy. Along the line the order had sped "to keep their spears at rest on the right shoulder until the bugle signal; then lower them for the charge, slow march, and even pace, no one to quicken into a run." Lastly, the watchword was passed, "Zeus the Saviour, Heracles our Guide." The enemy waited their approach, confident in the excellence of his position; but as they drew closer the Hellene light troops, with a loud alala! without waiting for the order, dashed against the foe. The latter, on their side, came forward eagerly to meet the charge, both the cavalry and the mass of the Bithynians; and these turned the peltasts. But when with counter-wave the phalanx of the heavy infantry rapidly advancing, faced them, and at the same time the bugle sounded, and the battle hymn rose from all lips, and after this a loud cheer rose, and at the same instant they couched their spears;--at this conjuncture the enemy no longer welcomed them, but fled. Timasion with his cavalry followed close, and, considering their scant numbers, they did great execution. It was the left wing of the enemy, in a line with which the Hellene cavalry were posted, that was so speedily scattered. But the right, which was not so hotly pursued, collected upon a knoll; and when the Hellenes saw them standing firm, it seemed the easiest and least dangerous course to go against them at once. Raising the battle hymn, they straightway fell upon them, but the others did not await their coming. Thereupon the peltasts gave chase until the right of the enemy was in its turn scattered, though with slight loss in killed; for the enemy's cavalry was numerous and threatening. But when the Hellenes saw the cavalry of Pharnabazus still standing in compact order, and the Bithynian horsemen massing together as if to join it, and like spectators gazing down from a knoll at the occurrences below; though weary, they determined to attack the enemy as best they could, and not suffer him to recover breath with reviving courage. So they formed in compact line and advanced. Thereupon the hostile cavalry turned and fled down the steep as swiftly as if they had been pursued by cavalry. In fact they sought the shelter of a gully, the existence of which was unknown to the Hellenes. The latter accordingly turned aside too soon and gave up the chase, for it was too late. Returning to the point where the first encounter took place they erected a trophy, and went back to the sea about sunset. It was something like seven miles to camp.

October 10, Friday   **<Diodorus November 8, Saturday>**

VI

After this the enemy confined themselves to their own concerns, and removed their households and property as far away as possible. The Hellenes, on their side, were still awaiting the arrival of Cleander with the ships of war and transports, which ought to be there soon. So each day they went out with the baggage animals and slaves and fearlessly brought in wheat and barley, wine and vegetables, millet and figs; since the district produced all good things, the olive alone excepted. When the army stayed in camp to rest, pillaging parties were allowed to go out, and those who went out appropriated the spoils; but when the whole army went out, if any one went off apart and seized anything, it was voted to be public property. Ere long there was an ample abundance of supplies of all sorts, for marketables arrived from Hellenic cities on all sides, and marts were established. Mariners coasting by, and hearing that a city was being founded and that there was a harbour, were glad to put in. Even the hostile tribes dwelling in the neighbourhood presently began to send envoys to Xenophon. It was he who was forming the place into a city, as they understood, and they would be glad to learn on what terms they might secure his friendship. He made a point of introducing these visitors to the soldiers.

October 16, Thursday   **<Diodorus November 14, Friday>**
Arrival of Cleander from Byzantium, Stoning of Dexippus and lay trial of Agasias

Meanwhile Cleander arrived with two ships of war, but not a single transport. At the moment of his arrival, as it happened, the army had taken the field, and a separate party had gone off on a pillaging expedition into the hills and had captured a number of small cattle. In this apprehension of being deprived of them, these same people spoke to Dexippus (this was the same man who had made off from Trapezus with the fifty-oared galley), and urged him to save their sheep for them. "Take some for yourself," said they, "and give the rest back to us." So, without more ado, he drove off the soldiers standing near, who kept repeating that the spoil was public property. Then off he went to Cleander. "Here is an attempt," said he, "at robbery." Cleander bade him to bring up the culprit to him. Dexippus seized on some one, and was for haling him to the Spartan governor. Just then Agasias came across him and rescued the man, who was a member of his company; and the rest of the soldiers present set to work to stone Dexippus, calling him "traitor." Things looked so ill that a number of the crew of the ships of war took fright and fled to the sea, and with the rest Cleander himself. Xenophon and the other generals tried to hold the men back, assuring Cleander that the affair signified nothing at all, and that the origin of it was a decree pased by the army. That was to blame, if anything. But Cleander, goaded by Dexippus, and personally annoyed at the fright which he had experienced, threatened to sail away and publish an interdict against them, forbidding any city to receive them, as being public enemies. For at this date the Lacedaemonians held sway over the whole Hellenic world. Thereat the affair began to wear an ugly look, and the Hellenes begged and implored Cleander to reconsider his intention. He replied that he would be as good as his word, and that nothing should stop him, unless the man who set the example of stoning, with the other who rescued the prisoner, were given up to him. Now, one of the two whose persons were thus demanded--Agasias--had been a friend to Xenophon throughout; and that was just why Dexippus was all the more anxious to accuse him. In their perplexity the generals summoned a full meeting of the soldiers, and some speakers were disposed to make very light of Cleander and set him at naught. But Xenophon took a more serious view of the matter; he rose and addressed the meeting thus: "Soldiers, I cannot say that I feel disposed to make light of this business, if Cleander be allowed to go away, as he threatens to do, in his present temper towards us. There are Hellenic cities close by; but then the Lacedaemonians are the lords of Hellas, and they can, any one of them, carry out whatever they like in the cities. If then the first thing this Lacedaemonian does is to close the gates of Byzantium, and next to pass an order to the other governors, city by city, not to receive us because we are a set of lawless ruffians disloyal to the Lacedaemonians; and if, further, this report of us should reach the ears of their admiral, Anaxibius, to stay or to sail away will alike be difficult. Remember, the Lacedaemonians at the present time are lords alike on land and on sea. For the sake then of a single man, or for two men's sake, it is not right that the rest of us should be debarred from Hellas; but whatever they enjoin we must obey. Do not the cities which gave us birth yield them obedience also? For my own part, inasmuch as Dexippus, I believe, keeps telling Cleander that Agasias would never have done this had not I, Xenophon, bidden him, I absolve you of all complicity, and Agasias too, if Agasias himself states that I am in any way a prime mover in this matter. If I have set the fashion of stone-throwing or any other sort of violence I condemn myself--I say that I deserve the extreme penalty, and I will submit to undergo it. I further say that if any one else is accused, that man is bound to surrender himself to Cleander for judgement, for by this means you will be absolved entirely from the accusation. But as the matter now stands, it is cruel that just when we were aspiring to win praise and honour throughout Hellas, we are destined to sink below the level of the rest of the world, banned from the Hellenic cities whose common name we boast." After him Agasias got up, and said, "I swear to you, sirs, by the gods and goddesses, verily and indeed, neither Xenophon nor any one else among you bade me rescue the man. I saw an honest man--one of my own company--being taken up by Dexippus, the man who betrayed you, as you know full well. That I could not endure; I rescued him, I admit the fact. Do not you deliver me up. I will surrender myself, as Xenophon suggests, to Cleander to pass what verdict on me he thinks right. Do not, for the sake of such a matter, make foes of the Lacedaemonians; rather God grant that (125) each of you may safely reach the goal of his desire. Only do you choose from among yourselves and send with me to Cleander those who, in case of any omission on my part, may by their words and acts supply what is lacking." Thereupon the army granted him to choose for himself whom he would have go with him and to go; and he at once chose the generals. After this they all set off to Cleander--Agasias and the generals and the man who had been rescued by Agasias--and the generals spoke as follows: "The army has sent us to you, Cleander, and this is their bidding: 'If you have fault to find with all, they say, you ought to pass sentence on all, and do with them what seems best; or if the charge is against one man or two, or possibly several, what they expect of these people is to surrender themselves to you for judgement.' Accordingly, if you lay anything to the charge of us generals, here we stand at your bar. Or do you impute the fault to some one not here? tell us whom. Short of flying in the face of our authority, there is no one who will absent himself."

At this point Agasias stepped forward and said: "It was I, Cleander, who rescued the man before you yonder from Dexippus, when the latter was carrying him off, and it was I who gave the order to strike Dexippus. My plea is that I know the prisoner to be an honest man. As to Dexippus, I know that he was chosen by the army to command a fifty-oared galley, which we had obtained by request from the men of Trapezus for the express purpose of collecting vessels to carry us safely home. But this same Dexippus betrayed his fellow-soldiers, with whom he had been delivered from so many perils, and made off into hiding like a runaway slave, whereby we have robbed the Trapezuntines of their frigate, and must needs appear as knaves in their eyes for this man's sake. As to ourselves, as far as he could, he has ruined us; for, like the rest of us, he had heard how all but impossible it was for us to retreat by foot across the rivers and to reach Hellas in safety. That is the stamp of man whom I robbed of his prey. Now, had it been you yourself who carried him off, or one of your emissaries, or indeed any one short of a runaway from ourselves, be sure that I should have acted far otherwise. Be assured that if you put me to death at this time you are sacrificing a good, honest man for the sake of a coward and a scamp." When he had listened to these remarks, Cleander replied that if such had been the conduct of Dexippus, he could not congratulate him. "But still," he added, turning to the generals, "were Dexippus ever so great a scamp he ought not to suffer violence; but in the language of your own demand he was entitled to a fair trial, and so to obtain his deserts. What I have to say at present therefore is: leave your friend here and go your way, and when I give the order be present at the trial. I have no further charge against the army or any one, since the prisoner himself admits that he rescued the man." Then the man who had been rescued said: "In behalf of myself, Cleander, if possibly you think that I was being taken up for some misdeed, it is not so; I neither struck nor shot; I merely said, 'The sheep are public property;' for it was a resolution of the soldiers that whenever the army went out as a body any booty privately obtained was to be public property. That was all I said, and thereupon yonder fellow seized me and began dragging me off. He wanted to stop our mouths, so that he might have a share of the things himself, and keep the rest for these buccaneers, contrary to the ordinance." In answer to that Cleander said: "Very well, if that is your disposition you can stay behind too, and we will take your case into consideration also." Thereupon Cleander and his party proceeded to breakfast; but Xenophon collected the army in assembly, and advised their sending a deputation to Cleander to intercede in behalf of the men. Accordingly it was resolved to send some generals and officers with Dracontius the Spartan, and of the rest those who seemed best fitted to go. The deputation was to request Cleander by all means to release the two men. Accordingly Xenophon came and addressed him thus: "Cleander, you have the men; the army has bowed to you and assented to do what you wished with respect to these two members of their body and themselves in general. But now they beg and pray you to give up these two men, and not to put them to death. Many a good service have these two wrought for our army in past days. Let them but obtain this from you, and in return the army promises that, if you will put yourself at their head and the gracious gods approve, they will show you how orderly they are, how apt to obey their general, and, with heaven's help, to face their foes unflinchingly. They make this further request to you, that you will present yourself and take command of them and make trial of them. 'Test us ourselves,' they say, 'and test Dexippus, what each of us is like, and afterwards assign to each his due.'" When Cleander heard these things, he answered: "Nay, by the twin gods, I will answer you quickly enough. Here I make you a present of the two men, and I will as you say present myself, and then, if the gods vouchsafe, I will put myself at your head and lead you into Hellas. Very different is your language from the tale I used to hear concerning you from certain people, that you wanted to withdraw the army from allegiance to the Lacedaemonians." After this the deputation thanked him and retired, taking with them the two men; then Cleander sacrificed as a preliminary to marching and consorted friendlily with Xenophon, and the two struck up an alliance.

October 17, Friday   <Diodorus November 15, Saturday>

When the Spartan saw with what good discipline the men carried out their orders, he was still more anxious to become their leader.

October 19, Sunday   <Diodorus November 17, Monday>

However, in spite of sacrifices repeated on three successive days, the victims steadily remained unfavourable. So he summoned the generals and said to them: "The victims smile not on me, they suffer me not to lead you home; but be not out of heart at that. To you it is given, as it would appear, to bring your men safe home. Forwards then, and for our part, whenever you come yonder, we will bestow on you as warm a welcome as we may." Then the soldiers resolved to make him a present of the public cattle, which he accepted, but again gave back to them.

October 20, Monday   <Diodorus November 18, Tuesday>

So he sailed away; but the soldiers made division of the corn which they had collected and of the other captured property, and commenced their homeward march through the territory of the Bithynians. At first they confined themselves to the main road; but not chancing upon anything whereby they might reach a friendly territory with something in their pockets for themselves, they resolved to turn sharp round, and marched for one day and night in the opposite direction.

October 25, Saturday   \<Diodorus November 23, Sunday\>
Arrival at Chrysopolis (Üsküdar in Turkey, formerly known as Scutari)

By this proceeding they captured many slaves and much small cattle; and on the sixth day reached Chrysopolis in Chalcedonia (126). Here they halted seven days while they disposed of their booty by sale.

BOOK VII (In the earlier portion of the narrative will be found a detailed history of the fortunes of the Hellenes during their march up country with Cyrus down to the date of the battle; and, subsequently to his death, until they reached the Euxine; as also of all their doings in their efforts to escape from the Euxine, partly by land marches and partly under sail by sea, until they found themselves outside the mouth of the Black Sea (south of the Bosphorus) at Chrysopolis in Asia.)

November 2, Sunday   \<Diodorus December 1, Monday\>
Anaxibius and Xenophon

I

At this point Pharnabazus, who was afraid that the army might undertake a campaign against his satrapy, sent to Anaxibius, the Spartan high admiral, who chanced to be in Byzantium, and begged him to convey the army out of Asia, undertaking to comply with his wishes in every respect. Anaxibius accordingly sent to summon the generals and officers to Byzantium, and promised that the soldiers should not lack pay for service, if they crossed the strait. The officers said that they would deliberate and return an answer. Xenophon individually informed them that he was about to quit the army at once, and was only anxious to set sail. Anaxibius pressed him not to be in so great a hurry: "Cross over with the rest," he said, "and then it will be time enough to think about quitting the army." This the other undertook to do. Now Seuthes the Thracian sent Medosades and begged Xenophon to use his influence to get the army across. "Tell Xenophon, if he will do his best for me in this matter, he will not regret it." Xenophon answered: "The army is in any case going to cross; so that, as far as that is concerned, Seuthes is under no obligation to me or to any one else; but as soon as it is once across, I personally shall be quit of it. Let Seuthes, therefore, as far as he may deem consistent with prudence, apply to those who are going to remain and will have a voice in affairs."

November 3, Monday   <Diodorus December 2, Tuesday>
Crossing the Bosphorus Waterway to Byzantium (modern day Istanbul in Turkey)

After this the whole body of troops crossed to Byzantium.

November 4, Tuesday   <Diodorus December 3, Wednesday>
Incident at Byzantium

But Anaxibius, instead of proceeding to give pay, made proclamation that, "The soldiers were to take up their arms and baggage and go forth," as if all he wished were to ascertain their numbers and bid them god-speed at the same moment. The soldiers were not well pleased at that, because they had no money to furnish themselves with provisions for the march; and they sluggishly set about getting their baggage together. Xenophon meanwhile, being on terms of intimacy with the governor, Cleander, came to pay his host a final visit, and bid him adieu, being on the point of setting sail. But the other protested; "Do not do so, or else," said he, "you will be blamed, for even now certain people are disposed to hold you to account because the army is so slow in getting under weigh." The other answered, "Nay, I am not to blame for that. It is the men themselves, who are in want of provisions; that is why they are out of heart at their exodus." "All the same," he replied, "I advise you to go out, as if you intended to march with them, and when you are well outside, it will be time enough to take yourself off." "Well then," said Xenophon, "we will go and arrange all this with Anaxibius." They went and stated the case to the admiral, who insisted that they must do as he had said, and march out, bag and baggage, by the quickest road; and as an appendix to the former edict, he added, "Any one absenting himself from the review and the muster will have himself to blame for the consequences." This was peremptory. So out marched, the generals first, and then the rest; and now, with the exception of here a man and there, they were all outside; it was a "clean sweep"; and Eteonicus stood posted near the gates, ready to close them, as soon as the men were fairly out, and to thrust in the bolt pin. Then Anaxibius summoned the generals and captains, and addressed them: "Provisions you had better get from the Thracian villages; you will find plenty of barley, wheat, and other necessaries in them; and when you have got them, off with you to the Chersonese, where Cyniscus will take you into his service." Some of the soldiers overheard what was said, or possibly one of the officers was the medium of communication; however it was, the news was handed on to the army. As to the generals, their immediate concern was to try and gain some information as to Seuthes: "Was he hostile or friendly? also, would they have to march through the Sacred mountain (127), or round about through the middle of Thrace?"

While they were discussing these points, the soldiers snatched up their arms and made a rush full speed at the gates, with the intention of getting inside the fortification again. But Eteonicus and his men, seeing the heavy infantry coming up at a run promptly closed the gates and thrust in the bolt pin. Then the soldiers fell to battering the gates, exclaiming that it was iniquitous to thrust them forth in this fashion into the jaws of their enemies. "If you do not of your own accord open the gates," they cried, "we will split them in half"; and another set rushed down to the sea, and so along the break-water and over the wall into the city; while a third set, consisting of those few who were still inside, having never left the city, seeing the affair at the gates, severed the bars with axes and flung the portals wide open; and the rest came pouring in. Xenophon, seeing what was happening, was seized with alarm lest the army betake itself to pillage, and ills incurable be wrought to the city, to himself, and to the soldiers. Then he set off, and, plunging into the throng, was swept through the gates with the crowd. The Byzantines no sooner saw the soldiers forcibly rushing in than they left the open square, and fled, some to the shipping, others to their homes, while those already indoors came racing out, and some fell to dragging down their ships of war, hoping possibly to be safe on board these; while there was not a soul who doubted but that the city was taken, and that they were all undone. Eteonicus made a swift retreat to the citadel. Anaxibius ran down to the sea, and, getting on board a fisherman's smack, sailed round to the acropolis, and at once sent off to fetch over the garrison troops from Chalcedon, since those already in the acropolis seemed hardly sufficient to keep the men in check. The soldiers, catching sight of Xenophon, threw themselves upon him, crying: "Now, Xenophon, is the time to prove yourself a man. You have got a city, you have got triremes, you have got money, you have got men; to-day, if you only chose, you can do us a good turn, and we will make you a great man." He replied: "Nay, I like what you say, and I will do it all; but if that is what you have set your hearts on, fall into rank and take up position at once." This he said, wishing to quiet them, and so passed the order along the lines himself, while bidding the rest to do the same: "Take up position; stand easy." But the men themselves, by a species of self-marshalling, fell into rank, and were soon formed, the heavy infantry eight deep, while the light infantry had run up to cover either wing. The Thracian Square, as it is called, is a fine site for manouvering, being bare of buildings and level. As soon as the arms were stacked and the men's tempers cooled, Xenophon called a general meeting of the soldiers, and made the following speech:-- "Soldiers, I am not surprised at your wrath, or that you deem it monstrous treatment so to be cheated; but consider what will be the consequences if we gratify our indignation, and in return for such deception, avenge ourselves on the Lacedaemonians here present, and plunder an innocent city. We shall be declared enemies of the Lacedaemonians and their allies; and what sort of war that will be, we need not go far to conjecture. I take it, you have not forgotten some quite recent occurrences. We Athenians entered into war against the Lacedaemonians and their allies with a fleet consisting of not less than three hundred line-of-battle ships, including those in dock as well as those afloat. We had vast treasures stored up in the city, and a yearly income which, derived from home or foreign sources, amounted to no less than a thousand talents. Our empire included all the islands, and we were possessed of numerous cities both in Asia and in Europe. Amongst others, this very Byzantium, where we are now, was ours; and yet in the end we were vanquished, as you all very well know. "What, must we anticipate, will now be our fate? The Lacedaemonians have not only their old allies, but the Athenians and those who were at that time allies of Athens are added to them. Tissaphernes and all the rest of the Asiatics on the seaboard are our foes, not to speak of our arch-enemy, the king himself, up yonder, whom we came to deprive of his empire, and to kill, if possible. I ask then, with all these banded together against us, is there any one so insensate as to imagine that we can survive the contest? For heaven's sake, let us not go mad or loosely throw away our lives in war with our own native cities--nay, our own friends, our kith and our kin; for in one or other of the cities they are all included. Every city will march against us, and not unjustly, if, after refusing to hold one single barbarian city by right of conquest, we seize the first Hellenic city that we come to and make it a ruinous heap. For my part, my prayer is that before I see such things wrought by you, I, at any rate, may lie ten thousand fathoms under ground! My counsel to you, as Hellenes, is to try and obtain your just rights, through obedience to those who stand at the head of Hellas; and if so be that you fail in those demands, why, being more sinned against than sinning, need we rob ourselves of Hellas too? At present, I propose that we should send to Anaxibius and tell him that we have made an entrance into the city, not meditating violence, but merely to discover if he and his will show us any good; for if so, it is well; but of otherwise, at least we will let him see that he does not shut the door upon us as dupes and fools. We know the meaning of discipline; we turn our backs and go." This resolution was passed, and they sent Hieronymus an Eleian, with two others, Eurylochus an Arcadian and Philesius an Achaean, to deliver the message. So these set off on their errand. But while the soldiers were still seated in conclave, Coeratadas, of Thebes, arrived. He was a Theban not in exile, but with a taste for generalship, who made it his business to see if any city or nation were in need of his services. Thus, on the present occasion, he presented himself, and begged to state that he was ready to put himself at their head, and lead them into the Delta of Thrace (128), as it is called, where they would find themselves in a land of plenty; but until they got there, he would provide them with meat and drink enough and to spare. While they were still listening to this tale, the return message from Anaxibius came. His answer was: "The discipline, they had spoken of, was not a thing they would regret; indeed he would report their behaviour to the authorities at home; and for himself, he would take advice and do the best he could for them." Thereupon the soldiers accepted Coeratadas as their general, and retired without the walls. Their new general undertook to present himself to the troops next day with sacrificial beasts and a soothsayer, with eatables also and drinkables for the army. Now, as soon as they were gone out, Anaxibius closed the gates and issued a proclamation to the effect that "any of the soldiers caught inside should be knocked down to the hammer and sold at once."

November 5, Wednesday   <Diodorus December 4, Thursday>

Next day, Coeratadas arrived with the victims and the soothsayer. A string of twenty bearers bearing barleymeal followed at his heels, succeeded by other twenty carrying wine, and three laden with a supply of olives, and two others carrying, the one about as much garlic as a single man could lift, and the other a similar load of onions. These various supplies he set down, apparently for distribution, and began to sacrifice. Now Xenophon sent to Cleander, begging him to arrange matters so that he might be allowed to enter the walls, with a view to starting from Byzantium on his homeward voyage. Cleander came, and this is what he said: "I have come; but I was barely able to arrange what you want. Anaxibius insisted: 'It was not convenient that Xenophon should be inside while the soldiers are close to the walls without; the Byzantines at sixes and sevens moreover; and no love lost between the one party of them and the other.' Still, he ended by bidding you to come inside, if you were really minded to leave the town by sea with himself." Accordingly Xenophon bade the soldiers good-bye, and returned with Cleander within the walls. To return to Coeratadas. The first day he failed to get favourable signs at the sacrifice, and never a dole of rations did he make to the soldiers.

November 6, Thursday   <Diodorus December 5, Friday>

On the second day the victims were standing ready near the altar, and so was Coeratadas, with chaplet crowned, all ready to sacrifice, when up comes Timasion the Dardanian, with Neon the Asinaean, and Cleanor of Orchomenus, forbidding Coeratadas to sacrifice: "He must understand there was an end to his generalship, unless he gave them provisions." The other bade them measure out the supplies, "Pray, dole them out." But when he found that he had a good deal short of a single day's provisions for each man, he picked up his paraphernalia of sacrifice and withdrew. As to being general, he would have nothing more to say to it.

November 7, Friday   <Diodorus December 6, Saturday>

II

Now these five were left--Neon the Asinaean, Phryniscus the Achaean, Philesius the Achaean, Xanthicles the Achaean, Timasion the Dardanian--at the head of the army, and they pushed on to some villages of the Thracians facing Byzantium, and there encamped. Now the generals could not agree. Cleanor and Phryniscus wished to march to join Seuthes, who had worked upon their feelings by presenting one with a horse and the other with a woman to wife. But Neon's object was to come to the Chersonese: "When we are under the wing of the Lacedaemonians," he thought, "I shall step to the front and command the whole army." Timasion's one ambition was to cross back again into Asia, hoping to be reinstated at home and end his exile. The soldiers shared the wishes of the last general. But, as time dragged on, many of the men sold their arms at different places and set sail as best they could; others (actually gave away their arms, some here, some there, and (129)) became absorbed in the cities. One man rejoiced. This was Anaxibius, to whom the break-up of the army was a blessing. "That is the way," he said to himself, "I can best gratify Pharnabazus."

November 10, Monday   <Diodorus December 9, Tuesday>
Events at Cyzicus (corresponding to the Erdek and Bandırma roads
on the southern coast of the sea of Marmara in Turkey – about 40km
north of where Alexander the Great later fought the Battle of
Granicus near the modern-day village of Ergili in Turkey)

But Anaxibius, while prosecuting his voyage from Byzantium, was met at
Cyzicus by Aristarchus, the new governor, who was to succeed Cleander at
Byzantium; and report said that a new admiral, Polus, if he had not actually
arrived, would presently reach the Hellespont and relieve Anaxibius. The
latter sent a parting injunction to Aristarchus to be sure and sell all the
Cyreian soldiers he could lay hands on still lingering in Byzantium; for
Cleander had not sold a single man of them; on the contrary, he had made
it his business to tend the sick and wounded, pitying them, and insisting on
their being received in the houses. Aristarchus changed all that, and was no
sooner arrived in Byzantium than he sold no less than four hundred of
them.

November 12, Wednesday   <Diodorus December 11, Thursday>
Events at Parium (corresponding to village of Kemer in the township
of Biga in Çanakkale province of Turkey)

Meanwhile Anaxibius, on his coasting voyage, reached Parium, and,
according to the terms of their agreement, he sent to Pharnabazus. But the
latter, learning that Aristarchus was the new governor at Byzantim, and that
Anixibius had ceased to be admiral, turned upon him a cold shoulder, and
set out concocting the same measures concerning the Cyreian army with
Aristarchus, as he had lately been at work upon with Anaxibius.

November 16, Sunday   <Diodorus December 15, Monday>

Anaxibius thereupon summoned Xenophon and bade him, by every
manner of means, sail to the army with the utmost speed, and keep it
together. "He was to collect the scattered fragments and march them down
to Perinthus, and thence convey them across to Asia without loss of time."
And herewith he put a thirty-oared galley at his service, and gave him a
letter of authority and an officer to accompany him, with an order to the
Perinthians "to escort Xenophon without delay on horseback to the army."

November 17, Monday   **<Diodorus December 16, Tuesday>**
Xenophon leaves Byzantium (Istanbul)

So it was that Xenophon sailed across

November 19, Wednesday   **<Diodorus December 18, Thursday>**
Xenophon rejoins the army on the north coast of the Sea of Marmara

and eventually reached the army. The soldiers gave him a joyous welcome, and would have been only too glad to cross from Thrace into Asia under his leadership.

November 23, Sunday   **<Diodorus December 22, Monday>**

But Seuthes, hearing that Xenophon had arrived,

November 26, Wednesday   **<Diodorus December 25, Thursday>**

sent Medosades again, by sea to meet him, and begged him to bring the army to him; and whatever he thought would make his speech persuasive, he was ready to promise him. But the other replied, that none of these things were open to him to do;

November 27, Thursday   **<Diodorus December 26, Friday>**

and with this answer Medosades departed,

November 28, Friday   **<Diodorus December 27, Saturday>**
Arrival at Perinthus (corresponds with with modern day Marmara Ereğlisi which is on the north side of the Sea of Marmara in Turkey)

and the Hellenes proceeded to Perinthus.

Here on arrival Neon withdrew his troops and encamped apart, having about eight hundred men; while the remainder of the army lay in one place under the walls of Perinthus.

November 29, Saturday   \<Diodorus December 28, Sunday\>

After this, Xenophon set himself to find vessels, so as to lose no time in crossing.

December 5, Friday   \<Diodorus January 3, Saturday\>

But in the interval Aristarchus, the governor from Byzantium, arrived with a couple of war-ships, being moved to do so by Pharnabazus. To make doubly sure, he first forbade the skippers and shipmasters to carry the troops across, and then he visited the camp and informed the soldiers that their passage into Asia was forbidden. Xenophon replied that he was acting under the orders of Anaxibius, who had sent him thither for this express purpose; to which Aristarchus retorted, "For the matter of that, Anaxibius is no longer admiral, and I am governor in this quarter; if I catch any of you at sea, I will sink you." With these remarks he retired within the walls of Perinthus.

December 6, Saturday   \<Diodorus January 4, Sunday\>

Next day, he sent for the generals and officers of the army. They had already reached the fortification walls, when some one brought word to Xenophon that if he set foot inside, he would be seized, and either meet some ill fate there or more likely be delivered up to Pharnabazus. On hearing this Xenophon sent forward the rest of the party, but for himself pleaded that there was a sacrifice which he wished to offer. In this way he contrived to turn back and consult the victims, "Would the gods allow him to try and bring the army over to Seuthes?" On the one hand it was plain that the idea of crossing over to Asia in the face of this man with his ships of war, who meant to bar the passage, was too dangerous. Nor did he altogether like the notion of being blocked up in the Chersonese with an army in dire need of everything; where, besides being at the beck and call of the governor of the place, they would be debarred from the necessities of life. While Xenophon was thus employed, the generals and officers came back with a message from Aristarchus, who had told them they might retire for the present, but in the afternoon he would expect them. The former suspicions of a plot had now ripened to a certainty. Xenophon meantime had ascertained that the victims were favourable to his project. He personally, and the army as a whole, might with safety proceed to Seuthes, they seemed to say. Accordingly, he took with him Polycrates, the Athenian captain, and from each of the generals, not including Neon, some one man whom they could in each case trust, and in the night they set off to visit the army of Seuthes, sixty furlongs distant.

December 7, Sunday   <Diodorus January 5, Monday>

As they approached, they came upon some deserted watch-fires, and their first impression was that Seuthes had shifted his position; but presently perceiving a confused sound (the voices of Seuthes' people signalling to one another), the explanation dawned on him: Seuthes kept his watch-fires kindled in front of, instead of behind, his night pickets, in order that the outposts, being in the dark, might escape notice, their numbers and position thus being a mystery; whilst any party approaching from the outside, so far from escaping notice, would, through the glare of the fire, stand out conspicuously. Perceiving how matters stood, Xenophon sent forward his interpreter, who was one of the party, and bade him inform Seuthes that Xenophon was there and craved conference with him. The others asked if he were an Athenian from the army yonder, and no sooner had the interpreter replied, "Yes, the same," than up they leapt and galloped off; and in less time than it takes to tell a couple of hundred peltasts had come up who seized and carried off Xenophon and those with him and brought them to Seuthes. The latter was in a tower right well guarded, and there were horses round it in a circle, standing all ready bitted and bridled; for his alarm was so great that he gave his horses their provender during the day (130), and during the nights he kept watch and ward with the brutes thus bitted and bridled. It was stated in explanation that in old days an ancestor of his, named Teres, had been in this very country with a large army, several of whom he had lost at the hands of the native inhabitants, besides being robbed of his baggage train. The inhabitants of the country are Thynians, and they are reputed to be far the most warlike set of fighters--especially at night. When they drew near, Seuthes bade Xenophon enter, and bring with him any two he might choose. As soon as they were inside, they first greeted one another warmly, and then, according to the Thracian custom, pledged themselves in bowls of wine. There was further present at the elbow of Seuthes, Medosades, who on all occasions acted as his ambassador-in-chief. Xenophon took the initiative and spoke as follows: "You have sent to me, Seuthes, once and again. On the first occasion you sent Medosades yonder, to Chalcedon, and you begged me to use my influence in favour of the army crossing over from Asia. You promised me, in return for this conduct on my part, various kindnesses; at least that is what Medosades stated"; and before proceeding further he turned to Medosades and asked, "Is not that so?" The other assented. "Again, on a second occasion, the same Medosades came when I had crossed over from Parium to rejoin the army; and he promised me that if I would bring you the army, you would in various respects treat me as a friend and brother. He said especially with regard to certain seaboard places of which you are the owner and lord, that you were minded to make me a present of them." At this point he again questioned Medosades, "Whether the words attributed to him were exact?" and Medosades once more fully assented. "Come now," proceeded Xenophon, "recount what answer I made you, and first at Chalcedon." "You answered that the army was, in any case, about to cross over to Byzantium; and as far as that went, there was no need to pay you or any one else anything; and for yourself, you added, that once across you were minded to leave the army, which thing came to pass even as you said." "Well! what did I say," he asked, "at your next visit, when you came to me in Selybria?" "You said that the proposal was impossible; you were all going to Perinthus to cross into Asia." "Good," said Xenophon, "and in spite of it all, at the present moment, here I am myself, and Phryniscus, one of my colleagues, and Polycrates yonder, a captain; and outside, to represent the other generals (all except Neon the Laconian), the trustiest men they could find to send. So that if you wish to give these transactions the seal of still greater security, you have nothing to do but to summon them also; and do you, Polycrates, go and say from me, that I bid them leave their arms outside, and you can leave your own sword outside before you enter with them on your return." When Seuthes had heard so far, he interposed: "I should never mistrust an Athenian, for we are relatives already (131), I know; and the best of friends, I believe, we shall be." After that, as soon as the right men entered, Xenophon first questioned Seuthes as to what use he intended to make of the army, and he replied as follows: "Maesades was my father; his sway extended over the Melanditae, the Thynians, and the Tranipsae. Then the affairs of the Odrysians took a bad turn, and my father was driven out of this country, and later on died himself of sickness, leaving me to be brought up as an orphan at the court of Medocus, the present king. But I, when I had grown to man's estate, could not endure to live with my eyes fixed on another's board. So I seated myself on the seat by him as a suppliant, and begged him to give me as many men as he could spare, that I might wreak what mischief I could on those who had driven us forth from our land; that thus I might cease to live in dependence upon another's board, like a dog watching his master's hand. In answer to my petition, he gave me the men and the horses which you will see at break of day, and nowadays I live with these, pillaging my own ancestral land. But if you would join me, I think, with the help of heaven, we might easily recover my empire. That is what I want of you." "Well then," said Xenophon, "supposing we came, what should you be able to give us? the soldiers, the officers, and the generals? Tell us that these witnesses may report your answer." And he promised to give "to the common soldiers a cyzicene (132), to a captain twice as much, and to a general four times as much, with as much land as ever they liked, some yoke of oxen, and a fortified place upon the seaboard." "But now supposing," said Xenophon, "we fail of success, in spite of our endeavours; suppose any intimidation on the part of the Lacedaemonians should arise; will you receive into your country any of us who may seek to find a refuge with you?" He answered: "Nay, not only so, but I shall look upon you as my brothers, entitled to share my seat, and the joint possessors of all the wealth which we may be able to acquire. And to you yourself, O Xenophon! I will give my daughter, and if you have a daughter, I will buy her in Thracian fashion; and I will give you Bisanthe as a dwelling-place, which is the fairest of all my possessions on the seaboard (133)."

III

After listening to these proposals, they gave and accepted pledges of good faith; and so the deputation rode off. Before day they were back again in camp, and severally rendered a report to those who sent them.

December 8, Monday   **<Diodorus January 6, Tuesday>**

At dawn Aristarchus again summoned the generals and officers, but the latter resolved to have done with the visit to Aristarchus, and to summon a meeting of the army. In full conclave the soldiers met, with the exception of Neon's men, who remained about ten furlongs off. When they were met together Xenophon rose, and made the following announcement: "Men, Aristarchus with his ships of war hinders us from sailing where we fain would go; it is not even safe to set foot on board a vessel. But if he hinders us here, he hastens us there. 'Be off to the Chersonese,' says he, 'force a passage through the Sacred mountain.' If we master it and succeed in getting to that place, he has something in store for us. He promises that he will not sell you any more, as he did at Byzantium; you shall not be cheated again; you shall have pay; he will no longer, as now, suffer you to remain in want of provisions. That is his proposal. But Seuthes says that if you will go to him he will treat you well. What you have now to consider is, whether you will stay to debate this question, or leave its settlement till we have gone up into a land of provisions. If you ask me my opinion, it is this: Since here we have neither money to buy, nor leave to take without money what we need, why should we not go up into these villages where the right to help ourselves is conferred by might? There, unhampered by the want of bare necessaries, you can listen to what this man and the other wants of you and choose whichever sounds best. Let those," he added, "who agree to this, hold up their hands." They all held them up. "Retire then," said he, "and get your kit together, and at the word of command, follow your leader."

December 9, Tuesday   <Diodorus January 7, Wednesday>
Dinner with Seuthes II, king of the Odrysian kingdom of Thrace

After this, Xenophon put himself at the head and the rest followed. Neon, indeed, and other agents from Aristarchus tried to turn them from their purpose, but to their persuasions they turned a deaf ear. They had not advanced much more than three miles, when Seuthes met them; and Xenophon, seeing him, bade him ride up. He wished to tell him what they felt to be conducive to their interests, and in the presence of as many witnesses as possible. As soon as he had approached, Xenophon said: "We are going where the troops will have enough to live upon; when we are there, we will listen to you and to the emissaries of the Laconian, and choose between you both whatever seems best. If then you will lead us where provisions are to be got in plenty, we shall feel indebted to you for your hospitality." And Seuthes answered: "For the matter of that, I know many villages, close-packed and stocked with all kinds of provisions, just far enough off to give you a good appetite for your breakfasts." "Lead on then!" said Xenophon. When they had reached the villages in the afternoon, the soldiers met, and Seuthes made the following speech: "My request to you, sirs, is that you will take the field with me, and my promise to you is that I will give every man of you a cyzicene, and to the officers and generals at the customary rate; besides this I will honour those who show special merit. Food and drink you shall get as now for yourselves from the country; but whatever is captured, I shall claim to have myself, so that by distribution of it I may provide you with pay. Let them flee, let them creep into hiding-places, we shall be able to pursue after them, we will track them out; or if they resist, along with you we will endeavour to subdue them to our hands." Xenophon inquired: "And how far from the sea shall you expect the army to follow you?" "Nowhere more than seven days' journey," he answered, "and in many places less." After this, permission was given for all who wished to speak, and many spoke, but ever to one and the same tune: "What Seuthes said, was very right. It was winter, and for a man to sail home, even if he had the will to do so, was impossible. On the other hand, to continue long in a friendly country, where they must depend upon what they could purchase, was equally beyond their power. If they were to wear away time and support life in a hostile country, it was safer to do so with Seuthes than by themselves, not to speak of all these good things; but if they were going to get pay into the bargain, that indeed was a godsend." To complete the proceedings, Xenophon said: "If any one opposes the measure, let him state his views; if not, let the officer put the proposition to the vote." No one opposed; they put it to the vote, and the resolution was carried; and without loss of time, he informed Seuthes that they would take the field with him. After this the troops messed in their separate divisions, but the generals and officers were invited by Seuthes to dinner at a neighbouring village which was in his possession. When they were at the doors, and on the point of stepping in to dinner, they were met by a certain Heracleides, of Maronea (134). He came up to each guest, addressing himself particularly to those who, as he conjectured, ought to be able to make a present to Seuthes. He addressed himself first to some Parians who were there to arrange a friendship with Medocus, the king of the Odrysians, and were bearers of presents to the king and to his wife. Heracleides reminded them: "Medocus is up country twelve days' journey from the sea; but Seuthes, now that he has got this army, will be lord on the sea-coast; as your neighbour, then, he is the man to do you good or do you ill. If you are wise, you will give him whatever he askes of you. On the whole, it will be laid out at better interest than if you have it to Medocus, who lives so far off." That was his mode of persuasion in their case. Next he came to Timasion the Dardanian, who, some one had told him, was the happy possessor of certain goblets and oriental carpets. What he said to him was: "It is customary when people are invited to dinner by Seuthes for the guests to make him a present; now if he should become a great person in these parts, he will be able to restore you to your native land, or to make you a rich man here." Such were the solicitations which he applied to each man in turn whom he accosted. Presently he came to Xenophon and said: "You are at once a citizen of no mean city, and with Seuthes also your own name is very great. Maybe you expect to obtain a fort or two in this country, just as others of your countrymen have done (135), and territory. It is only right and proper therefore that you should honour Seuthes in the most magnificent style. Be sure, I give this advice out of pure friendliness, for I know that the greater the gift that you are ready to bestow on him, the better the treatment you will receive at his hands." Xenophon, on hearing this, was in a sad dilemma, for he had brought with him, when he crossed from Parium, nothing but one boy and just enough to pay his travelling expenses. As soon as the company, consisting of the most powerful Thracians there present, with the generals and captains of the Hellenes, and any embassy from a state which might be there, had arrived, they were seated in a circle, and the dinner was served. Thereupon three-legged stools were brought in and placed in front of the assembled guests. They were laden with pieces of meat, piled up, and there were huge leavened-loaves fastened on to the pieces of meat with long skewers. The tables, as a rule, were set beside the guests at intervals. That was the custom; and Seuthes set the fashion of the performance. He took up the loaves which lay by his side and broke them into little pieces, and then threw the fragments here to one and there to another as seemed to him good; and so with the meat likewise, leaving for himself the merest taste. Then the rest fell to following the fashion set them, those that is who had tables placed beside them. Now there was an Arcadian, Arystas by name, a huge eater; he soon got tired of throwing the pieces about, and seized a good three-quarters loaf in his two hands, placed some pieces of meat upon his knees, and proceeded to discuss his dinner. Then beakers of wine were brought round, and every one partook in turn; but when the cupbearer came to Arystas and handed him the bowl, he looked up, and seeing that Xenophon had done eating: "Give it him," quoth he, "he is more at leisure. I have something better to do at present." Seuthes, hearing a remark, asked the cupbearer what was said, and the cupbearer, who knew how to talk Greek, explained. Then followed a peal of laughter. When the drinking had advanced somewhat, in came a Thracian with a white horse, who snatched the brimming bowl and said: "Here's a health to thee, O Seuthes! Let me present thee with this horse. Mounted on him, thou shalt capture whom thou choosest to pursue, or retiring from battle, thou shalt not dread the foe." He was followed by one who brought in a boy, and presented him in proper style with "Here's a health to thee, O Seuthes!" A third had "clothes for his wife." Timasion, the Dardanian, pledged Seuthes, and presented a silver bowl (136) and a carpet worth ten minae. Gnesippus, an Athenian, got up and said: "It was a good old custom, and a fine one too, that those who had, should give to the king for honour's sake, but to those who had not, the king should give; whereby, my lord," he added, "I too may one day have the wherewithal to give thee gifts and honour." Xenophon the while was racking his brains what he was to do; he was not the happier because he was seated in the seat next Seuthes as a mark of honour; and Heracleides bade the cupbearer hand him the bowl. The wine had perhaps a little mounted to his head; he rose, and manfully seized the cup, and spoke: "I also, Seuthes, have to present you with myself and these my dear comrades to be your trusty friends, and not one of them against his will. They are more ready, one and all, still more than I, to be your friends. Here they are; they ask nothing from you in return, rather they are forward to labour in your behalf; it will be their pleasure to bear the brunt of battle in voluntary service. With them, God willing, you will gain vast territory; you will recover what was once your forefathers'; you will win for yourself new lands; and not lands only, but horses many, and of men a multitude, and many a fair dame besides. You will not need to seize upon them in robber fashion; it is your friends here who, of their own accord, shall take and bring them to you, they shall lay them at your feet as gifts." Up got Seuthes and drained with him the cup, and with him sprinkled the last drops fraternally (137).

At this stage entered musicians blowing upon horns such as they use for signal calls, and trumpeting on trumpets, made of raw oxhide, tunes and airs, like the music of the double-octave harp (138). Seuthes himself got up and shouted, trolling forth a war song; then he sprang from his place and leapt about as though he would guard himself against a missile, in right nimble style. Then came in a set of clowns and jesters.

December 10, Wednesday   <Diodorus January 8, Thursday>

But when the sun began to set, the Hellenes rose from their seats. It was time, they said, to place the night sentinels and to pass the watchword; further, they begged of Seuthes to issue an order that none of the Thracians were to enter the Hellenic camp at night, "since between your Thracian foes and our Thracian friends there might be some confusion." As they sallied forth, Seuthes rose to accompany them, like the soberest of men. When they were outside, he summoned the generals apart and said: "Sirs, our enemies are not aware as yet of our alliance. If, therefore, we attack them before they take precautions not to be caught, or are prepared to repel assault, we shall make a fine haul of captives and other stock." The generals fully approved of these views, and bade him lead on. He answered: "Prepare and wait; as soon as the right time comes I will be with you. I shall pick up the peltasts and yourselves, and with the help of the gods, I will lead on." "But consider one point," urged Xenophon; "if we are to march by night, is not the Hellenic fashion best? When marching in the daytime that part of the army leads the van which seems best suited to the nature of the country to be traversed--heavy or light infantry, or cavalry; but by night our rule is that the slowest arm should take the lead. Thus we avoid the risk of being pulled to pieces: and it is not so easy for a man to give his neighbour the slip without intending, whereas the scattered fragments of an army are apt to fall foul of one another, and to cause damage or incur it in sheer ignorance." To this Seuthes replied: "You reason well, and I will adopt your custom. I will furnish you with guides chosen from the oldest experts of the country, and I will myself follow with the cavalry in the rear; it will not take me long, if need be, to present myself at the front." Then, for kinship's sake, they chose "Athenaia (139)" as their watchword. With this, they turned and sought repose.

December 11, Thursday   \<Diodorus January 9, Friday\>

It was about midnight when Seuthes presented himself with his cavalry troopers armed with corselets, and his light infantry under arms. As soon as he had handed over to them the promised guides, the heavy infantry took the van, followed by the light troops in the centre, while the cavalry brought up the rear. At daybreak Seuthes rode up to the front. He complimented them on their method: so often had he himself, while marching by night with a mere handful of men, been separated with his cavalry from his infantry. "But now," said he, "we find ourselves at dawn of day all happily together, just as we ought to be. Do you wait for me here," he proceeded, "and recruit yourselves. I will take a look round and rejoin you." So saying he took a certain path over hill and rode off. As soon as he had reached deep snow, he looked to see whether there were footprints of human beings leading forward or in the opposite direction; and having satisfied himself that the road was untrodden, back he came, exclaiming: "God willing, sirs, it will be all right; we shall fall on the fellows, before they know where they are. I will lead on with the cavalry; so that if we catch sight of any one, he shall not escape and give warning to the enemy. Do you follow, and if you are left behind, keep to the trail of the horses. Once on the other side of the mountains, we shall find ourselves in numerous thriving villages." By the middle of the day he had already gained the top of the pass and looked down upon the villages below. Back he came riding to the heavy infantry and said: "I will at once send off the cavalry into the plain below, and the peltasts too, to attack the villages. Do you follow with what speed you may, so that in case of resistance you may lend us your aid." Hearing this, Xenophon dismounted, and the other asked: "Why do you dismount just when speed is the thing we want?" The other answered: "But you do not want me alone, I am sure. The hoplites will run all the quicker and more cheerily if I lead them on foot." Thereupon Seuthes went off, and Timasion with him, taking the Hellene squadron of something like forty troopers. Then Xenophon passed the order: the active young fellows up to thirty years of age from the different companies to the front; and off with these he went himself, bowling along (140); while Cleanor led the other Hellenes.

When they had reached the villages, Seuthes, with about thirty troopers, rode up, exclaiming: "Well, Xenophon, this is just what you said! the fellows are caught, but now look here. My cavalry have gone off unsupported; they are scattered in pursuit, one here, one there, and upon my word, I am more than half afraid the enemy will collect somewhere and do them a mischief. Some of us must remain in the villages, for they are swarming with human beings." "Well then," said Xenophon, "I will seize the heights with the men I have with me, and do you bid Cleanor extend his line along the level beside the villages." When they had done so, there were enclosed--of captives for the slave market, one thousand; of cattle, two thousand; and of other small cattle, ten thousand. For the time being they took up quarters there.

December 12, Friday   **<Diodorus January 10, Saturday>**

IV

But the next day Seuthes burnt the villages to the ground; he left not a single house, being minded to inspire terror in the rest of his enemies, and to show them what they also were to expect, if they refused obedience; and so he went back again. As to the booty, he sent off Heracliedes to Perinthus to dispose of it, with a view to future pay for the soldiers. But for himself he encamped with the Hellenes in the lowland country of the Thynians, the natives leaving the flats and betaking themselves in flight to the uplands. There was deep snow, and cold so intense that the water brought in for dinner and the wine within the jars froze; and many of the Hellenes had their noses and ears frost-bitten. Now they came to understand why the Thracians wear fox-skin caps on their heads and about their ears; and why, on the same principle, they are frocked not only about the chest and bust but so as to cover the loins and thighs as well; and why on horseback they envelop themselves in long shawls which reach down to the feet, instead of the ordinary short rider's cloak. Seuthes sent off some of the prisoners to the hills with a message to say that if they did not come down to their homes, and live quietly and obey him, he would burn down their villages and their corn, and leave them to perish with hunger. Thereupon down they came, women and children and the older men; the younger men preferred to quarter themselves in the villages on the skirts of the hills. On discovering this, Seuthes bade Xenophon take the youngest of the heavy infantry and join him on an expedition.

December 13, Saturday   **<Diodorus January 11, Sunday>**

They rose in the night, and by daybreak had reached the villages; but the majority of the inhabitants made good their escape, for the hills were close at hand. Those whom he did catch, Seuthes unsparingly shot down. Now there was a certain Olynthian, named Episthenes; he was a great lover of boys, and seeing a handsome lad, just in the bloom of youth, and carrying a light shield, about to be slain, he ran up to Xenophon and supplicated him to rescue the fair youth. Xenophon went to Seuthes and begged him not to put the boy to death. He explained to him the disposition of Episthenes; how he had once enrolled a company, the only qualification required being that of personal beauty; and with these handsome young men at his side there were none so brave as he. Seuthes put the question, "Would you like to die on his behalf, Episthenes?" whereat the other stretched out his neck, and said, "Strike, if the boy bids you, and will thank his preserver." Seuthes, turning to the boy, asked, "Shall I smite him instead of you?" The boy shook his head, imploring him to slay neither the one nor the other, whereupon Episthenes caught the lad in his arms, exclaiming, "It is time you did battle with me, Seuthes, for my boy; never will I yield him up," and Seuthes laughed: "what must be must," and so consented. In these villages he decided that they must bivouac, so that the men on the mountains might be still further deprived of subsistence. Stealthily descending he himself found quarters in the plain; while Xenophon with his picked troops encamped in the highest village on the skirts of the hills,; and the rest of the Hellenes hard by, among the highland Thracians (141), as they are called.

December 17, Wednesday   **<Diodorus January 15, Thursday>**

After this, not many days had idly slipt away before the Thracians from the mountains came down and wished to arrange with Seuthes for terms of truce and hostages. Simultaneously came Xenophon and informed Seuthes that they were camped in bad quarters, with the enemy next door; "it would be pleasanter too," he added, "to bivouac in a strong position in the open, than under cover on the edge of destruction." The other bade him take heart and pointed to some of their hostages, as much as to say "Look there!" Parties also from the mountaineers came down and pleaded with Xenophon himself, to help arrange a truce for them. This he agreed to do, bidding them to pluck up heart, and assuring them that they would meet with no mischief, if they yielded obedience to Seuthes. All their parleying, however, was, as it turned out, merely to get a closer inspection of things. This happened in the day, and in the following night the Thynians descended from the hill country and made an attack. In each case, the guide was the master of the house attacked; otherwise it would have taxed their powers to discover the houses in the dark, which, for the sake of their flocks and herds, were palisaded all round with great stockades. As soon as they had reached the doors of any particular house, the attack began, some hurling in their spears, others belabouring with their clubs, which they carried, it was said, for the purpose of knocking off the lance points from the shaft. Others were busy setting the place on fire; and they kept calling Xenophon by name: "Come out, Xenophon, and die like a man, or we will roast you alive inside." By this time too the flames were making their appearance through the roof, and Xenophon and his followers were within, with their coats of mail on, and big shields, swords, and helmets. Then Silanus, a Macistian (142), a youth of some eighteen years, signalled on the trumpet; and in an instant, out they all leapt with their drawn swords, and the inmates of other quarters as well. The Thracians took to their heels, according to their custom, swinging their light shields round their backs. As they leapt over the stockade some were captured, hanging on the top with their shields caught in the palings; others missed the way out, and so were slain; and the Hellenes chased them hotly, till they were outside the village.

A party of Thynians turned back, and as the men ran past in bold relief against a blazing house, they let fly a volley of javelins, out of the darkness into the glare, and wounded two captains, Hieronymus, an Euodean (143), and Theogenes, a Locrian. No one was killed, only the clothes and baggage of some of the men were consumed in the flames. Presently up came Seuthes to the rescue with seven troopers, the first to hand, and his Thracian trumpeter by his side. Seeing that something had happened, he hastened to the rescue, and ever the while his bugler wound his horn, which music added terror to the foe. Arrived at length, he greeted them with outstretched hand, exclaiming, "I thought to find you all dead men."

After that, Xenophon begged him to hand over the hostages to himself, and if so disposed, to join him on an expedition to the hills, or if not, to let him go alone.

December 18, Thursday   \<Diodorus January 16, Friday\>

Accordingly the next day Seuthes delivered up the hostages. They were men already advanced in years, but the pick of the mountaineers, as they themselves gave out. Not merely did Seuthes do this, but he came himself, with his force at his back (and by this time he had treble his former force, for many of the Odrysians, hearing of his proceedings, came down to join in the campaign); and the Thynians, espying from the mountains the vast array of heavy infantry and light infantry and cavalry, rank upon rank, came down and supplicated him to make terms. "They were ready," they professed, "to do all that he demanded; let him take pledges of their good faith." So Seuthes summoned Xenophon and explained their proposals, adding that he should make no terms with them, if Xenophon wished to punish them for their night attack. The latter replied: "For my part, I should think their punishment is great enough already, if they are to be slaves instead of free men; still," he added, "I advise you for the future to take as hostages those who are most capable of doing mischief, and to let the old men abide in peace at home." So to a man they gave in their adhesion in that quarter of the country.

December 23, Tuesday   <Diodorus January 21, Tuesday>
Crossing the delta and arrival at the land of the Odrysians (corresponds to the river delta near Çerkezköy in the district of Tekirdağ Province in the Marmara Region of Turkey)

V

Crossing over in the direction of the Thracians above Byzantium, they reached the Delta, as it is called. Here they were no longer in the territory of the Maesades, but in the country of Teres the Odrysian (an ancient worthy (144)). Here Heracleides met them with the proceeds of the spoil, and Seuthes picked out three pairs of mules (there were only three, the other teams being oxen); then he summoned Xenophon and bade him take them, and divide the rest between the generals and officers, to which Xenophon replied that for himself, he was content to receive his share another time, but added: "Make a present of these to my friends here, the generals who have served with me, and to the officers." So of the pairs of mules Timasion the Dardanian received one, Cleanor the Orchomenian one, and Phryniscus the Achaean one. The teams of oxen were divided among the officers. Then Seuthes proceeded to remit pay due for the month already passed, but all he could give was the equivalent of twenty days. Heracleides insisted that this was all he had got by his trafficking. Whereupon Xenophon with some warmth exclaimed: "Upon my word, Heracleides, I do not think you care for Seuthes' interest as you should. If you did, you have been at pains to bring back the full amount of the pay, even if you had had to raise a loan to do so, and, if by no other means, by selling the coat off your own back."

What he said annoyed Heracleides, who was afraid of being ousted from the friendship of Seuthes, and from that day forward he did his best to calumniate Xenophon before Seuthes. The soldiers, on their side, laid the blame of course on Xenophon: "Where was their pay?" and Seuthes was vexed with him for persistently demanding it for them. Up to this date he had frequently referred to what he would do when he got to the seaboard again; how he intended to hand over to him Bisanthe, Ganos, and Neontichos (145). But from this time forward he never mentioned one of them again. The slanderous tongue of Heracleides had whispered him:--it was not safe to hand over fortified towns to a man with a force at his back.

Consequently Xenophon fell to considering what he ought to do as regards marching any further up the country; and Heracleides introduced the other generals to Seuthes, urging them to say that they were quite as well able to lead the army as Xenophon, and promising them that within a day or two they should have full pay for two months, and he again implored them to continue the campaign with Seuthes. To which Timasion replied that for his part he would continue no campaign without Xenophon; not even if they were to give him pay for five months; and what Timasion said, Phryniscus and Cleanor repeated; the views of all three coincided. Seuthes fell to upbraiding Heracleides in round terms. "Why had he not invited Xenophon with the others?" and presently they invited him, but by himself alone. He, perceiving the knavery of Heracleides, and that his object was to calumniate him with the other generals, presented himself; but at the same time he took care to bring all the generals and the officers.

December 24, Wednesday   \<Diodorus January 22, Wednesday\>

After their joint consent had been secured, they continued the campaign. Keeping the Pontus on their right, they passed through the millet-eating (146) Thracians, as they are called,

December 27, Saturday   \<Diodorus January 25, Saturday\>
Arrival at Salmydessus (modern-day Kıyıköy in Turkey)

and reached Salmydessus. This is a point at which many trading vessels bound for the Black Sea run aground and are wrecked, owing to a sort of marshy ledge or sandbank which runs out for a considerable distance into the sea (147). The Thracians, who dwell in these parts, have set up pillars as boundary marks, and each set of them has the pillage of its own flotsom and jetsom; for in old days, before they set up these landmarks, the wreckers, it is said, used freely to fall foul of and slay one another. Here was a rich treasure trove, of beds and boxes numberless, with a mass of written books, and all the various things which mariners carry in their wooden chests.

December 31, Wednesday   **<Diodorus January 29, Wednesday>**

Having reduced this district,

January 3, Saturday   **<Diodorus February 1, Saturday>**
Arrival back at the land of the Odrysians (corresponds to the river delta near Çerkezköy in the district of Tekirdağ Province in the Marmara Region of Turkey)

they turned round and went back again. By this time the army of Seuthes had grown to be considerably larger than the Hellenic army; for on the one hand, the Odrysians flocked down in still larger numbers, and on the other, the tribes which gave in their adhesion from time to time were amalgamated with his armament. They got into quarters on the flat country above Selybria at about three miles (148) distance from the sea. As to pay, not a penny was as yet forthcoming, and the soldiers were cruelly disaffected to Xenophon, whilst Seuthes, on his side, was no longer so friendlily disposed. If Xenophon ever wished to come face to face with him, want of leisure or some other difficulty always seemed to present itself.

VI

At this date, when nearly two months had already passed, an embassy arrived. These were two agents from Thibron--Charminus, a Lacedaemonian, and Polynicus. They were sent to say that the Lacedaemonians had resolved to open a campaign against Tissaphernes, and that Thibron, who had set sail to conduct the war, was anxious to avail himself of the troops. He could guarantee that each soldier should receive a daric a month as pay, the officers double pay, and the generals quadruple. The Lacedaemonian emissaries had no sooner arrived than Heracleides, having learnt that they had come in search of the Hellenic troops, goes off himself to Seuthes and says: "The best thing that could have happened; the

Lacedaemonians want these troops and you have done with them, so that if you hand over the troops to them, you will do the Lacedaemonians a good turn and will cease to be bothered for pay any more. The country will be quit of them once and for ever." On hearing this Seuthes bade him introduce the emissaries. As soon as they had stated that the object of their coming was to treat for the Hellenic troops, he replied that he would willingly give them up, that his one desire was to be the friend and ally of Lacedaemon. So he invited them to partake of hospitality, and entertained them magnificently; but he did not invite Xenophon, nor indeed any of the other generals. Presently the Lacedaemonians asked: "What sort of man is Xenophon?" and Seuthes answered: "Not a bad fellow in most respects; but he is too much the soldiers' friend; and that is why it goes ill with him." They asked: "Does he play the popular leader?" and Heracleides answered: "Exactly so." "Well then," said they, "he will oppose our taking away the troops, will he not?" "To be sure he will," said Heracleides; "but you have only to call a meeting of the whole body, and promise them pay, and little further heed will they pay to him; they will run off with you." "How then are we to get them collected?" they asked. "Early to-morrow," said Heracleides, "we will bring you to them; and I know," he added once more, "as soon as they set eyes on you, they will flock to you with alacrity." Thus the day ended.

January 4, Sunday   <Diodorus February 2, Sunday>

The next day Seuthes and Heracleides brought the two Laconian agents to the army, and the troops were collected, and the agents made a statement as follows: "The Lacedaemonians have resolved on war with Tissaphernes, who did you so much wrong. By going with us therefore you will punish your enemy, and each of you will get a daric a month, the officers twice that sum, and the generals quadruple." The soldiers lent willing ears, and up jumped one of the Arcadians at once, to find fault with Xenophon. Seuthes also was hard by, wishing to know what was going to happen. He stood within ear shot, and his interpreter by his side; not but what he could understand most of what was said in Greek himself. At this point the Arcadian spoke: "For the matter of that, Lacedaemonians, we should have been by your sides long ago, if Xenophon had not persuaded us and brought us hither. We have never ceased campaigning, night and day, the dismal winter through, but he reaps the fruit of our toils. Seuthes has enriched him privately, but deprives us of our honest earnings; so that, standing here as I do to address you first, all I can say is, that if I might see the fellow stoned to death as a penalty for all the long dance he has led us, I should feel I had got my pay in full, and no longer grudge the pains we have undergone." The speaker was followed by another and then another in the same strain; and after that Xenophon made the following speech:-- "True is the old adage; there is nothing which mortal man may not expect to see. Here am I being accused by you to-day, just where my conscience tells me that I have displayed the greatest zeal on your behalf. Was I not actually on my road home when I turned back? Not, God knows, because I learned that you were in luck's way, but because I heard that you were in sore straits, and I wished to help you, if in any way I could. I returned, and Seuthes yonder sent me messenger after messenger, and made me promise upon promise, if only I could persuade you to come to him. Yet, as you yourselves will bear me witness, I was not to be diverted. Instead of setting my hand to do that, I simply led you to a point from which, with least loss of time, I thought you could cross into Asia. This I believed was the best thing for you, and you I knew desired it. "But when Aristarchus came with his ships of war and hindered our passage across, you will hardly quarrel with me for the step I then took in calling you together that we might advisedly consider our best course. Having heard both sides--first Aristarchus, who ordered you to march to the Chersonese, then Seuthes, who pleaded with you to undertake a campaign with himself--you all proposed to go with Seuthes; and you all gave your votes to that effect. What wrong did I commit in bringing you, whither you were eager to go? If, indeed, since the time when Seuthes began to tell lies and cheat us about the pay, I have supported him in this, you may justly find fault with me and hate me. But if I, who at first was most of all his friend, to-day am more than any one else at variance with him, how can I, who have chosen you and rejected Seuthes, in fairness be blamed by you for the very thing which has been the ground of quarrel between him and me? But you will tell me, perhaps, that I get from Seuthes what is by right yours, and that I deal subtly by you? But is it not clear that, if Seuthes has paid me anything, he has at any rate not done so with the intention of losing by what he gives me, whilst he is still your debtor? If he gave to me, he gave in order that, by a small gift to me, he might escape a larger payment to yourselves. But if that is what you really think has happened, you can render this whole scheme of ours null and void in an instant by exacting from him the money which is your due. It is clear, Seuthes will demand back from me whatever I have got from him, and he will have all the more right to do so, if I have failed to secure for him what he bargained for when I took his gifts. But indeed, I am far removed from enjoying what is yours, and I swear to you by all the gods and goddesses that I have not taken even what Seuthes promised me in private. He is present himself and listening, and he is aware in his own heart whether I swear falsely. And what will surprise you the more, I can swear besides, that I have not received even what the other generals have received, no, nor yet what some of the officers have received. But how so? why have I managed my affairs no better? I thought, sirs, the more I helped him to bear his poverty at the time, the more I should make him my friend in the day of his power. Whereas, it is just when I see the star of his good fortune rising, that I have come to divine the secret of his character. "Some one may say, are you not ashamed to be so taken in like a fool? Yes, I should be ashamed, if it had been an open enemy who had so deceived me. But, to my mind, when friend cheats friend, a deeper stain attaches to the perpetrator than to the victim of deceit. Whatever precaution a man may take against his friend, that we took in full. We certainly gave him no pretext for refusing to pay us what he promised. We were perfectly upright in our dealings with him. We did not dawdle over his affairs, nor did we shrink from any work to which he challenged us. "But you will say, I ought to have taken security of him at the time, so that had he fostered the wish, he might have lacked the ability to deceive. To meet that retort, I must beg you to listen to certain things, which I should never have said in his presence, except for your utter want of feeling towards me, or your extraordinary ingratitude. Try and recall the posture of your affairs, when I extricated you and brought you to Seuthes. Do you not recollect how at Perinthus Aristarchus shut the gates in your faces each time you offered to approach the town, and how you were driven to camp outside under the canopy of heaven? It was midwinter; you were thrown upon the resources of a market wherein few were the articles offered for sale, and scanty the wherewithal to purchase them. Yet stay in Thrace you must, for there were ships of war riding at anchor in the bay, ready to hinder your passage across; and what did that stay imply? It meant being in a hostile country, confronted by countless cavalry, legions of light infantry. And what had we? A heavy infantry force certainly, with which we could have dashed at villages in a body possibly, and seized a modicum of food at most; but as to pursuing the enemy with such a force as ours, or capturing men or cattle, the thing was out of the question; for when I rejoined you your original cavalry and light infantry divisions had disappeared. In such sore straits you lay! "Supposing that, without making any demands for pay whatever, I had merely won for you the alliance of Seuthes--whose cavalry and light infantry were just what you needed--would you not have thought that I had planned very well for you? I presume, it was through your partnership with him and his that you were able to find such complete stores of corn in the villages, when the Thracians were driven to take to their heels in such hot haste, and you had so large a share of captives and cattle. Why! from the day on which his cavalry force was attached to us, we never set eyes on a single foeman in the field, though up to that date the enemy with his cavalry and his light infantry used undauntedly to hang on our heels, and effectually prevented us from scattering in small bodies and reaping a rich harvest of provisions. But if he who partly gave you this security has failed to pay in full the wages due to you therefrom, is not that a terrible misfortune? So monstrous indeed that you think I ought not to go forth alive (149).

"But let me ask you, in what condition do you turn your backs on this land to-day? Have you not wintered here in the lap of plenty? Whatever you have got from Seuthes has been surplus gain. Your enemies have had to meet the bill of your expenses, whilst you led a merry round of existence, in which you have not once set eyes on the dead body of a comrade or lost one living man. Again, if you have achieved any, (or rather many) noble deeds against the Asiatic barbarian, you have them safe. And in addition to these to-day you have won for yourselves a second glory. You undertook a campaign against the European Thracians, and have mastered them. What I say then is, that these very matters which you make a ground of quarrel against myself, are rather blessings for which you ought to show gratitude to heaven. "Thus far I have confined myself to your side of the matter. Bear with me, I beg you, while we examine mine. When I first essayed to part with you and journey homewards, I was doubly blest. From your lips I had won some praise, and, thanks to you, I had obtained glory from the rest of Hellas. I was trusted by the Lacedaemonians; else would they not have sent me back to you. Whereas to-day I turn to go, calumniated before the Lacedaemonians by yourselves, detested in your behalf by Seuthes, whom I meant so to benefit, by help of you, that I should find in him a refuge for myself and for my children, if children I might have, in after time. And you the while, for whose sake I have incurred so much hate, the hate of people far superior to me in strength, you, for whom I have not yet ceased to devise all the good I can, entertain such sentiments about me. Why? I am no renegade or runaway slave, you have got hold of. If you carry out what you say, be sure you will have done to death a man who has passed many a vigil in watching over you; who has shared with you many a toil and run many a risk in turn and out of turn; who, thanks to the gracious gods! has by your side set up full many a trophy over the barbarian; who, lastly, has strained every nerve in his body to protect you against yourselves. And so it is, that to-day you can move freely, where you choose, by sea or by land, and no one can say you nay; and you, on whom this large liberty dawns, who are sailing to a long desired goal, who are sought after by the greatest of military powers, who have pay in prospect, and for leaders these Lacedaemonians, our acknowledged chiefs: now is the appointed time, you think, to put me to a speedy death. But in the days of our difficulties it was very different, O ye men of marvellous memory! No! in those days you called me 'father!' and you promised you would bear me ever in mind, 'your benefactor.' Not so, however, not so ungracious are those who have come to you to-day; nor, if I mistake not, have you bettered yourselves in their eyes by your treatment of me." With these words he paused, and Charminus the Lacedaemonian got up and said: "Nay, by the Twins, you are wrong, surely, in your anger against this man; I myself can bear testimony in his favour. When Polynicus and I asked Seuthes, what sort of a man he was? Seuthes answered:--he had but one fault to find with him, that he was too much the soldiers' friend, which also was the cause why things went wrong with him, whether as regards us Lacedaemonians or himself, Seuthes." Upon that Eurylochus of Lusia, an Arcadian, got up and said (addressing the two Lacedaemonians), "Yes, sirs; and what strikes me is that you cannot begin your generalship of us better than by exacting from Seuthes our pay. Whether he like it or no, let him pay in full; and do not take us away before." Polycrates the Athenian, who was put forward by Xenophon, said: "If my eyes do not deceive me, sirs, there stands Heracleides, yonder, the man who received the property won by our toil, who took and sold it, and never gave back either to Seuthes or to us the proceeds of the sale, but kept the money to himself, like the thief he is. If we are wise, we will lay hold of him, for he is no Thracian, but a Hellene; and against Hellenes is the wrong he has committed." When Heracleides heard these words, he was in great consternation; so he came to Seuthes and said: "If we are wise we will get away from here out of reach of these fellows." So they mounted their horses and were gone in a trice, galloping to their own camp. Subsequently Seuthes sent Abrozelmes, his private interpreter, to Xenophon, begging him to stay behind with one thousand heavy troops; and engaging duly to deliver to him the places on the seaboard, and the other things which he had promised; and then, as a great secret, he told him, that he had heard from Polynicus that if he once got into the clutches of the Lacedaemonians, Thibron was certain to put him to death. Similar messages kept coming to Xenophon by letter or otherwise from several quarters, warning him that he was calumniated, and had best be on his guard. Hearing which, he took two victims and sacrificed to Zeus the King: "Whether it were better and happier to stay with Seuthes on the terms proposed, or depart with the army?" The answer he received was, "Depart."

January 5, Monday   **<Diodorus February 3, Monday>**
Move to the outskirts of Perinthus (corresponding to Marmara Ereglisi in modern-day Turkey)

VII

After this, Seuthes removed his camp to some considerable distance; and the Hellenes took up their quarters in some villages, selecting those in which they could best supply their commissariat, on the road to the sea.

January 8, Thursday   **<Diodorus February 6, Thursday>**
Negotiations with Seuthes

Now these particular villages had been given by Seuthes to Medosades. Accordingly, when the latter saw his property in the villages being expended by the Hellenes, he was not over well pleased; and taking with him an Odrysian, a powerful person amongst those who had come down from the interior, and about thirty mounted troopers, he came and challenged Xenophon to come forth from the Hellenic host. He, taking some of the officers and others of a character to be relied upon, came forward. Then Medosades, addressing Xenophon, said: "You are doing wrong to pillage our villages; we give you fair warning--I, in behalf of Seuthes, and this man by my side, who comes from Medocus, the king up country--to begone out of the land. If you refuse, understand, we have no notion of handing it over to you; but if you injure our country we will retaliate upon you as foes." Xenophon, hearing what they had to say, replied: "Such language addressed to us by you, of all people, is hard to answer. Yet for the sake of the young man with you, I will attempt to do so, that at least he may learn how different your nature is from ours. We," he continued, "before we were your friends, had the free run of this country, moving this way or that, as it took our fancy, pillaging and burning just as we chose; and you yourself, Medosades, whenever you came to us on an embassy, camped with us, without apprehension of any foe. As a tribe collectively you scarcely approached the country at all, or if you found yourselves in it, you bivouacked with your horses bitted and bridled, as being in the territory of your superiors. Presently you made friends with us, and, thanks to us, by God's help you have won this country, out of which to-day you seek to drive us; a country which we held by our own strength and gave to you. No hostile force, as you well know, was capable of expelling us. It might have been expected of you personally to speed us on our way with some gift, in return for the good we did you. Not so; even though our backs are turned

188

to go, we are too slow in our movements for you. You will not suffer us to take up quarters even, if you can help it, and these words arouse no shame in you, either before the gods, or this Odrysian, in whose eyes to-day you are man of means, though until you cultivated our friendship you lived a robber's life, as you have told us. However, why do you address yourself to me? I am no longer in command. Our generals are the Lacedaemonians, to whom you and yours delivered the army for withdrawal; and that, without even inviting me to attend, you most marvellous of men, so that if I lost their favour when I brought you the troops, I might now win their gratitude by restoring them." As soon as the Odrysian had heard this statement, he exclaimed: "For my part, Medosades, I sink under the earth for very shame at what I hear. If I had known the truth before, I would never have accompanied you. As it is, I return at once. Never would King Medocus applaud me, if I drove forth his benefactors." With these words, he mounted his horse and rode away, and with him the rest of his horsemen, except four or five. But Medosades, still vexed by the pillaging of the country, urged Xenophon to summon the two Lacedaemonians; and he, taking the pick of his men, came to Charminus and Polynicus and informed them that they were summoned by Medosades; probably they, like himself, would be warned to leave the country; "if so," he added, "you will be able to recover the pay which is owing to the army. You can say to them, that the army has requested you to assist in exacting their pay from Seuthes, whether he like it or not; that they have promised, as soon as they get this, cheerfully to follow you; that the demand seems to you to be only just, and that you have accordingly promised not to leave, until the soldiers have got their dues." The Lacedaemonians accepted the suggestion: they would apply these arguments and others the most forcible they could hit upon; and with the proper representatives of the army, they immediately set off. On their arrival Charminus spoke: "If you have anything to say to us, Medosades, say it; but if not, we have something to say to you." And Medosades submissively made answer: "I say," said he, "and Seuthes says the same: we think we have a right to ask that those who have become our friends should not be ill-treated by you; whatever ill you do to them you really do to us, for they are a part of us." "Good!" replied the Lacedaemonians, "and we intend to go away as soon as those who won for you the people and the territory in question have got their pay. Failing that, we are coming without further delay to assist them and to punish certain others who have broken their oaths and done them wrong. If it should turn out that you come under this head, when we come to exact justice, we shall begin with you." Xenophon added: "Would you prefer, Medosades, to leave it to these people themselves, in whose country we are (your friends, since this is the designation you prefer), to decide by ballot, which of the two should leave the country, you or we?" To that proposal he shook his head, but he trusted the two Laconians might be induced to go to Seuthes about the pay, adding, "Seuthes, I am sure, will lend a willing ear;" or if they could not go, then he prayed them to send Xenophon with himself, promising to lend the latter all the aid in his power, and finally he begged them not to burn the villages. Accordingly they sent Xenophon, and with him a serviceable staff. Being arrived, he addressed Seuthes thus:-- "Seuthes, I am here to advance no claims, but to show you, if I can, how unjust it was on your part to be angered with me because I zealously demanded of you on behalf of the soldiers what you promised them. According to my belief, it was no less to your interest to deliver it up, than it was to theirs to receive it. I cannot forget that, next to the gods, it was they who raised you up to a conspicuous eminence, when they made you king of large territory and many men, a position in which you cannot escape notice, whether you do good or do evil. For a man so circumstanced, I regarded it as a great thing that he should avoid the suspicion even of ungrateful parting with his benefactors. It was a great thing, I thought, that you should be well spoken of by six thousand human beings; but the greatest thing of all, that you should in no wise discredit the sincerity of your own word. For what of the man who cannot be trusted? I see that the words of his mouth are but vain words, powerless, and unhonoured; but with him who is seen to regard truth, the case is otherwise. He can achieve by his words what another achieves by force. If he seeks to bring the foolish to their senses--his very frown, I perceive, has a more sobering effect than the chastisement inflicted by another. Or in negotiations the very promises of such an one are of equal weight with the gifts of another. "Try and recall to mind in your own case, what advance of money you made to us to purchase our alliance. You know you did not advance one penny. It was simply confidence in the sincerity of your word which incited all these men to assist you in your campaign, and so to acquire for you an empire, worth many times more than thirty talents, which is all they now claim to receive. Here then, first of all, goes the credit which won for you your kingdom, sold for so mean a sum. Let me remind you of the great importance which you then attached to the acquisition of your present conquests. I am certain that to achieve what stands achieved to-day, you would willingly have foregone the gain of fifty times that paltry sum. To me it seems that to lose your present fortune were a more serious loss than never to have won it; since surely it is harder to be poor after being rich than never to have tasted wealth at all, and more painful to sink to the level of a subject, being a king, then never to have worn a crown. "You cannot forget that your present vassals were not persuaded to become your subjects out of love for you, but by sheer force; and but for some restraining dread they would endeavour to be free again to-morrow. And how do you propose to stimulate their sense of awe, and keep them in good behaviour towards you? Shall they see our soldiers so disposed towards you that a word on your part would suffice to keep them now, or if necessary would bring them back again to-morrow? while others hearing from us a hundred stories in your praise, hasten to present themselves at your desire? Or will you drive them to conclude adversely, that through mistrust of what has happened now, no second set of soldiers will come to help you, for even these troops of ours are more their friends than yours? And indeed it was not because they fell short of us in numbers that they became your subjects, but from lack of proper leaders. There is a danger, therefore, now lest they should choose as their protectors some of us who regard ourselves as wronged by you, or even better men than us-- the Lacedaemonians themselves; supposing our soldiers undertake to serve with more enthusiasm, if the debt you owe to them be first exacted; and the Lacedaemonians, who need their services, consent to this request. It is plain, at any rate, that the Thracians, now prostrate at your feet, would display far more enthusiasm in attacking, than in assisting you; for your mastery means their slavery, and your defeat their liberty. "Again, the country is now yours, and from this time forward you have to make provision for what is yours; and how will you best secure it an immunity from ill? Either these soldiers receive their dues and go, leaving a legacy of peace behind, or they stay and occupy an enemy's country, whilst you endeavour, by aid of a still larger army, to open a new campaign and turn them out; and your new troops will also need provisions. Or again, which will be the greater drain on your purse? to pay off your present debt, or, with that still owing, to bid for more troops, and of a better quality? "Heracleides, as he used to prove to me, finds the sum excessive. But surely it is a far less serious thing for you to take and pay it back to-day than it would have been to pay the tithe of it, before we came to you; since the limit between less and more is no fixed number, but depends on the relative capacity of payer and recipient, and your yearly income now is larger than the whole property which you possessed in earlier days. "Well, Seuthes, for myself these remarks are the expression of friendly forethought for a friend. They are expressed in the double hope that you may show yourself worthy of the good things which the gods have given you, and that my reputation may not be ruined with the army. For I must assure you that to-day, if I wished to injure a foe, I could not do so with this army. Nor again, if I wished to come and help you, should I be competent to the task; such is the disposition of the troops towards me. And yet I call you to witness, along with the gods who know, that never have I received anything from you on account of the soldiers. Never to this day have I, to my private gain, asked for what was theirs, nor even claimed the promises which were made to myself; and I swear to you, not even had you proposed to pay me my dues, would I have accepted them, unless the soldiers also had been going to receive theirs too; how could I? How shameful it would have been in me, so to have secured my own interests, whilst I disregarded the disastrous state of theirs, I being so honoured by them. Of course to the mind of Heracleides this is all silly talk; since the one great object is to keep money by whatever means. That is not my tenet, Seuthes. I believe that no fairer or brighter jewel can be given to a man, and most of all a prince, than the threefold grace of valour, justice, and generosity. He that possesses these is rich in the multitude of friends which surround him; rich also in the desire of others to be included in their number. While he prospers, he is surrounded by those who will rejoice with him in his joy; or if misfortune overtake him, he has no lack of sympathisers to give him help. However, if you have failed to learn from my deeds that I was, heart and soul, your friend; if my words are powerless to reveal the fact to-day, I would at least direct your attention to what the soldiers said; you were standing by and heard what those who sought to blame me said. They accused me to the Lacedaemonians, and the point of their indictment was that I set greater store by yourself than by the Lacedaemonians; but, as regards themselves, the charge was that I took more pains to secure the success of your interests than their own. They suggested that I had actually taken gifts from you. Was it, do you suppose, because they detected some ill-will in me towards you that they made the allegation? Was it not rather, that they had noticed my abundant zeal on your behalf? "All men believe, I think, that a fund of kindly feeling is due to him from whom we accept gifts. But what is your behaviour? Before I had ministered to you in any way, or done you a single service, you welcomed me kindly with your eyes, your voice, your hospitality, and you could not sate yourself with promises of all the fine things that were to follow. But having once achieved your object, and become the great man you now are, as great indeed as I could make you, you can stand by and see me degraded among my own soldiers! Well, time will teach you--that I fully believe--to pay whatever seems to you right, and even without the lessons of that teacher you will hardly care to see whose who have spent themselves in benefiting you, become your accusers. Only, when you do pay your debt, I beg of you to use your best endeavour to right me with the soldiers. Leave me at least where you found me; that is all I ask." After listening to this appeal, Seuthes called down curses on him, whose fault it was, that the debt had not long ago been paid, and, if the general suspicion was correct, this was Heracleides. "For myself," said Seuthes, "I never had any idea of robbing you of your just dues. I will repay." Then Xenophon rejoined: "Since you are minded to pay, I only ask that you will do so through me, and will not suffer me on your account to hold a different position in the army from what I held when we joined you." He replied: "As far as that goes, so far from holding a less honoured position among your own men on my account, if you will stay with me, keeping only a thousand heavy infantry, I will deliver to you the fortified places and everything I promised." The other answered: "On these terms I may not accept them, only let us go free." "Nay, but I know," said Seuthes, "that it is safer for you to bide with me than to go away." Then Xenophon again: "For your forethought I thank you, but I may not stay. Somewhere I may rise to honour, and that, be sure, shall redound to your gain also." Thereupon Seuthes spoke: "Of silver I have but little; that little, however, I give to you, one talent; but of beeves I can give you six hundred head, and of sheep four thousand, and of slaves six score. These take, and the hostages besides, who wronged you, and begone." Xenophon laughed and said: "But supposing these all together do not amount to the pay; for whom is the talent, shall I say? It is a little dangerous for myself, is it not? I think I had better be on the look-out for stones when I return. You heard the threats?" So for the moment he stayed there,

January 9, Friday   **<Diodorus February 7, Friday>**

but the next day Seuthes gave up to them what he had promised, and sent an escort to drive the cattle. The soldiers at first maintained that Xenophon had gone to take up his abode with Seuthes, and to receive what he had been promised; so when they saw him they were pleased, and ran to meet him. And Xenophon, seeing Charminus and Polynicus, said: "Thanks to your intervention, this much has been saved for the army. My duty is to deliver this fraction over to your keeping; do you divide and distribute it to the soldiers." Accordingly they took the property and appointed official vendors of the booty, and in the end incurred considerable blame. Xenophon held aloof. In fact it was no secret that he was making his preparations to return home, for as yet the vote of banishment had not been passed at Athens (150). But the authorities in the camp came to him and begged him not to go away until he had conducted the army to its destination, and handed it over to Thibron.

January 11, Sunday   **<Diodorus February 9, Sunday>**
Arrival at Lampascus (near Lapseki in Çanakkale Province of modern day Turkey – Alexander the Great passed here just before the Battle of Granicus)

VIII

From this place they sailed across to Lampsacus, and here Xenophon was met by Eucleides the soothsayer, a Phliasian, the son of Cleagoras, who painted "the dreams (151)" in the Lycium. Eucleides congratulated Xenophon upon his safe return, and asked him how much gold he had got? and Xenophon had to confess: "Upon my word, I shall have barely enough to get home, unless I sell my horse, and what I have about my person." The other could not credit the statement. Now when the Lampsacenes sent gifts of hospitality to Xenophon, and he was sacrificing to Apollo, he requested the presence of Eucleides; and the latter, seeing the victims, said: "Now I believe what you said about having no money. But I am certain," he continued, "if it were ever to come, there is an obstacle in the way. If nothing else, you are that obstacle yourself." Xenophon admitted the force of that remark. Then the other: "Zeus Meilichios (152) is an obstacle to you, I am sure," adding in another tone of voice, "have you tried sacrificing to that god, as I was wont to sacrifice and offer whole burnt offerings for you at home?" Xenophon replied that since he had been abroad, he had not sacrificed to that god. Accordingly Eucleides counselled him to sacrifice in the old customary way: he was sure that his fortune would improve.

January 12, Monday   **<Diodorus February 10, Monday>**

The next day Xenophon went on to Ophrynium and sacrificed, offering a holocaust of swine, after the custom of his family, and the signs which he obtained were favourable. That very day Bion and Nausicleides arrived laden with gifts for the army. These two were hospitably entertained by Xenophon, and were kind enough to repurchase the horse he had sold in Lampsacus for fifty darics; suspecting that he had parted with it out of need, and hearing that he was fond of the beast they restored it to him, refusing to be remunerated.

January 14, Wednesday   **<Diodorus February 12, Wednesday>**

From that place they marched through the Troad, and,

January 16, Friday   **<Diodorus February 14, Friday>**
Crossing Mount Ida (Kazdagi or Goose Mountain, 20 miles southeast of Troy)

crossing Mount Ida,

399 BC

January 19, Monday   **<Diodorus February 17, Tuesday>**
Arrival at Antandrus (corresponding to the area of the Devren hill between the village of Avcılar and the town of Altınoluk in the Edremit district of Balıkesir Province of modern-day Turkey)

arrived at Antandrus,

January 21, Wednesday   **<Diodorus February 19, Thursday>**
Passing the coast of north-eastern Aegean Sea (including Edremit Bay) to the plain of Thebe (near modern-day Yabancılar in Balıkesir Province Turkey)

and then pushed along the seaboard of Mysia to the plain of Thebe (153).

January 23, Friday   **<Diodorus February 21, Saturday>**
Passing through Kaïkos (modern-day river area of Bakırçay between the Temnus mountains and Elaitic Gulf encompassing Lydia, Mysia, and Aeolis) and arriving at Pergamus (northwest of the modern city of Bergama)

Thence they made their way through Adramytium and Certonus (154) by Atarneus, coming into the plain of the Caicus, and so reached Pergamus in Mysia.

Here Xenophon was hospitably entertained at the house of Hellas, the wife of Gongylus the Eretrian (155), the mother of Gorgion and Gongylus. From her he learnt that Asidates, a Persian notable, was in the plain. "If you take thirty men and go by night, you will take him prisoner," she said, "wife, children, money, and all; of money he has a store;" and to show them the way to these treasures, she sent her own cousin and Daphnagoras, whom she set great store by. So then Xenophon, with these two to assist, did sacrifice; and Basias, an Eleian, the soothsayer in attendance, said that the victims were as promising as could be, and the great man would be an easy prey. Accordingly, after dinner he set off, taking with him the officers who had been his staunchest friends and confidants throughout; as he wished to do them a good turn. A number of others came thrusting themselves on their company, to the number of six hundred, but the officers repelled them: "They had no notion of sharing their portion of the spoil," they said, "just as though the property lay already at their feet."

January 24, Saturday   \<Diodorus February 22, Sunday\>
(Crossing the Carcasus possibly Bakırçay river south of Pergamus towards the area of Parthenium and Apollonia, the latter which is on the route to Sardis/ modern-day Sart)

About midnight they arrived. The slaves occupying the precincts of the tower, with the mass of goods and chattles, slipped through their fingers, their sole anxiety being to capture Asidates and his belongings. So they brought their batteries to bear, but failing to take the tower by assault (since it was high and solid, and well supplied with ramparts, besides having a large body of warlike defenders), they endeavoured to undermine it. The wall was eight clay bricks thick, but by daybreak the passage was effected and the wall undermined. At the first gleam of light through the aperture, one of the defendants inside, with a large ox-spit, smote right through the thigh of the man nearest the hole, and the rest discharged their arrows so hotly that it was dangerous to come anywhere near the passage; and what with their shouting and kindling of beacon fires, a relief party at length arrived, consisting of Itabelius at the head of his force, and a body of Assyrian heavy infantry from Comania, and some Hyrcanian cavalry (156), the latter also being mercenaries of the king. There were eighty of them, and another detachment of light troops, about eight hundred, and more from Parthenium, and more again from Apollonia and the neighbouring places, also cavalry.

It was now high time to consider how they were to beat a retreat. So seizing all the cattle and sheep to be had, with the slaves, they put them within a hollow square and proceed to drive them off. Not that they had a thought to give to the spoils now, but for precaution's sake and for fear lest if they left the goods and chattels behind and made off, the retreat would rapidly degenerate into a stampede, the enemy growing bolder as the troops lost heart. For the present then they retired as if they meant to do battle for the spoils. As soon as Gongylus espied how few the Hellenes were and how large the attacking party, out he came himself, in spite of his mother, with his private force, wishing to share in the action. Another too joined in the rescue--Procles, from Halisarna and Teuthrania, a descendant of

Damaratus. By this time Xenophon and his men were being sore pressed by the arrows and slingstones, though they marched in a curve so as to keep their shields facing the missiles, and even so, barely crossed the river Carcasus, nearly half of them wounded. Here it was that Agasias the Stymphalian, the captain, received his wound, while keeping up a steady unflagging fight against the enemy from beginning to end. And so they reached home in safety with about two hundred captives, and sheep enough for sacrifices.

January 25, Sunday   <Diodorus February 23, Monday>

The next day Xenophon sacrificed and led out the whole army under the cover of night, intending to pierce far into the heart of Lydia with a view to lulling to sleep the enemy's alarm at his proxmity, and so in fact to put him off his guard. But Asidates, hearing that Xenophon had again sacrificed with the intention of another attack, and was approaching with his whole army, left his tower and took up quarters in some villages lying under the town of Parthenium.

January 26, Monday   <Diodorus February 24, Tuesday>
Return to Pergamus (northwest of the modern city of Bergama in Turkey)

Here Xenophon's party fell in with him, and took him prisoner, with his wife, his children, his horses, and all that he had; and so the promise of the earlier victims was literally fulfilled. After that they returned again to Pergamus, and here Xenophon might well thank God with a warm heart, for the Laconians, the officers, the other generals, and the soldiers as a body united to give him the pick of horses and cattle teams, and the rest; so that he was now in a position himself to do another a good turn. Meanwhile Thibron arrived and received the troops which he incorporated with the rest of his Hellenic forces, and so proceeded to prosecute a war against Tissaphernes and Pharnabazus (157).

5 ORIGINAL REFERENCES

(1) Parrhasia, a district and town in the south-west of Arcadia.

(2) A Persian gold coin = 125.55 grains of gold.

(3) Lit. "guest-friend." Aristippus was, as we learn from the "Meno" of Plato, a native of Larisa, of the family of the Aleuadae, and a pupil of Gorgias. He was also a lover of Menon, whom he appears to have sent on this expedition instead of himself.

(4) Lit. "into the country of the Pisidians."

(5) Of Stymphalus in Arcadia.

(6) "Targeteers" armed with a light shield instead of the larger one of the hoplite, or heavy infantry soldier. Iphicrates made great use of this arm at a later date.

(7) The Persian "farsang" = 30 stades, nearly 1 league, 3 1/2 statute miles, though not of uniform value in all parts of Asia.

(8) "Two plethra": the plethron = about 101 English feet.

(9) Lit. "inhabited," many of the cities of Asia being then as now deserted, but the suggestion is clearly at times "thickly inhabited," "populous."

(10) Lit. "paradise," an oriental word = park or pleasure ground.

(11) Perhaps this should be Agias the Arcadian, as Mr. Macmichael suggests. Sophaenetus has already been named above.

(12) The Lycaea, an Arcadian festival in honour of Zeus {Arcaios}, akin to the Roman Lupercalia, which was originally a shepherd festival, the introduction of which the Romans ascribe to the Arcadian Evander.

(13) Lit. "plain of the Cayster," like Ceramon-agora, "the market of the Ceramians" above, the name of a town.

(14) I.e. ready for action, c.f. "bayonets fixed".

(15) Lit. "into the country of the barbarian."

(16) Or "how he insisted that he was not going up."

(17) Cf. Plat. "Alcib." i. 123 B. "Why, I have been informed by a credible person, who went up to the king (at Susa), that he passed through a large tract of excellent land, extending for nearly a day's journey, which the people of the country called the queen's girdle, and another which they called her veil," etc. Olympiodorus and the Scholiast both think that Plato here refers to Xenophon and this passage of the "Anabasis." Grote thinks it very probable that Plato had in his mind Xenophon (either his "Anabasis" or personal communications with him).

(18) The choenix = about 1 quart (or, according to others, 1 1/2 pint). It was the minimum allowance of corn for a man, say a slave, per diem. The Spartan was allowed at the public table 2 choenices a day.

(19) For "the wall of Media" see Grote, "Hist. of Greece," vol. ix. p. 87 and foll. note 1 (1st ed.), and various authorities there quoted or referred to. The next passage enclosed in ( ) may possibly be a commentator's or editor's note, but, on the whole, I have thought it best to keep the words in the text instead of relegating them, as heretofore, to a note. Perhaps some future traveller may clear up all difficulties.

(20) I.e. between 9 and 10 A.M.

(21) The MSS. add, "to expose oneself to the risks of war bareheaded is, it is said, a practice common to the Persians," which I regard as a commentator's note, if not an original marginal note of some early editor, possibly of the author himself. The "Cyropaedeia" is full of such comments, "pieces justificatives" inserted into the text.

(22) I.e. the omens from inspecting the innards of the victims, and the omens from the acts and movements of the victims.

(23) Some critics regard this sentence as an editor's or commentator's note.

(24) "Ctesias, the son of Ctesiochus, was a physician of Cnidos. Seventeen years of his life were passed at the court of Persia, fourteen in the service of Darios, three in that of Artaxerxes; he returned to Greece in 398 B.C.," and "was employed by Artaxerxes in diplomatic services." See Mure; also Ch. Muller, for his life and works. He wrote (1) a history on Persian affairs in three parts--Assyrian, Median, Persian--with a chapter "On Tributes;" (2) a history of Indian affairs (written in the vein of Sir John Maundeville, Kt.); (3) a Periplus; (4) a treatise on Mountains; (5) a treatise on Rivers.

(25) The character now to be drawn is afterwards elaborated into the Cyrus of the Cyropaedeia.

(26) The elder Cyrus, when a boy, kills not a bear but a boar.

(27) The Spartan king who was deposed in B.C. 491, whereupon he fled to King Darius, and settled in south-western Mysia. See Herod. vi. 50, 61-70. We shall hear more of his descendant, Procles, the ruler of Teuthrania, in the last chapter of this work.

(28) 10 A.M.

(29) So the best MSS. Others read "Xenophon," which Kruger maintains to be the true reading. He suggests that "Theopompus" may have crept into the text from a marginal note of a scholiast, "Theopompus" (the historian) "gives the remark to Proxenus."

(30) The MSS. add the words, "The total distance of the route, taking Ephesus in Ionia as the starting point up to the field of battle, consisted of 93 stages, 535 parasangs, or 16,050 furlongs; from the battle-field to Babylon (reckoned a three days' journey) would have been another 360 stades," which may well be an editor's or commentator's marginal note.

(31) It is a question whether the words "a wolf" ought not to be omitted.

(32) I.e. the cabbage-like crown.

(33) Possibly Xenophon himself.

(34) The Greater Zab, which flows into the Tigris near a town now called Senn, with which most travellers identify Caenae.

(35) We learn from Diodorus Siculus, xiv. 35, that the Egyptians had revolted from the Persians towards the end of the reign of Darius.

(36) The famous rhetorician of Leontini, 485-380 B.C. His fee was 100 minae.

(37) Proxenus, like Cyrus, is to some extent a prototype of the Cyrus of the "Cyropaedia." In other words, the author, in delineating the portrait of his ideal prince, drew from the recollection of many princely qualities observed by him in the characters of many friends. Apart from the intrinsic charm of the story, the "Anabasis" is interesting as containing the raw material of experience and reflection which "this young scholar or philosopher," our friend, the author, will one day turn to literary account.

(38) For a less repulsive conception of Menon's character, however unhistorical, see Plato's "Meno," and Prof. Jowlett's Introduction, "Plato," vol. i. p. 265: "He is a Thessalian Alcibiades, rich and luxurious--a spoilt child of fortune."

(39) The reader should turn to Grote's comments on the first appearance of Xenophon. He has been mentioned before, of course, more than once before; but he now steps, as the protagonist, upon the scene, and as Grote says: "It is in true Homeric vein, and in something like Homeric language, that Xenophon (to whom we owe the whole narrative of the expedition) describes his dream, or the intervention of Oneiros, sent by Zeus, from which this renovating impulse took its rise."

(40) So it is said of the Russian General Skobelef, that he had a strange custom of going into battle in his cleanest uniform, perfumed, and wearing a diamond-hilted sword, "in order that," as he said, "he might die in his best attire."

(41) For this ancient omen see "Odyssey," xvii. 541: "Even as she spake, and Telemachus sneezed loudly, and around the roof rung wondrously. And Penelope laughed."... "Dost thou not mark how my son has sneezed a blessing on all my words?"

(42) See Herod. vi. 114; the allusion is to the invasion of Greece by

Datis and Artaphernes, and to their defeat at Marathon, B.C. 490. "Heredotus estimates the number of those who fell on the Persian side at 6400 men: the number of Athenian dead is accurately known, since all were collected for the last solemn obsequies--they were 192."--Grote, "Hist. of Greece," vol. v. p. 475.

(43) Then = at Salamis, B.C. 480, and at Plataea and Mycale, B.C. 479, on the same day.

(44) See "Odyssey," ix. 94, "ever feeding on the Lotus and forgetful of returning."

(45) Here seems to be the germ--unless, indeed, the thought had been conceived above--here at any rate the first conscious expression of the colonisation scheme, of which we shall hear more below, in reference to Cotyora; the Phasis; Calpe. It appears again fifty years later in the author's pamphlet "On Revenues," chapters i. and vi. For the special evils of the fourth century B.C., and the growth of pauperism between B.C. 401 and 338, see Jebb, "Attic Orators," vol i. p. 17.

(46) Can this be the same man whose escape is so graphically described above?

(47) These words sound to me like an author's note, parenthetically, and perhaps inadvertently, inserted into the text. It is an "aside" to the reader, which in a modern book would appear as a footnote.

(48) Larissa, on the side of the modern Nimrud (the south-west corner, as is commonly supposed, of Nineveh).

The name is said to mean "citadel," and is given to various Greek cities (of which several occur in Xenophon).

(49) I.e. Cyrus the Great.

(50) Opposite Mosul, the north-west portion of the ancient Nineveh, about eighteen miles above Larissa. The circuit of Nineveh is said to have been about fifty-six miles. It was overthrown by Cyrus in B.C. 558.

(51) The wife of Astyages, the last king of Media. Some think "the wall of Media" should be "Medea's wall," constructed in the period of Queen Nitocris, B.C. 560.

(52) The best MSS read {Skuthai}, Scythians; if this is correct, it is only the technical name for "archers." Cf. Arrian, "Tact." ii. 13. The police at Athens were technically so called, as being composed of Scythian slaves. Cf. Aristoph. "Thesm." 1017.

(53) I.e., in practising, in order to get the maximum range they let fly the arrows, not horizontally, but up into the air. Sir W. Raleigh (Hist. of the World, III. x. 8) says that Xenophon "trained his archers to short compass, who had been accustomed to the point blank," but this is surely not Xenophon's meaning.

(54) In the passage above I have translated {lokhoi} companies, and, as usual, {lokhagoi} captains. The half company is technically called a pentecostys, and a quarter company an enomoty, and the officers in charge of them respectively penteconter and enomotarch. These would be equivalent nearly to our subalterns and sergeants, and in the evolutions described would act as guides and markers in charge of their sections. Grote thinks there were six companies formed on each flank--twelve in all. See "Hist. of Greece," vol. ix. p. 123, note (1st ed.)

(55) I.e. the Persian leaders were seen flogging their men to the attack. Cf. Herod. vii. 22. 3.

(56) Lit. "a mere nail tip."

(57) Some think that these three hundred are three of the detached companies described above; others, that they were a picked corps in attendance on the commander-in-chief.

(58) Some MSS. "and the men behind to pass him by, as he could but ill keep up the pace."

(59) See Dr. Kiepert, "Man. Anc. Geog." (Mr. G. A. Macmillan) iv. 47. The Karduchians or Kurds belong by speech to the Iranian stock, forming in fact their farthest outpost to the west, little given to agriculture, but chiefly to the breeding of cattle. Their name, pronounced Kardu by the ancient Syrians and Assyrians, Kordu by the Armenians (plural Kordukh), first appears in its narrower sense in western literature in the pages of the eye-witness Xenophon as {Kardoukhoi}. Later writers knew of a small kingdom here at the time of the Roman occupation, ruled by native princes, who after Tigranes II (about 80 B.C.) recognised the overlordship of the Armenian king. Later it became a province of the Sassanid kingdom, and as such was in 297 A.D. handed over among the regiones transtigritanae to the

Roman empire, but in 364 was again ceded to Persia.

(60) I.e. several ton weight.

(61) Or, "mamelon."

(62) To take up position.

(63) I.e. of Lusi (or Lusia), a town (or district) in Northern Arcadia.

(64) I.e. the Eastern Tigris.

(65) It is impossible to give the true sense and humour of the passage in English, depending, as it does, on the double meaning of {diabainein} (1) to cross (a river), (2) to stride or straddle (of the legs). The army is unable to cross the Centrites; Xenophon dreams that he is fettered, but the chains drop off his legs and he is able to stride as freely as ever; next morning the two young men come to him with the story how they have found themselves able to walk cross the river instead of having to swim it. It is obvious to Xenophon that the dream is sent from Heaven.

(66) Or, "having doffed it," i.e. the wreath, an action which the soldiers would perform symbolically, if Grote is right in his interpretation of the passage, "Hist. of Greece," vol. ix. p. 137.

(67) Lit. "comrade-women."

(68) Or, "to stick tight to them and not to be outdone"; or, as others understand, "the (infantry) soldiers clamoured not to be left behind, but to follow them up into the mountains."

(69) Or, as we should say, "in his shirt sleeves." Doubtless he lay with his {imation} or cloak loosely wrapped round him; as he sprang to his feet he would throw it off, or it would fall off, and with the simple inner covering of the {khiton} to protect him, and arms free, he fell to chopping the wood, only half clad.

(70) Reading {Temeniten}, i.e. a native of Temenus, a district of Syracuse; al. {Temniten}, i.e. from Temnus in the Aeolid; al. {Temeniten}, i.e. from Temenum in the Argolid.

(71) Al. "ten," al. "five."

(72) Hug, after Rehdantz, would omit the words "in the plenitude of health and strength."

(73) Or, "the invalids."

(74) Probably a tributary of the Araxes = modern Pasin-Su.

(75) Or, more lit., "with the head a mark for missiles."

(76) These are the Armeno-Chalybes, so called by Pliny in contradistinction to another mountain tribe in Pontus so named, who were famous for their forging, and from whom steel received its Greek name {khalups}. With these latter we shall make acquaintance later on.

(77) I.e. with a single point or spike only, the Hellenic spear having a spike at the butt end also.

(78) Gymnias is supposed (by Grote, "Hist. of Greece," vol. ix. p. 161) to be the same as that which is now called Gumisch-Kana--perhaps "at no great distance from Baibut," Tozer, "Turkish Armenia," p.432. Others have identified it with Erzeroum, others with Ispir.

(79) Some MSS. give "the sacred mountain." The height in question has been identified with "the ridge called Tekieh-Dagh to the east of Gumisch-Kana, nearer to the sea than that place" (Grote, ib. p.162), but the exact place from which they caught sight of the sea has not been identified as yet, and other mountain ranges have been suggested.

(80) For this formation, see "The Retreat of the Ten Thousand; a military study for all time," by Lieut.-General J. L. Vaughan, C.B.

(81) Or, "we will gobble them up raw." He is thinking of the Homeric line ("Iliad", iv. 35) "Perchance wert thou to enter within the gates and long walls and devour Priam raw, and Priam's sons and all the Trojans, then mightest thou assuage thine anger."--Leaf.

(82) This suggests 1800 as the total of the peltasts, 8000 as the total of the hoplites, but the companies were probably not limited to 100, and under "peltasts" were probably included other light troops.

(83) "Modern travellers attest the existence, in these regions, of honey intoxicating and poisonous.... They point out the Azalea Pontica as the flower from which the bees imbibe this peculiar quality."--Grote, "Hist. of

Greece," vol. ix. p. 155.

(84) Trebizond.

(85) Or, "to sacrifice to Zeus the Preserver, and to Heracles thank-offerings for safe guidance," Heracles "the conductor" having special sympathy with wanderers.

(86) The pankration combined both wrestling and boxing.

(87) A native of the country parts of Laconia.

(88) Lit. "{Musos} (Mysus), a Mysian by birth, and {Musos} (Mysus) by name."

(89) I.e. of Asine, perhaps the place named in Thuc. iv. 13, 54; vi. 93 situated on the western side of the Messenian bay. Strabo, however, speaks of another Asine near Gytheum, but possibly means Las. See Arnold's note to Thuc. iv. 13, and Smith's "Dict. Geog. (s.v.)"

(90) Cf. Herod. i. 14; Strabo. ix. 420 for such private treasuries at Delphi.

(91) I.e. in the year B.C. 394. The circumstances under which Agesilaus was recalled from Asia, with the details of his march and the battle of Coronea, are described by Xenophon in the fourth book of the "Hellenica."

(92) Scillus, a town of Triphylia, a district of Elis. In B.C. 572 the Eleians had razed Pisa and Scillus to the ground. But between B.C. 392 and 387 the Lacedaemonians, having previously (B.C. 400, "Hell." III. ii. 30) compelled the Eleians to renounce their supremacy over their dependent cities, colonised Scillus and eventually gave it to Xenophon, then an exile from Athens. Xenophon resided here from fifteen to twenty years, but was, it is said, expelled from it by the Eleians soon after the battle of Leuctra, in B.C. 371.--"Dict. Geog. (s.v.)" The site of the place, and of Xenophon's temple, is supposed to be in the neighbourhood of the modern village of Chrestena, or possibly nearer Mazi. To reach Olympia, about 2 1/2 miles distant, one must cross the Alpheus.

(93) Pholoe. This mountain (north of the Alpheus) is an offshoot of Erymanthus, crossing the Pisatis from east to west, and separating the waters of the Peneus and the Ladon from those of the Alpheus --"Dict. Geog." (Elis).

(94) I.e. dwellers in mossyns, or wooden towers. See Herod. iii. 94; vii. 78. Cf. also Strabo, xi. 41.

(95) Or, "consul."

(96) I.e. "chestnuts."

(97) The MSS. here read, "Up to this point the expedition was conducted on land, and the distance traversed on foot from the battle-field near Babylon down to Cotyora amounted to one hundred and twenty-two stages--that is to say, six hundred and twenty parasangs, or eighteen thousand stades, or if measured in time, an eight months' march." The words are probably the note of some editor or commentator, though it is quite likely that the author himself may have gone through such calculations and even have inserted them as a note to his text.

(98) Lit. "harmost". The term, denoting properly a governor of the islands and foreign cities sent out by the Lacedaemonians during their supremacy, came, it would seem, to be adopted by other Greek communities under somewhat similar circumstances. Cotyora receives a harmost from her mother-city, Sinope. For the Greek colonies here mentioned, see Kiepert's "Man. Anct. Geog." (Engl. tr., Mr. G. A. Macmillan), p. 63.

(99) Cf. Plato, "Theages," 122.

(100) A cyzicene stater = twenty-eight silver drachmae of Attic money B.C. 335, in the time of Demosthenes; but, like the daric, this gold coin would fluctuate in value relatively to silver. It contained more grains of gold than the daric.

(101) Of Dercylidas we hear more in the "Hellenica." In B.C. 411 he was harmost at Abydos; in B.C. 399 he superseded Thimbron in Asia Minor; and was himself superseded by Agesilaus in B.C. 396.

(102) The word {masteuein} occurs above, and again below, and in other writings of our author. It is probably Ionic or old Attic, and occurs in poetry.

(103) Aeetes is the patronym of the kings of Colchis from mythical times onwards; e.g. Medea was the daughter of Aeetes.

(104) Whether this was a local saying or a proverb I cannot say. The

words have a poetical ring about them: "When Borrhas blows, fair voyages to Hellas."

(105) I.e. a board of judges or jurors.

(106) See the "Dict. of Antiq." 622 a. HYBREOS GRAPHE. In the case of common assaults as opposed to indecent assault, the prosecution seems to have been allowable only when the object of a wanton attack was a free person. Cf. Arist. "Rhet." ii. 24.

(107) I.e. the national Thracian hymn; for Sitalcas the king, a national hero, see Thuc. ii. 29.

(108) The Aenianians, an Aeolian people inhabiting the upper valley of the Sperchius (the ancient Phthia); their capital was Hypata. These men belonged to the army collected by Menon, the Thessalian. So, doubtless, did the Magnesians, another Aeolian tribe occupying the mountainous coast district on the east of Thessaly. See Kiepert's "Man. Anct. Geog." (Macmillan's tr.), chap. vi.. 161, 170.

(109) See Plato, "Rep." 400 B, for this "war measure"; also Aristoph. "Clouds," 653.

(110) For this famous dance, supposed to be of Doric (Cretan or Spartan) origin, see Smith's "Dict. of Antiquities," "Saltatio"; also Guhl and Koner, "The Life of the Greeks and Romans," Eng. tr.

(111) Harmene, a port of Sinope, between four and five miles (fifty stades) west of that important city, itself a port town. See Smith, "Dict. Geog.," "Sinope"; and Kiepert, op. cit. chap. iv. 60.

(112) Cf. "Cyrop." II. i. 1; an eagle appears to Cyrus on the frontiers of Persia, when about to join his uncle Cyaxares, king of Media, on his expedition against the Assyrian.

(113) It is important to note that the Greek word {oionos}, a solitary or lone-flying bird, also means an omen. "It was a mighty bird and a mighty omen."

(114) I have left this passage in the text, although it involves, at first sight, a topographical error on the part of whoever wrote it, and Hug and other commentators regard it as spurious. Jason's beach (the modern Yasoun Bouroun) and the three first-named rivers lie between Cotyora and

Sinope. Possibly the author, or one of his editors, somewhat loosely inserted a recapitulatory note concerning the scenery of this coasting voyage at this point. "By the way, I ought to have told you that as they coasted along," etc.

(115) One of the most powerful of commercial cities, distinguished as Pontica (whence, in the middle ages, Penteraklia), now Eregli. It was one of the older Greek settlements, and, like Kalchedon (to give that town its proper name), a Megaro-Doric colony. See Kiepert, op. cit. chap. iv. 62.

(116) According to another version of the legend Heracles went down to bring up Cerberus, not here, but at Taenarum.

(117) The total now amounted to 8640 and over.

(118) The Haven of Calpe = Kirpe Liman or Karpe in the modern maps. The name is interesting as being also the ancient name of the rock fortress of Gibraltar.

(119) Some MSS. here read, "In the prior chapter will be found a description of the manner in which the absolute command of Cheirisophus was abruptly terminated and the army of the Hellenes broken up. The sequel will show how each of these divisions fared." The passage is probably one of those commentators' notes, with which we are now familiar.

(120) Lit. "marched and fought," as did the forlorn hope under Sir C. Wilson making its way from Abu Klea to the Nile in Jan. 1885.

(121) I.e. "his society was itself a passport to good fortune."

(122) "Cenotaph", i.e. "an empty tomb." The word is interesting as occurring only in Xenophon, until we come to the writers of the common dialect. Compare "hyuscyamus," hogbean, our henbane, which we also owe to Xenophon. "Oecon." i. 13, see Sauppe, "Lexil. Xen." s.vv.

(123) This I take to be the meaning of the words, which are necessarily ambiguous, since {pharmakon}, "a drug," also means "poison." Did Cheirisophus conceivably die of fever brought on by some poisonous draught? or did he take poison whilst suffering from fever? or did he die under treatment?

(124) Lit. "had they wound off thread by thread"; the metaphor is from

unwinding a ball of wool.

(125) Reading with the best MSS., {sozoisthe}. Agasias ends his sentence with a prayer. Al. {sozesthe}, "act so that each," etc.

(126) The name should be written "Calchedonia." The false form drove out the more correct, probably through a mispronunciation, based on a wrong derivation, at some date long ago. The sites of Chrysopolis and Calchedon correspond respectively to the modern Scutari and Kadikoi.

(127) So the mountain-range is named which runs parallel to the Propontis (Sea of Marmora) from lat. 41 degrees N. circa to lat. 40 degrees 30'; from Bisanthe (Rhodosto) to the neck of the Chersonese (Gallipoli).

(128) The exact locality, so called, is not known; doubtless it lay somewhere between Byzantium and Salmydessus, possibly at Declus (mod. Derkos); or possibly the narrow portion of Thrace between the Euxine, Bosphorus, and Propontis went by this name. See note in Pretor ad. loc., and "Dict. Geog." "Thracia."

(129) The MSS. give the words so rendered--{oi de kai (didontes ta opla kata tous khorous)}, which some critics emend {diadidontes}, others bracket as suspected, others expunge.

(130) I.e. "instead of letting them graze."

(131) Tradition said that the Thracians and Athenians were connected, through the marriage of a former prince Tereus (or Teres) with Procne, the daughter of Pandion. This old story, discredited by Thucydides, ii. 29, is referred to in Arist. "Birds," 368 foll. The Birds are about to charge the two Athenian intruders, when Epops, king of the Birds, formerly Tereus, king of Thrace, but long ago transformed into a hoopoe, intercedes in behalf of two men, {tes emes gunaikos onte suggene kai phuleta}, "who are of my lady's tribe and kin." As a matter of history, the Athenians had in the year B.C. 431 made alliance with Sitalces, king of the Odrysians (the son of Teres, the first founder of their empire), and made his son, Sadocus, an Athenian citizen. Cf. Thuc. ib.; Arist. Acharnians, 141 foll.

(132) A cyzicene monthly is to be understood.

(133) Bisanthe, one of the Ionic colonies founded by Samos, with the Thracian name Rhaedestus (now Rodosto), strongly placed so as to command the entrance into the Sacred mountain.

(134) A Greek colony in Thrace. Among Asiatico-Ionian colonies were Abdera, founded by Teos, and Maroneia, celebrated for its wine, founded by Chios about 540 B.C.--Kiepert, "Man. Anct. Geog." viii. 182.

(135) Notably Alcibiades, who possessed two or three such fortresses.

(136) Or rather "saucer" ({phiale}).

(137) For the Thracian custom, vide Suidas, s.v. {kataskedazein}.

(138) Or, "magadis." This is said to have been one of the most perfect instruments. It comprised two full octaves, the left hand playing the same notes as the right an octave lower. Guhl and Koner, p. 203, Engl. transl. See also "Dict. Antiq." "Musica"; and Arist. "Polit." xix. 18, {Dia ti e dia pason sumphonia adetai mone; magasizousi gar tauten, allen de oudemian}, i.e. "since no interval except the octave ({dia pason}) could be 'magidised' (the effect of any other is well known to be intolerable), therefore no other interval was employed at all."

(139) "Our Lady of Athens."

(140) {etropkhaze}, a favourite word with our author. Herodotus uses it; so does Aristot.; so also Polybius; but the Atticists condemn it, except of course in poetry.

(141) Cf. "Highlanders."

(142) "Of Macistus," a town in the Triphylia near Scillus.

(143) If this is the same man as Hieronymus of Elis, who has been mentioned two or three times already, possibly the word {Euodea} points to some town or district of Elis; or perhaps the text is corrupt.

(144) See above re previous Teres. The words "an ancient worthy" may possibly be an editor's or commentator's note.

(145) For Bisanthe see above. Ganos, a little lower down the coast, with Neontichos once belonged to Alcibiades, if we may believe Cornelius Nepos, "Alc." vii. 4, and Plutarch, "Alc." c. 36. See above.
(146) Or, "the Melinophagi."

(147) See, for a description of this savage coast, Aesch. "Prom." vinc. 726, etc.--"{trakheia pontou Salmudesia gnathosekhthroxenos nautaisi,

metruia neon.}" "The rugged Salmudesian jaw of the Black Sea, Inhospitable to sailors, stepmother of ships." But the poet is at fault in his geography, since he connects "the Salmydesian jaw" with the Thermodon.

(148) Lit. "thirty stades." Selybria is about fourty-four miles from Byzantium, two-thirds of the way to Perinthus.

(149) I.e. the fate of a scape-goat is too good for me.

(150) I.e. "at this moment the vote of banishment had not been passed which would prevent his return to Athens." The natural inference from these words is, I think, that the vote of banishment was presently passed, at any rate considerably earlier than the battle of Coronea in B.C. 394, five years and a half afterwards.

(151) Reading {ta enupnia}, or if {ta entoikhia} with Hug and others, translate "the wall-paintings" or the "frescoes." Others think that a writing, not a painting, is referred to.

(152) Zeus Meilichios, or the gentle one. See Thuc. i. 126. The festival of the Diasia at Athens was in honour of that god, or rather of Zeus under that aspect. Cf. Arist. "Clouds," 408.

(153) Thebe, a famous ancient town in Mysia, at the southern foot of Mt. Placius, which is often mentioned in Homer ("Il." i. 366, vi. 397, xxii. 479, ii. 691). See "Dict. Geog." s.v. The name {Thebes pedion} preserves the site. Cf. above {Kaustrou pedion}, and such modern names as "the Campagna" or "Piano di Sorrento."

(154) The site of Certonus is not ascertained. Some critics have conjectured that the name should be Cytonium, a place between Mysia and Lydia; and Hug, who reads {Kutoniou}, omits {odeusantes par 'Atanea}, "they made their way by Atarneus," as a gloss.

(155) Cf. Thuc. i. 128; also "Hell." III. i. 6.

(156) The Hyrcanian cavalry play an important part in the "Cyropaedeia." They are the Scirites of the Assyrian army who came over to Cyrus after the first battle. Their country is the fertile land touching the south-eastern corner of the Caspian. Cf. "Cyrop." IV. ii. 8, where the author (or an editor) appends a note on the present status of the Hyrcanians.

(157) The MSS. add: "The following is a list of the governors of the

several territories of the king which were traversed by us during the expedition: Artimas, governor of Lydia; Artacamas, of Phrygia; Mithridates, of Lycaonia and Cappadocia; Syennesis, of Cilicia; Dernes, of Phoenicia and Arabia; Belesys, of Syria and Assyria; Rhoparas, of Babylon; Arbacus, of Media; Tiribazus, of the Phasians and Hesperites. Then some independent tribes--the Carduchians or Kurds, and Chalybes, and Chaldaeans, and Macrones, and Colchians, and Mossynoecians, and Coetians, and Tibarenians. Then Corylas, the governor of Paphlagonia; Pharnabazus, of the Bithynians; Seuthes, of the European Thracians. The entire journey, ascent and descent, consisted of two hundred and fifteen stages = one thousand one hundred and fifty-five parasangs = thirty-four thousand six hundred and fifty stades. Computed in time, the length of ascent and descent together amounted to one year and three months." The annotator apparently computes the distance from Ephesus to Cotyora.

ABOUT THE AUTHOR

Dr Hutan Ashrafian, BSc Hons, MBBS, MRCS, MBA, PhD is a scientist, surgeon, philosopher and historian.

He is currently lecturer in surgery at Imperial College London and senior surgeon registrar at Chelsea and Westminster Hospital in London. Awarded the Arris and Gale Lectureship by the Royal College of Surgeons of England and the Hunterian Prize, he leads a team focusing on the development of innovative technological, pharmaceutical and economic strategies to resolve the global healthcare burden of obesity, metabolic syndrome and cancer.

His historical and paleopathological work spans the classical era exploring preeminent leadership styles notable in Alexander the Great, Xenophon, Hannibal Barca and Julius Caesar. His investigations into ancient innovation include the earliest world literature from the Ancient Near East and the integration of science with art in the renaissance focusing on the work of Leonardo da Vinci, Raphael and Michelangelo. As an Egyptologist, he has offered the first pathological analysis of the Great Sphinx and his analysis of the death of Tutankhamun and 18th Dynasty Pharaohs received world-wide attention through documentaries on the BBC, National Geographic and the Smithsonian Channel. He is founder and executive chair of the Institute of Civilisation.

www.ingramcontent.com/pod-product-compliance
Lightning Source LLC
Chambersburg PA
CBHW070557100426
42744CB00006B/316